RESCUING
a BROKEN
AMERICA

*Why America Is Deeply Divided
and How to Heal it Constitutionally*

MICHAEL COFFMAN, PH.D.

RESCUING A BROKEN AMERICA

Why America is Deeply Divided and
How We Can Heal It Constitutionally

by MICHAEL COFFMAN, Ph.D.

ISBN 978-160037-822-5 (paperback)
Library of Congress Control Number: 2010930397

Published by:

MORGAN JAMES PUBLISHING
1225 Franklin Ave. Ste 325
Garden City, NY 11530-1693
Toll Free 800-485-4943
www.MorganJamesPublishing.com

Cover Design by:
Rachel Lopez
rachel@r2cdesign.com

Interior Design by:
Bonnie Bushman
bbushman@bresnan.net

In an effort to support local communities, raise awareness and funds, Morgan James Publishing donates one percent of all book sales for the life of each book to Habitat for Humanity.
Get involved today, visit **www.HelpHabitatForHumanity.org.**

Dedication

To my wife Susan,
whose tireless support
made this book possible.

Acknowledgments

I greatly appreciate the research,

advice, time and support from

Becky McGlauflin and Kristie Pelletier.

Contents

PART II
HOW DID IT HAPPEN?

PART III
TAKING BACK AMERICA

Table of Contents

Foreword

"THEY CALL IT THE AMERICAN DREAM FOR A *REASON*: Because it is *American.* It is unique to this land. Of all the countries in the world, it is America - and ONLY America - that embodies the cherished principle that every human being has a "right to life, liberty, and the pursuit of happiness," and that those rights come from our Creator and not from government. I don't know what the Chinese Dream would be – to have the government not censor their internet and not tell them how many children they can have. It's the American Dream that cherishes liberty and it's the reason why we're going to lead the world for decades to come.

As you know, America started out with a Tea Party…and that spirit of liberty and individualism has never died out. Our Founding Fathers risked their lives, their property, and their honor to create a country founded on these principles. And they crafted a brilliant Constitution that has preserved those rights for over 200 years.

According to legend, on the day the Constitutional Convention adjourned, Benjamin Franklin walked through the streets of Philadelphia, where a crowd gathered around him. A woman in the crowd asked him, "Well, Dr. Franklin, what kind of government have you given us?"

Franklin replied, "A Republic, if you can keep it."

Today the Tea Party movement optimizes the spirit of the original Founders. But to succeed in any debate, the debater needs to know the facts. *Rescuing a Broken America* provides the background and solutions needed to take back America and once again establish the American Dream.

— Congresswoman Cathy McMorris Rodgers,
U.S. House of Representatives, May 27, 2010.

Preface

IN ANOTHER LIFE, OR SO IT SEEMS, I was once a college professor and a research scientist. Never in my wildest imagination did I believe that I would ever have a need to write a book like this. On the other hand, never in my wildest imagination did I believe the American culture would ever become corrupted by an ideology so dangerous that it could destroy America as free society.

I was leading a multimillion dollar research effort on the effects of acid rain and global warming on our nation's ecosystems in the late 1980s and 1990s when I began to realize that science was being ignored or politicized for a purpose. Congress spent approximately a billion dollars on research defining various aspects of acid rain and global warming before passing a draconian reauthorization of the Clean Air Act. I was shocked that the severe restrictions were not justified by the science. Worse, a lot of science was taken totally out of context in order to justify the new draconian regulations.

It occurred to me then, that I could be the best scientist in the world and it would make no difference in policy formulation. Science was either ignored or twisted to mean something that the science itself never supported. I began to "follow the money trail" to try to determine what was driving this madness.

It did not take long to realize there was a huge agenda behind these policy decisions. It soon became crystal clear that part of this agenda was to shift the power away from the people and center it in the government. My generation is probably the last one that was taught the true basis of our Constitutional Republic in public school. What we have today is almost opposite of what our Constitution was supposed to protect us from. Another aspect of the agenda was to create a world government (now called global governance).

Many who pick up this book to read will be deeply offended because it will challenge their core beliefs; their worldview; their reality. It is my hope and prayer that most Americans will be open-minded enough to continue reading to find out how they have been indoctrinated into believing a lie, and perhaps for the first time begin to understand why the Founders organized our government and limited its power by the Constitution.

This was so serious I eventually quit my well-paying job to try to alert the American people to the deception that was occurring. As has happened for many others who have tried, my efforts have only been partially successful. As time has progressed, I, and others, have pieced together a clear picture of what has and is happening. I wrote an 850-page book detailing what I had discovered in 2005, but even that did not cover all the details of this horrendous agenda. The book was never published because it was too long for the average person to read. When I was drawn back into the global warming debate the book languished. Finally, a group of people convinced me to shorten the original book substantially so that the interested person would not be intimidated by its size.

Although this book is now readable by any interested American, it is woefully lacking in detail, examples and supporting material. As such, the knowledgeable reader will find it lacking in many historical and current facts. Nonetheless, it does provide the broad sweep of the agenda and why it is extremely dangerous. For the first time, the reader will understand why America is so deeply divided and what is behind the mind-bending machinations of the last several administrations. It is not about political parties, it is about two warring worldviews to create global governance.

America is at a major turning point in its history. We either reverse this progression of destruction starting in the 2010 elections, or we will lose the freedoms and the standard of living our Founders began for us. There is simply no other alternative. It must start this year.

The book is divided into three parts. The first part defines the deep cultural division in America and its extreme danger to the future of America. The second part defines the deliberate and systematic effort that has successfully created that division, and how it was accomplished. The third part identifies what we must do to stop, and then reverse this agenda. A very successful and proven strategy is provided to utilize Constitution protections embedded in federal and state law to stop the encroachment of the government into our lives.

The increasing vigor of the Tea Party Movement and the dramatic increase in ratings of the conservative news media and talk show hosts give me hope that Americans can save America. Whenever Americans are faced with a clear and imminent danger they have always arisen to the occasion. Those who are pushing this agenda are very powerful and will fight back—hard. Be forewarned, but also know those who would destroy America are no match against America's people. Let this book help in this process.

— Michael S. Coffman, Ph.D.

PART I

WHAT'S HAPPENING TO AMERICA

1

A War of World Views

During much of the twentieth century, America increasingly replaced Constitutional governance with another form of governance— one that systematically destroyed the very principle that has made America the greatest nation in the history of the world.

AMERICA IS DEEPLY DIVIDED. Although the division has been happening incrementally for decades, it became starkly apparent during the 2000 Presidential Campaign. Pundits claimed that the Florida voting recount, scandals, hanging chads and all, caused the division. It did not. Division was threatening our nation *before* the election occurred. The U.S. Supreme Court was deeply divided *before* the Court ruled in favor of George Bush in the Florida vote count. The election merely revealed its stark ugliness in ways that we could no longer ignore.

The now famous "red" map published by *USA Today* following the 2000 election clearly showed that the urban/suburban areas voted for Gore while the more rural counties voted for Bush. The mainstream media explained away this phenomenon with simplistic reasoning like "liberal strongholds" versus "conservative strongholds," or it was a contrast of "urban values" versus "rural values." Hidden within these simplistic explanations was the subtle implication that the hicks from the country do not have the sophistication needed to vote intelligently.

Bigotry and elitism aside, these one-dimensional explanations contain an element of truth. Tragically, however, they gloss over a disturbing fact: a major schism exists between worldviews as America drifts away from the foundation of governance that guarantees each citizen "life, liberty and the pursuit of happiness." The story is the same throughout rural America; a growing realization that the urban-suburban citizen's political power has been plundering their rural brethren for decades. It is not unlike what King George did to the colonists in the 1700s. Now, in the twenty-first century, those who would desire to rule the world are even plundering urbanites through programs like smart growth.

The polarization in America became progressively worse in the years following the 2000 election. As the 2008 election grew near, Democrats generally hated President George Bush with a passion. Contrary to previous elections, however, Independents were also fed up with Bush's big spending programs and increasing federal control. Even many Republicans were disillusioned by a feeling that Bush had betrayed them, especially in rural America. The general underlying feeling was that *anyone* would be better than Bush and his destructive policies. Very few understood why they felt that way. They just knew what Bush had done was not good for the country.

The country was ripe for a major change. Change was what Candidate Barack Obama's campaign was all about, especially after the financial collapse that started in mid September. While the two presidential candidates were exceptionally civil, their adherents became bitterly partisan. For most conservatives, Obama's message of change did not ring true. They were very nervous about what candidate Obama meant by change. It seemed far too socialistic for them. His association with the likes of William Ayers greatly disturbed conservatives. Ayers is an unrepentant convicted felon and co-founder of the extremely radical, communist Weather Underground.[1] On the other hand, conservatives weren't all that enamored with candidate John McCain either. He seemed far too liberal. But he was at least better in their view than Obama. In spite of Obama's radically left political history, mainstream political analysts assured likely Obama supporters that he would govern from the middle as President Clinton had done in the 1990s. In spite

4

of Obama's dubious past, the mainstream media provided a Teflon coating that deflected the otherwise very serious concerns of his radical beliefs.

The prevailing attitude of the mainstream media was that the country was sick of President Bush and wanted any kind of change. Besides, study after study has shown that the mainstream media were mostly progressive liberals who agreed with, and solidly supported Obama. NBC's Chris Matthews typified this mainstream ideology when he told his audience on February 13, 2008 of his admiration for Obama by saying "It's part of reporting this case, this election, the feeling most people get when they hear Barack Obama's speech. My, I felt this thrill going up my leg. I mean, I don't have that too often."[2]

Obama's socialist views came blazing to the forefront on October 12, 2008, when he was unknowingly caught on video responding to Sam Wurzelbacher, more popularly known as "Joe the Plumber." Sam was a plumber who was concerned some of Obama's ideas would greatly increase his taxes and perhaps put him out of business. Caught by ABC News cameraman Scott Shulman, the world saw and heard Barack Obama's response;

> It's not that I want to punish your success. I just want to make sure that everybody who is behind you, that they've got a chance at success too… and I think when you spread the wealth around, it is good for everybody.[3]

While the comment was reported by every news organization, and ignited a firestorm with conservatives, the general attitude of the mainstream media was, "so what, what's wrong with that?" Again, the mainstream media protected him from any damage that would have meant certain political death if he had said the same things 25 years earlier.

Candidate Obama never did define what he meant by change. He did, however, repeatedly identify himself with progressive ideology. Obama also gave America a disturbing warning just before Election Day, "we are five days away from fundamentally transforming the United States of America."[4] That's very strong language. What did that mean? Not surprisingly, no one in the mainstream media asked that simple question. In hindsight, it may well be the biggest understatement in the twenty-first century.

What is this fundamental transformation and how does it affect the average American? Americans quickly began to find out during the first year of President Obama's tenure. Massive spending bills were quickly passed by a Democrat controlled Congress. In addition to the massive takeover of America's health care and higher education systems, this will add over eight *trillion* dollars of new debt (or $26,000 per person), a banking and automobile bailout and takeover. Yet, that was just the start.

All this pales in comparison to proposed economically devastating cap and trade legislation which allegedly "solves" the global warming catastrophe. Senator James Inhofe (R-OK) claimed that cap and trade was "the largest tax increase in the history of America."[5] Worse, it would essentially put federal bureaucrats in charge of the American economy by deciding who gets carbon credits and who does not.[6] Although the cap and trade legislation was stalled, it clearly shows the magnitude of the government takeover Obama visualizes.

Democrats and progressives claim that all this is necessary to save the nation and the world from the catastrophic damage allegedly done during the eight-year Bush administration. As successive one to two thousand page bills costing hundreds of billion of dollars each were passed during Obama's first year *without even being read* by the democratic majority, millions of Americans began to protest. By mid-summer hundreds of unplanned "Tea Party" rallies around the country were held to protest the excessive spending and intrusion into their private lives and finances. The rallies quickly evolved into a massive libertarian-leaning Tea Party movement.

Although attacked, scorned, denigrated and ignored by the mainstream media, a stunning NBC/Wall Street Journal Poll on December 16, 2009 found that 41 percent of the American people viewed the Tea Party movement favorably, compared to only 23 percent who did not. Conversely the Democrat Party only had a 35 percent favorable/45 percent unfavorable rating, and the Republican

Party a 28 percent favorable/43 percent unfavorable rating.[7] Yet, the mainstream media continued to act as if the movement did not even exist.

If the Tea Party and Republican polls are added together, a whopping 69 percent of the American people tend to favor fiscally conservative governance. This is probably overstated because many Republicans are liberal-leaning, not true conservatives. Nonetheless, the conservative-leaning citizens see that what the Democrats are doing is socialistic and bankrupting the country. This was made apparent in the January 19, 2010 Senate election of conservative Scott Brown in Massachusetts to replace liberal Ted Kennedy. Yet, the Democrats say it is not socialism, but "social and economic justice," an end to racism, and environmental protection that they are attempting to accomplish. These goals, they claim, are both noble and necessary to attain equality.

Both sides accuse the other of being un-American, bigots, fear mongers and racists. It is just as racist and bigoted for a progressive liberal to assume automatically that someone who is opposed to President Obama, or another black leader, is opposed because he or she hates blacks. These progressive liberals have deliberately created class and gender warfare, urban vs. rural schisms, and federal verses state power struggles.

A January 25, 2010 Gallup Poll found President Obama is the most divisive first-year president in United States history.[8] We are becoming more and more divided at an ever accelerating rate. Why? Who is right? Why is it tearing the very fabric of America apart? An April 18, 2010 Pew Research Center Poll found that nearly 80 percent of Americans were frustrated or angry with the federal government.[9] Why? As important, how can this schism be fixed and how can communities and individuals protect themselves?

The War on the Constitution

What makes America so deeply divided? What happened to the God-given right to "life, liberty and the pursuit of happiness" as penned by Thomas Jefferson in the Declaration of Independence? Where has the principle of a government of the people, by the people, and for the people gone? Why are Americans losing the American Dream?

The answer lies in understanding that America is mired in a war of worldviews. Its people no longer understand the principles of unalienable rights and self-government as envisioned by the founding fathers. Children no longer learn the foundations of freedom in public schools. Consequently, they no longer understand the God-given rights that protect each individual from the plundering by others and by their government.

During much of the twentieth century, America increasingly replaced Constitutional governance with another form of governance—one that systematically destroyed the very principle that has made America the greatest nation in the history of the world. The deep divisions in America are the result of an all-out war between the axiom of freedom and mutual respect best laid down by John Locke (1632-1704) in his *Two Treatises on Government* (1689), and that of Jean Jacques Rousseau in his *Social Contract* (1762) and *Discourse on the Origin of Inequality* (1754).

While other writers/philosophers also supported one philosophy or the other, this book uses the writings of these two authors to show the contrast between the two philosophies. Also, most historical writings compare the similarities, not the differences between the writings of the two men. While there are important similarities, the two models are diametrically opposed to each other in actual application. These foundational differences are rarely mentioned.

Locke's writings were refined by Sir William Blackstone (1723-1780) and others until Thomas Jefferson made them the cornerstone of the Declaration of Independence. Jefferson claimed the Declaration is based entirely on the "Laws of Nature and of Nature's God." Conversely, Rousseau provided the foundational philosophy that spawned the bloody French Revolution and inspired the writings of Immanuel Kant, Georg W. F. Hegel, Karl Marx[10] and many others. Most of Europe has been infected with the Rousseau model, including England.

Government's purpose, according to Locke, is to join with others to "unite, for the mutual preservation of their lives, liberties and estate, which I call by the general name, property."[11] According to Locke, the primary reason for government "is the *preservation of their property*" (Italics added). Most Americans today would be amazed to learn that the free right to own property represents the foundation upon which life and liberty depend.

This fundamental principle became the cornerstone of the Declaration of Independence of 1776 and the United States Constitution; "We hold these truths to be self-evident, that all men are created equal, that they are endowed by their Creator with certain unalienable Rights, that among these are Life, Liberty and the pursuit of Happiness…" This clause lays out the critical understanding that every citizen has "equal *opportunity*" to succeed (or fail), not equal results.

The Founders did not establish the Constitution to *grant rights*. Rather, they established this government of laws (not a government of men) in order to **secure** each person's Creator *endowed rights* to life, liberty, and property. These rights are not granted by government, which can take away what it grants. Instead they are granted by God, which makes them eternal and not subject to change. Even so, the Founders recognized that rights, though endowed by the Creator as unalienable and eternal, could not be sustained in society unless they were protected under a code of law which was itself in harmony with a higher law. They called it "natural law," "Nature's law" or "God's law."[12]

The drafters of the Declaration (which also included John Adams and Benjamin Franklin) used Natural Law instead of natural-rights theory, substituting "the pursuit of happiness" for "property" in the trinity of unalienable rights. There are several reasons for the substitution. To many people, the term property means an object like land and goods that can be bought and sold. Property as Locke used it meant far more; such as the sovereignty of one's self and the right to personal well being that tangible property can bring. "Life, Liberty and Property" is still used in the Fifth and Fourteenth Amendments of the U.S. Constitution.

The Declaration of Independence established the premise that in America each person has all the rights "to which the laws of Nature and Nature's God entitle them." In other words, God's law is the ultimate source and established limit for all of man's laws. It is intended to protect each of these natural rights for all of mankind.

Central to natural law is the right to use one's own property in the pursuit of happiness. Most people do not understand that the right to use their own property or "property rights" is far more important than "democracy" in maintaining liberty and building wealth. Thomas Sowell, senior fellow at the Hoover Institution, stated the utter truth of this fundamental principle in his book *The Quest for Cosmic Truth*, "In India the electoral franchise is wide and elections have long been regular, but property rights are weak. For most of the post-World War II era, in contrast, Hong Kong had no democracy, but property rights there have been among the strongest the world has ever seen. Indians are poor and shackled by a massively corrupt state; the people of Hong Kong are wealthy and free."[13]

Why are property rights so critically important? The Fraser Institute of Canada publishes an annual Economic Freedom of the World report.[14] One of the components of the report is an index of legally protected private property rights based on things like impartial courts, judicial independence, integrity of the legal system, protection of property rights, legal enforcement of contracts, and regulatory restriction on the sale of real property. Although somewhat subjective, when this index is compared with the per capita Gross Domestic Product (GDP) determined by the World Bank,[15] an enlightening curve results. (see graph) The lower the protection of property rights the lower reduced per capita GDP.

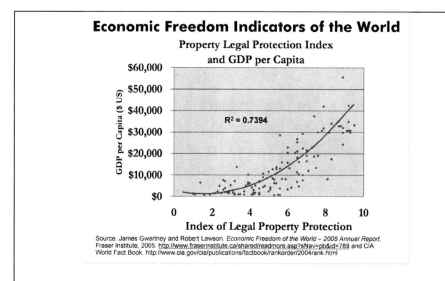

Economic Freedom Indicators of the World

Property Legal Protection Index and GDP per Capita

$R^2 = 0.7394$

GDP per Capita ($ US)

Index of Legal Property Protection

Source: James Gwartney and Robert Lawson. *Economic Freedom of the World – 2005 Annual Report.* Fraser Institute, 2005. http://www.fraserinstitute.ca/shared/readmore.asp?sNav=pb&id=789 and CIA World Fact Book. http://www.cia.gov/cia/publications/factbook/rankorder/2004rank.html

The basis of wealth creation for every nation is legally protected private property rights. The better the legal protection, the greater the wealth of the nation.

Conversely, the higher the protection of property rights, the higher the per capita gross domestic product. While not statistically significant, the graph clearly shows that well defined, legal property rights are critical in a nation's ability to create wealth.

As important as legally protected private property rights are, however, there are a myriad of other factors that influence the per capita GDP, including deceptive accounting practices, size of government, discrimination, corruption and others. For example, Canada has a protected private property index of 8.5 and a per capita GDP of $36,444, while the United States has a lower protected private property protection index of 7.9 but has a per capita GDP of $46,716, almost a third higher than Canada. The Fraser Institute provides a chilling warning for the disparity:

Canada's fiscal federalism…transfers money from rich to poor provinces. Since economic freedom spurs prosperity and growth, fiscal federalism in effect transfers money from relatively free provinces to relatively unfree provinces, muting the impact of economic freedom and perversely creating incentives for provincial politicians to limit economic freedom and, thus, economic growth since this increases the flow of federal transfers, which are directly controlled by these politicians. This enhances their power and their ability to reward friends and penalize enemies.[16]

This observation must be taken seriously. It is exactly what candidate Obama said we must do; massive income redistribution. Another way to look at this phenomenon is that Canada's model for governance is beginning to look more like the Jean Jacques Rousseau model than the John Lock model. It is increasingly true for the United States as well.

Rousseau attacked Locke's model, arguing that individuality and property rights divide man by focusing on self-interest and greed rather than the good of society. He argues in his *Social Contract* for the creation of an abstract common good.[17] It is not surprising that Rousseau's model has led to a severe distrust of capitalism, the free market, and paranoia to put property rights under direct government control. That belief is still held by the progressive liberals today.

Rousseau's ideas were molded by the abuses he saw in the nobility that still ruled France in a feudalistic manner. While nobility still existed in England when Locke wrote his treatises (and still does), the evolution of the Magna Charta through the centuries had already broken the back of feudalism in England if not the Colonies. Therefore, Rousseau's focus was on limiting the power of the nobility—something that had already happened in England centuries before. That difference had a huge impact on the model Rousseau proposed in his writings.

Rousseau sees "man as a malleable creature" to be molded by an enlightened government. Rather than privileged nobility, he "favors primitive man, the noble savage who lives in simple equality with his fellow man, with few needs, a limited appetite, over man in civilized society."[18] Rousseau seeks to achieve this equality through a vague socialist metaphysical concept called the "general will."[19] The general will allegedly overcomes the tension between individual interests and the community, by making community rights superior to the individual rights. The general will supposedly free from our subjective selves and personal interests.

In the *Social Contract*, individuals are part of a "collective body" that is called a "State" or "Sovereign." Citizens "share in the sovereign power, and subjects [are] under the laws of the State."[20] Rousseau goes on to say that raw force can bring consent to the general will; "That whoever refuses to obey the general will shall be constrained to do so by the whole body.... In this lies the key to the working of the political machine; this alone legitimises civil undertakings."[21] In doing so, Rousseau states the individual is supposedly "forced to be free" from his own selfishness.[22] Does this sound like the United States today?

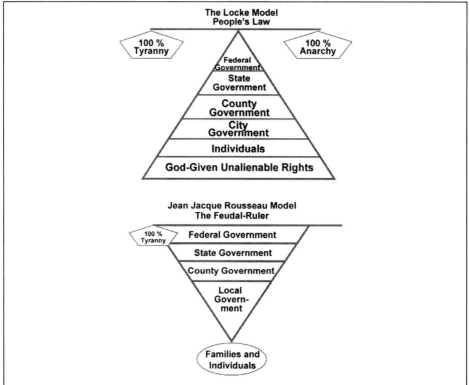

Top: In the Locke Model, sovereignty lies with the individual with decreasing power up the levels of government until the federal government has the least power of all. This provides a balance between anarchy and tyranny. Jefferson called this the People's Law. **Bottom:** In the Rousseau Model sovereignty supposedly lies with the individual, but in practice lies in the federal government. Power decreases down until families and individuals only have the power granted by the governments overseeing them. Jefferson called this the feudal-Ruler law that lead's to tyranny. He saw this in France. *Source: W. Cleon Skousen. The Making of America, the Substance and Meaning of the Constitution. The National Center for Constitutional Studies, Washington, D.C. 1986.*

In fairness, Rousseau was attempting to reign in the power of the nobility. Unfortunately, once the nobility was gone, all power was vested in the government with no real checks and balances. This difference between Locke and Rousseau is enormous, and results in two diametrically opposed forms of government. It is rarely mentioned in the glamorized comparisons between Locke and Rousseau.

It must be repeated; it is the enlightened state which determines the general will, or common good of the people in Rousseau's model. So while both Locke and Rousseau believed that a just government derives its power from the "consent of the governed," in application all rights are embodied in the State with Rousseau's model, while all rights belong to the individual in Locke's model.

The second major difference between Locke and Rousseau is property rights. Once again, Rousseau penned his writings *before* the French Revolution. Feudalism still ruled France and only a few wealthy noblemen could own property—who forced serfs to work the land for a pittance. Thus, Rousseau saw private property as an evil that repressed man. So much was Rousseau against property rights that he stated that no one should own anything; "You are undone if you forget that the fruits of the earth belong to us all, and the earth itself to no one!"[23] The rich, claimed Rousseau, designed property rights to place:

> new fetters on the poor, and gave new powers to the rich; which irretrievably destroyed natural liberty, eternally fixed the law of property and inequality, converted clever usurpation into unalterable right, and, for the advantage of a few ambitious individuals, subjected all mankind to perpetual labour, slavery and wretchedness.[24]

To avoid this perceived wretchedness, Rousseau insists that the public good is served only when the state owns or controls all land. It is small wonder that Karl Marx was a student of Rousseau's writings. However, there is a terrible flaw in the Rousseau/Marx logic. A major problem arises from government ownership of land. Everyone shares land owned by the government, but no one is responsible to take care of it. This principle is known as the law of the commons.

Without pride of ownership, there is no motivation to care for or optimize property held in common with the millions of other citizens. Everyone sinks to the lowest common denominator, the economic structure stagnates, and the infrastructure collapses. Although private property owners receive the blame for environmental destruction, ironically, Americans polluted their air and waterways because *no one owned* them.

The inevitable adverse consequence of common ownership to a large degree explains why Communism and Marxism, both products of Rousseau ideology, have been such dismal failures.[25] The environmental devastation found in Eastern Europe and Russia as the Iron Curtain and the Soviet Union collapsed in the early 1990s evidences a lack of motivation to protect the environment. America's waterways and air, unlike its land, are not under Locke's model of property rights. Consequently, like Eastern Europe and the former Soviet Union, America's air and water suffered the same fate of the tragedy of the commons.

In speaking before the Virginia State Constitutional Convention, James Madison warned about the danger of putting raw power in the hands of government, "The essence of Government is power; and power, lodged as it must be in human hands, will ever be liable to abuse."[26] Power in the hands of an unaccountable bureaucracy will always stomp on the rights of the people. For example, wetlands regulations have been used by government bureaucrats to heavily fine, and even put landowners in jail for minor or even questionable violations of the Clean Water Act. Worse, the Clean Water Act was never intended to include wetlands. It was intended only for navigable waters of the United States. In other words, it had to float a canoe to be within the jurisdiction of the law. Yet the brute force of this law has stripped hundreds of thousands of people of their property rights (except for paying taxes) on land that had no standing water.

In just one of thousands of examples of the abuse of this law, 70 year-old John Rapanos was found guilty of moving clean sand from one end of his property to another, according to Judge Lawrence Zatkoff of the Federal District Court in Michigan. Some of Rapanos' 54 acres had saturated soil part of the year while only a small area was actually marshy. Rapanos did not touch the marshy area but did move some sand to the area that had saturated soil part of the year and drained it.

The U.S. Army Corps of Engineers charged Rapanos with a wetlands violation without ever demonstrating that the impacted area was even legally wetlands. Judge Zatkoff was forced, by law to sentence Rapanos to 200 hours of community service and $185,000.[27] Rapanos was fortunate. The federal prosecutor wanted him sentenced to five years in prison and $13 million in fines. The case went to the U.S. Supreme Court[28] in 2006 and eventually sent the case back to District Court. Rapanos ultimately paid $150,000 in fines and $750,000 to mitigate the "damage" done to the 54 acres.[29]

Others, like Ocie Mills in Florida have received the five-year prison sentence that Rapanos was able to avoid. Is this a just law? It is the natural, yet chilling result of a concept called positive rights. It is diametrically opposed to the Founders original intent of the Constitution.

Contrast Between Locke and Rousseau
Models of Governance

Locke	Rousseau
The individual is sovereign. Unalienable individual rights form the basis of the U.S. Constitution and private property rights. Focuses on self-government where all men are created equal and have equal *opportunity*. Limits the right of government to intervene in the lives of individuals Administered by a minimum of government.	The government is sovereign. The "general will" (public good) as defined by the state (Nation). All people supposedly share equally in the wealth called social justice today. Based on positive rights that are defined by the government. Administered by collectivist and ever-growing government.

A War of World Views

Locke	Rousseau
Power to make decisions primarily in the hands of the people thereby encouraging risk-taking. The only laws needed are those to enforce the golden rule that no person can conduct activities that cause harm to another person or their property. Creativity to find new and better ways of doing things is encouraged by minimal regulatory structure.	Power to make most decisions primarily in the hands of government and bureaucrats. It is a breeding ground for government corruption and arbitrary enforcement of ever expanding regulations. Stifles creativity to find new and better ways to do things because there is no incentive. Considers capitalism and profits as wrong, even evil.
Establishes and protects private property rights which allows the creation of needed capital and provides the *only* proven way to eliminate poverty. It is why capitalism works in Western nations and doesn't within centrally controlled nations.	Minimizes property rights to only those allowed by the state to reduce *all* risk. Places nature's perceived needs ahead of man's real needs. By controlling property rights there is little incentive to build a better widget.
Encourages protection of asset value of privately owned property because of pride of ownership and the need to maintain environmental health for continued production or use.	Invokes the Law of the Commons where property is held in common by the state through deed or regulation. No one person, family or organization has a vested interest in protecting the property for the benefits it can provide.
Depends on free markets with minimum of regulations to create incentives to maximize efficiencies of production through creativity and entrepreneurship.	Depends on controlled markets by government to achieve predetermined social and environmental goals based on precautionary principle which, in turn, stifles creativity and entrepreneurship.

2

Constitutional Rights
VS Positive Rights

Make no mistake, it is an all-out war against the founding principles enshrined in the Declaration of Independence, U.S. Constitution, and Bill of Rights[30]

THERE WILL BE MANY WHO WILL STRONGLY DISAGREE with the conclusion that Rousseau's philosophy leads to a repressive government; even militant fascism and communism. The reader may even be deeply offended. That makes it even more imperative this book be read because America is at the tipping point. We either decide to return to Constitutional civil rights and liberties which have been proven to bring prosperity and freedom, or we fully embrace the Rousseau model which has repeatedly shown at best to stifle economic growth, prosperity and job creation, and at worst lead to abusive tyranny.

Rousseau's model is based on "positive rights;" i.e. rights granted *by* the government. Positive rights spell out what the government must do for the people and what the people can and cannot do. Positive rights were the basis of the Soviet Union's Constitution. History has not been kind to the actual practice of positive rights.

Conversely the Locke/Constitutional model is based on negative rights or natural rights that *limit* what the government can do. As an example, positive rights include the right of every citizen to have a job, or if not, have the government provide them a base income. This is a *government right* to happiness. On the other hand, the Locke model holds that everyone has a *God given right* to seek the best job they can, free from government interference in the *pursuit* of their happiness. It is imperfect because people are imperfect, but it is the best form of government possible.

The concept of "positive" rights is easily accepted by people because it sounds…, well, so positive! It is almost always based on emotion and feelings. Yet it is invariably destructive. The positive right theory grants the right to a job or welfare, even if the person is unemployable because he or she is lazy, on drugs, or any self-inflicted destructive behavior. In other words, positive rights inevitably *reinforce* bad behavior because it protects an individual from the *consequences* of his or her actions. Worse, it takes or steals from the productive members of society to give to the consciously unproductive members.

Progressive liberals immediately attack anyone holding such beliefs as cruel, heartless and without compassion—again targeting emotion and feelings. However, just like an emerging butterfly must struggle to break free of its cocoon or it will die, so too must people learn from their mistakes to properly mature and become productive members of society. As noble as are the progressive liberal's goals, their very efforts to help people invariably cause far more damage and harm than they help. There are consequences to bad behavior and choices, and we all need to learn from them.

Starr Parker, the young black author of *Uncle Sam's Plantation* who was a mother on welfare, shares how the progressive social programs have utterly failed;

Instead of solving economic problems, government welfare socialism created monstrous moral and spiritual problems. [These] kind of problems…are inevitable when individuals turn responsibility for their lives over to others. The legacy of American socialism is our blighted inner cities, dysfunctional inner city schools, and broken black families. Through God's grace, I found my way out. It was then that I understood what freedom meant and how great this country is.[31]

Even so, progressives are correct that a society must provide the means for citizens to learn how to help themselves. That was the original intent of public education. As will be discussed later, that is not what public education does today. In any event, it is unrealistic to assume "rights" whereby government must provide everything. History has shown that personal responsibility is the only way to a vibrant, healthy and prosperous society.

Unfortunately, we currently are in a generation that increasingly protects its children from any consequences of bad behavior or the trials of life. Certainly there are times when a child must be protected. However, when a child gets into trouble or has a problem today there is a growing tendency to tell them it is someone or something else's fault and "fix" it for them. Increasingly, children suffer no consequences for wrong behavior, or are not taught how to deal with life's inevitable problems. They are often told it is not their fault. It is little wonder that as these children become adults, they have difficulty in assuming responsibility for their actions. Instead, they want the government to do whatever they want and then protect them from their wrong decisions.

In the political realm, the inevitable failure of a program based on positive rights is never the fault of the Rousseau progressive liberal. It is always the fault of something or someone else. *Always*. The almost bizarre blame game and excuses by President Obama and Congress for their failures and problems in 2009-10 could well become classic examples. No matter what it is, it is President Bush's fault. Or, Obama failed to explain something like health care well enough for the apparently stupid people to understand. It never occurs to progressive liberals that maybe they are wrong and the people are right.

An April 22, 2010 Fox News poll found that 66 percent of the American people were fed up with the "blame Bush" excuse and that it was time for Obama to start taking responsibility for his own actions.[32]

After forty years of observing the shocking difference of these two diametrically opposed models of governance, author and psychiatrist Lyle Rossiter, M.D. Provides insight into what the liberal mind is passionate about. They generally view reality as,

A world filled with pity, sorrow, neediness, misfortune, poverty, suspicion, mistrust, anger, exploitation, discrimination, victimization, alienation and injustices. Those who occupy this world are "workers," "minorities," "the little guy," "women," and the "unemployed." They bear no responsibility for their problems. None of their agonies are attributable to faults or failings of their own; not to poor choices, bad habits, faulty judgment, wishful thinking, lack of ambition, low frustration tolerance, mental illness or defects in character.... Instead the "root causes" of all this pain lie in faulty social condition: poverty, disease, war, ignorance, unemployment, racial prejudice, ethnic and gender discrimination, modern technology, capitalism, globalization and imperialism.... "Big business," "Big Corporations," "greedy capitalists," "U.S. Imperialists," "the oppressors, the rich," "the wealthy," "the powerful," and " "the selfish."[33]

Certainly these are generalizations. Regardless, the root of Rousseau ideology is that man will do the right thing if given the chance. They are prevented from doing the right thing because of evil big corporations and greedy capitalists. The people are victims. Victimization is constantly exploited and reinforced. Therefore, individuals are not responsible for the bad consequences of their behavior and should not suffer from them. The solution is common for every progressive liberal: a very large authoritarian government having large social programs and choking regulations, all paid for with huge taxes; especially for corporations and the rich.

At the international level, global ills are the fault of the United States and its arrogance and bad behavior. Hence, if we just treat rogue nations like Iran, or Islamic Jihadists' with respect they will no longer hate the U.S. and we can negotiate a lasting peace. That explains why President Obama appears to be soft on terrorism and keeps holding out olive branches to Iran while letting ultimatums pass without doing anything. Progressive liberals literally cannot see that Jihadist terrorism or Iran's rush to become a nuclear power is not the result of bad U.S. policy, but a radical religious ideology of world domination that even most Muslims reject.

Progressive liberals can never understand why their ideas always fail. It's always the fault of conservatives, or wrong Constitutional principles or some outside obstruction. It is never because their basic worldview is wrong and will always lead to the wrong conclusions and solutions. Their worldview is based on emotions and feelings, not reality. They believe their failed program just needs more government control or more money and it will surely work. Benjamin Franklin called this belief insane when he purportedly said, "the definition of insanity is doing the same thing over and over and expecting different results."[34] By Franklin's definition, progressive liberal solutions are often insane.

Perhaps the clearest recent progressive liberal disconnect from reality was the demonization of Arizona's illegal immigration bill passed on April 24, 2010. The Arizona law was in response to a total lack of assistance by the Obama administration when runaway murders, crime and social costs resulting from illegals were reaching intolerable levels in Arizona. Incredibly, the Obama administration refused to even acknowledge Arizona's requests for help.

Yet, in classic progressive response, President Obama, Attorney General Holder, Homeland Security Janet Napolitano, and even Mexico's President Calderon viciously condemned the Arizona immigration law as being discriminatory that encouraged racial profiling. None of them have accepted the responsibility that both U.S. and Mexican federal governments had failed miserably to uphold the rule of law.

With the possible exception of President Obama, none of these leaders had even read the Arizona law which was only 18 pages long.[35] Then again, no one should be surprised after the progressive liberals passed bill after bill costing trillions of dollars in 2009 without even reading them. The Arizona law clearly states in four places that police could ask for proof of citizenship only when the person was stopped for another infraction or crime. Even then, the police could not do this unless there was reason to suspect he or she was an illegal alien.

It turns out that both the U.S. federal illegal immigration and the Mexican immigration laws are far tougher than the one passed by Arizona. The U.S. federal law has been on the books for 70 years. Entering Mexico illegally is a felony sporting up to 2 years in prison and up to 5,000 pesos, whereas Arizona's law is a misdemeanor. If caught a second time an illegal in Mexico can receive a prison sentence of 10 years.[36] Both Mexican and U.S. Federal law allow federal agents to detain any suspected illegal alien at any time and any place on a mere suspicion of being an illegal. President Calderon's condemnation of Arizona's law was not only a breach of protocol, but utterly hypocritical.

Around 70 percent of the American people agreed with Arizona's law.[37] Americans were generally incredulous of the president's position, given that the long-standing federal law is far more dangerous. It was even more shocking when progressive congressmen and women stood up in mass wildly applauding Mexican President Calderon when he gave a scathing condemnation of the Arizona law before Congress on May 20, 2010.[38]

President Obama was finally forced to send 1200 National Guard troops to Arizona in a supporting role when Senators McCain and Kyle (R-AZ) threatened to introduce legislation mandating him to do it. Most analysts called the token effort helpful, but to little to late.[39] While part of the progressive's over-the-top reaction was political grandstanding (illegals make excellent pawns that will vote for progressives after being given amnesty), much of it is a complete disassociation from reality.

Dr. Rossiter explains this irrationality by saying; "...*under careful scrutiny, liberalism's distortions of the normal ability to reason can only be understood as a product of psychopathology...The modern liberal mind, its distorted perceptions and its destructive agenda are the product of disturbed personalities.*"[40] (Italics original)

This does not portend well for America's future. America can never spend enough money to correct all the social evils progressive liberals perceive because with every correction, they create even more inequity that needs to be corrected. It never ends. Progressives either don't see or don't care that their environmental laws have destroyed the lives of hundreds of thousands of rural citizens with little to no real benefit to the environment. Nor can they see that constant compromise with terrorist organizations or evil leaders of nations is viewed by these leaders as weakness and just encourages more evil behavior.

Progressive liberals are not necessarily inherently evil. Yet, their actions, however noble, often produce evil results. Social laws and international negotiations must be based on a realistic worldview that truly understands the dynamics of human nature. That is why the Founders put severe limits on government in the Constitution.

The "tax the rich" ploy has been used by progressive liberals for decades to engender class warfare and create their version of social justice. The problem is that the "rich" are already taxed at substantially higher rates than any other nation in the world except for Japan. The tax rate for U.S. corporations is 39.1 percent and that for Japan is 39.5 percent.

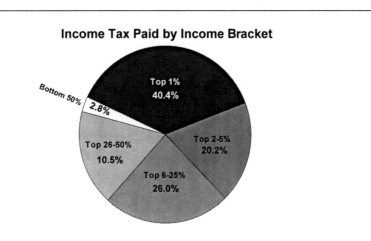

Income Tax Paid by Income Bracket

Bottom 50% — 2.8%
Top 1% — 40.4%
Top 2-5% — 20.2%
Top 6-25% — 26.0%
Top 26-50% — 10.5%

There is little to gain by taxing the richest people in the U.S. even more. The top 1% of Americans pay 40% of all income tax paid already and the top 5 percent pay over 60 %. Further taxation only takes money away from creating new jobs, or sends it overseas.

The Organization for Economic Cooperation and Development reports that tax rates for all member nations (minus the U.S.) averages only 26.5 percent.[41] In 2007, the top 0.1 percent of all incomes paid 20 percent of the nation's federal individual income taxes. The top 1 percent (including the 0.1 percent) paid a whopping 40.4 percent of all income taxes paid, and the top 25 percent paid 87 percent. The bottom 50 percent of taxpayers only pays 3 percent.[42] Is it any wonder middle class jobs are moving offshore? We are penalizing the very people and businesses that create jobs! The entire idea of taxing the rich even more is a red herring. Its sole purpose is to elicit class warfare.

The Robin Hood mentality of the Rousseau progressive liberals inevitably takes the money that would otherwise be used to create jobs in the private sector and squanders it in government programs. These programs do not create more wealth, nor do they create more private sector jobs.

The progressive liberals can continue to do this with near impunity because the bottom 50 percent can continue to demand more benefits. They don't have to pay for them. In doing so, the progressive liberals have literally turned the Constitution upside down. James Madison, when addressing the Constitutional Convention on June 6, 1787 said, "In all cases where a majority is united by a common interest or passion, the rights of the minority are in danger. What motives are to restrain them?"[43] Likewise, John Adams warned:

Unbridled passions produce the same effects, whether in a king, nobility, or a mob. The experience of all mankind has proved the prevalence of a disposition to use power wantonly. It is therefore as necessary to defend an individual against the majority (in a democracy) as against the king in a monarchy.[44]

Giving the majority free benefits ensures the reelection of progressive liberals, because they can say that they are looking out for the "little guy." What the "little guy" doesn't know is they are killing the goose that laid the golden egg. Higher and higher costs of production are forcing companies out of the United States, along with the "little guy's" jobs. The Founders understood the reality of this bedrock principle. Tragically, progressive liberals are shattering this reality and putting America on a very destructive path.

Progressives invariably suffer from the "pie syndrome." Since they have little economic sense due to their view that capitalism and the free market are primary evils in the world, they view the economy as a pie that has to be cut up fairly between the rich and poor—redistribution of wealth. That means more government control and more government jobs. It is no accident that government jobs have outnumbered private sector jobs since 2007.[45] Likewise, the 2009 stimulus bill has created or saved far more government jobs than private sector jobs, with most of those in heavily Democrat Districts.

Since Rousseau progressives believe big corporations, capitalism and the wealthy are the root of all evil, their wealth must be taken from them and given to the victimized downtrodden masses. However, the government cannot give anything to anybody that the government does not first take from somebody else. The corporations or the wealthy no longer can use that money to invest in activities that create new jobs.

The Robin Hood ideology of the progressives also hides the reality that when corporations and small businesses are punished by taxing them more heavily, those costs are inevitably passed on to the downtrodden masses in higher prices. Progressive liberalism is irrational. It actually hurts the people it is supposed to help.

Conversely, natural rights are based on the realization man is not guiltless; he is flawed and prone to do evil. Consequently, natural rights allow the person to suffer consequences for bad decisions or behavior, which in turn, helps the person learn what not to do in the future to be successful. Natural rights protect people *from* government intrusion so they can seek employment, make a better widget, make investments or otherwise build wealth that is essential for life, liberty and the pursuit of happiness. In other words, the pie is expanded so everyone prospers. Dr. Rossiter notes;

Competent people know that they can direct their own lives and provide for their own security through voluntary cooperation, and because they love a world of freedom in which to live as they choose they have no need for, and indeed vehemently reject, the oppressive intrusions of liberal government. What the competent citizen wants, in contrast to the modern liberal, is a coherent and dependable structure for ordered liberty; secured by a limited government that respects the autonomy and sovereignty of the individual and protects his property rights against the constant invasions of collectivism.[46] (Italics original)

The Rousseau liberal model does not work because it is based on positive rights and the impossible belief that the right government program can solve all the social and economic ills created by the Founding Fathers in the Constitution and the free market. President Obama, a self avowed progressive, made this very clear in a January 18, 2001 radio interview on Public Radio WBEZ FM in Chicago:

If you look at the victories and failures of the Civil Rights Movement, and its litigation strategy in the courts, I think where it succeeded was to the best formal rights in previously disposed peoples… The Supreme Court never ventured into the issues of redistribution of wealth [a positive right] and serves more basic issues of *political and economic justice* in this society. To that extent, as radical as people tried to characterize the Warren Court, it wasn't that radical. It didn't break free from the *essential constraints placed by the Founding Fathers in the Constitution*; at least as it has been interpreted, and the Warren Court interpreted it in the same way, that generally the *Constitution is a charter of negative liberties*. It says what the states can't do to you; states what the federal government can't do to you, but it doesn't say what the federal government or the state government *must do on your behalf* [positive rights]…. The tragedies of the Civil Rights Movement was because the Civil Rights Movement became so Court focused I think there was a tendency to lose track of the *political and community organizing activities* on the ground that are able to put together the actual coalitions of power through which you bring about redistributive change. [47]

This interview gives clear insight into the "*CHANGE*" Obama promised in his presidential campaign. Rather than upholding the United States Constitution as he promised under oath at his inauguration, he always intended to *radically change* the Constitution to reflect positive, rather than Constitutional rights. He believes the Founding Fathers were wrong when they based civil rights on negative rights, i.e. limiting what the government can do. That he surrounded himself with like-minded Czars, some of whom proclaimed they are communists or supported communism, and others who claimed China's butcher Mao Zedong as role models,[48] is no accident. For instance, Obama's Regulation Czar, Cass Sunstein has openly advocated amending the Constitution to include President Roosevelt's Second Bill of Rights.[49]

Roosevelt's Second Bill of Rights included the positive rights concept of 1) a job with a living wage, 2) freedom from unfair competition and monopolies, 3) a home, 4) medical care, 5) education, and 6) recreation. These same positive rights were also spelled out in the Soviet Union's Constitution. The whole world saw how well that worked out. Positive rights are government rights which the government can ignore.

Although President Obama is the most obvious politician to push a positive rights agenda, he is not the first to push for this anti-constitutional Rousseau model. The effort to implement positive rights goes back a hundred years to the progressive movement at the beginning of the twentieth century. The gradual erosion of Constitutional protections has been underway for a long time in both the Democrat and Republican parties. The only difference between the parties is that Democrats tend to favor communism and the Republicans tend to favor fascism, both of which are different versions of the Rousseau model.

Unfortunately, the positive rights model actually stifles the means of accomplishing the very thing they desire. The more progressive liberals try to solve an ill through programs, entitlements, regulations and taxation the worse it becomes. Dr. Rossiter explains the reason:

> *The enforcement of any positive right means that somebody's time, energy, money, intelligence, labor and property must be confiscated in the process, a clear violation of rights basic to liberty and therefore a clear case of injustice.* [50] (Italics original)

As previously discussed, Rousseau's model of positive rights and forced compliance through unending regulation stifles productivity and the wealth creation that provides jobs. Yet, it has formed the basis of all social and environmental laws in America since the 1960s. Rather than protecting the rights of others so wealth and jobs are created, as is the case with the Locke model, the Rousseau model encourages the majority (i.e. those in power) to dictate the rights of the minority. The term "public good" has replaced Rousseau's "General Will," but the results are the same, a stifled economy and joblessness.

Also discussed previously, Rousseau progressive liberals have a very warped view of human nature; they refuse to accept responsibility. After spending trillions of dollars trying to reduce poverty, for instance, the percentage of people below the poverty line has stayed between 12 and 15 percent since President Johnson instituted his Great Society.[51] There are certainly those who cannot help themselves because of mental or physical limitations. Yet, welfare programs provide no incentive to get out of poverty, despite claims to the contrary. Welfare enslaves those who could otherwise work into poverty and beholding to the government and progressive politicians who continue to provide them benefits at someone else's expense. Benjamin Franklin observed this defect in human nature in England back in 1766:

> In my youth I travelled much, and I observed in different countries, that the more public provisions were made for the poor, the less they provided for themselves, and of course became poorer. And, on the contrary, the less was done for them, the more they did for themselves, and became richer.... The day you passed that act, you took away from before their eyes the greatest of all inducements to

industry, frugality, and sobriety, by giving them a dependence on somewhat else than a careful accumulation during youth and health, for support in age or sickness. In short, you offered a premium for the encouragement of idleness, and you should not now wonder that it has had its effect in the increase of poverty.[52]

The same is true today. In America, at least, poverty is a defect of human nature which plagues us all. Welfare programs cannot work because, with but a few exceptions, most of the poor are not poor in America because of evil corporations or people; they are poor because of their own destructive decisions. Or, it is because the *culture* they are brought up in actively represses anyone who wants to break out of poverty. It creates perpetual victims. Yet, progressive liberals refuse to acknowledge human nature. They will never admit that their ideology is wrong. They claim the problem is that they did not spend enough money or restrict the evils of corporations and the free market sufficiently through federal entitlements and restrictive regulations.

Yet, the progressive liberals will never admit that their ideology is wrong. They claim the problem is that they did not spend enough money or restrict the evils of corporations and the free market sufficiently through federal entitlements and restrictive regulations.

Dr. Rossiter puts it this way. The progressive liberal is,

Willing to use any foundations of civilized freedom, in order to get what he demands. He seeks through the state that degree of coercion needed to redress the trauma, injustice, helplessness and humiliation [that he sees]. He hopes to do this by passing laws that indulge his impulses and exempt him from the proper obligations of mature adulthood.

President Obama's comment to "Joe the Plumber" during the 2009 campaign about "spreading the wealth" reflects the pure Rousseau mentality of "social justice." The same is true of his intrusion into compensation of senior banking officials, and the near fascist takeover of the college loan program, GM, Chrysler, Fannie Mae and Freddie Mac. In the case of GM's bankruptcy, Obama voided legal contracts (a form of property rights) by giving the unions a larger settlement than creditors, which had superior contractual rights.

In another example, the 2,300 page health care legislation passed on March 21, 2010 is a totally unworkable boondoggle that will exponentially expand the reach of government, dramatically increase medical costs and reduce medical care, especially for those seniors on Medicare. The so-called deficit neutral claim was based entirely on best case scenarios and mind-bendingly creative accounting that by the end of April, 2010 were exposed as fraudulent. The only thing that would have been better for progressives would have been a government run, single payer system. Yet the progressive liberal mind literally cannot see the failure that has happened in every other nation that has it.

The health care bill has been the holy grail of progressives for decades. The contortions the progressive liberals went through to get this bill passed defy every definition of sanity. Two weeks after passing the bill, 52 percent of likely voters want it repealed verses 42 percent who oppose repealing it.[53] Thirty-eight states are considering or intend to consider legislation using the Tenth Amendment to ban the mandatory provisions of federal health care in their state. Virginia, Idaho, and a growing number of states are suing the federal government on the grounds the legislation is unconstitutional.

Progressive liberals absolutely believe they are right even when the rest of the country correctly believes they are living in the twilight zone. Yet, the progressive liberals continue to lie, cheat, bribe, and intimidate anyone and everyone in a desperate attempt to pass the legislation before they lose their majority in the 2010 elections. They are willing to sacrifice themselves to get what they believe is absolutely the right thing to do. They apparently believe the American people are just too stupid to understand what is good for them. The end justifies the means.

As America moves toward the Rousseau model of governance, a hemorrhage of individual liberties is occurring that all Americans once took for granted. In the process, the American Dream is vanishing.

Consequences of the Rousseau Model on America

Through systematic indoctrination in U.S. public schools and the mainstream media, a large segment of society loosely ascribes to these beliefs today. That doesn't mean most liberals suffer from the ideology described above. What it means is their understanding is skewed by what they have been taught. They are open minded and can still make rational decisions.

Only a small minority believe in the Rousseau progressive liberalism as an absolute worldview. Yet they are in positions of incredible power. Their worldview dictates how they view reality. Nothing is likely to change their minds. For instance, gun control is a mantra of the Rousseau progressive liberals. This mantra cannot be shaken by the multitude of historical data which reveals that crime and murder rates go up when gun control laws are imposed. It is irrational. Yet, so locked into their belief is this minority, that they will often develop creative statistics to hide the escalation of crime or any evidence that disproves their belief.

It is this Rousseau blend of socialistic and fascist ideology that has driven the alleged "need" for the avalanche of restrictive and intrusive laws passed over the past thirty years. It is a worldview that is totally alien to the Founding Fathers' vision for America. Our Founders didn't choose the Locke model because they were ignorant of Rousseau. Remember, they were contemporaries of Rousseau and while they were somewhat sympathetic to Rousseau's ideas, fully embraced the concepts of Locke.

What we are witnessing today is not the "equal opportunity" that was the basis of the Declaration of Independence and established in the Constitution, but a total substitution by Rousseau ideology of "equal results" or "social justice." Make no mistake; it is an all-out war against the founding principles enshrined in the Declaration of Independence, U.S. Constitution, and Bill of Rights.

Today the Rousseau model has nearly subverted the Locke-based foundation of the U.S. Constitution, to the detriment of the very concept of liberty. It has most obviously hit rural residents the hardest. Constantly increasing, questionable government environmental regulations have destroyed rural resource-based family businesses, even entire communities; sometimes viciously. That is the primary reason rural counties voted for George Bush in both his presidential elections.

The abuse in rural America has been so bad that rural citizens often believe government bureaucrats who enforce the Rousseau regulations are evil. Most bureaucrats are not. In fact, most believe they are quite normal Americans. Rather, Rousseau socialism has elevated environmental protection to a moral imperative, while desensitizing critical thinking skills of the progressive liberal. You cannot have critical thinking if your education has been void of the importance of individual liberty and property rights.

Consequently, government regulatory bureaucrats actually believe they are serving the "public good" (Rousseau's General Will) by destroying the lives of rural citizens. They may not like it, but they see themselves as morally justified by a higher purpose. Most would be horrified if they ever realized they had been deliberately indoctrinated to follow the Rousseau ideology.

Those who are advancing the Rousseau model for America are glad to tell anyone who will listen that the U.S. Constitution is a living document, intended to change with "enlightenment." Their version of "enlightenment" is always more Rousseau oriented laws and regulations. Yet, the reason the United States is the most successful government in the history of the world is because the Founders never intended the Constitution to be a living document subject to change by the capricious and self-centered nature of man.

Rather, the Constitution centers on the principle of God-given natural law, which is eternal, not subject to the whims of men. It protects the individual against the *natural* desire that resides in every person, including destroying the Constitution—to control their own lives by controlling *everything* and *everyone* around them.

Constitutional Rights VS Positive Rights

The Constitution is timeless because it keeps in check the root cause of evil—the accumulation of power to control the lives and actions of others. The John Locke model of governance depends on checks and balances to prevent accumulation of power. In contrast, the Jean Jacques Rousseau model *depends* on the accumulation of power in the hands of a largely unaccountable government to enforce the "general will" or "public good." Tragically, as British historian and liberal philosopher Lord John Emerich Edward Dalberg Acton said, "Power tends to corrupt; absolute power corrupts absolutely."

Congress has become a cesspool of corruption as the Rousseau philosophy has penetrated both parties. The machinations exposed in the health care debate in 2009 and 2010 clearly show the Rousseau progressive liberal drive to win at any cost, regardless what is best for the nation, or that 60 percent of the American people strongly opposed it while only 35-40 percent favored it. It doesn't matter to the progressive liberal what the American people want, they are going to ram it down their throats anyway because they "know" what is best. Incredibly, the progressives claim they passed health care because it is what the "American people wanted!"

Perhaps nothing exemplifies this better than the proclamation of House Majority Leader Nancy Pelosi following the Senatorial loss in Massachusetts to the conservative Scott Brown;

> It means we will move on many fronts, any front we can. We will go through the gate. If the gate is closed, we will go over the fence. If the fence is too high, we will pole vault in. If that doesn't work, we will parachute in. But we are going to get health care reform passed for the American people for their own personal health and economic security and for the important role that it will play in reducing the deficit.[54]

That is exactly what she did. The arrogance of Rousseau progressives is mindboggling. Pelosi basically said that the progressives are right and the stupid American people be damned. The Rousseau progressives always know what is best. Truth no longer is important. Political power is the ultimate goal.

Although a perceived or created "need" is used to justify legislation like health care reform, the actual legislation is horribly corrupted by payoffs, special interest favoritism and agendas by the time it emerges as law. Such corruption was especially obvious to get health care legislation passed.

The switch from a no to a yes vote by House anti-abortionists led by Bart Stupak (D-MI) the day of the vote on March 21, 2010 is a classic example. They allegedly switched because President Obama signed an executive order preventing the use of federal funds for abortion.[55] Whatever your position on abortion, the switch from no to yes by these Democrats was a farce. Either Stupak or the others were woefully ignorant of the law, or they lied to the American people. An executive order cannot overrule legislative language. Obama's executive order would stand only until challenged in court. The judge would have no choice but to rule in favor of the legislative language and against the Obama executive order. The fact that this was discussed openly well in advance of Stupak's decision, strongly suggests these Congressmen were hiding behind the executive order.

Stupak paid a high price for what his constituents believed was a sellout of his conservative values to partisanship. The Tea Party targeted his district on April 9, 2010 during their Tea Party Express to Washington, and he announced his retirement the same day. Stupak said the Tea Party had nothing to do with his decision, and that he had planned to retire for some time. Most analysts felt, however, that the announcement was because of the pressure brought by the Tea Party. They raised the question of why Stupak was campaigning for reelection if he was going to retire.[56]

In a more direct lie to the American people, the progressive liberals tout that the Congressional Budget Office (CBO) scored the bill as reducing the deficit by $132 billion over ten years. Setting aside the fact that the costs of past social programs have always been grossly underestimated, the prediction by the CBO depends on cutting Medicare by $500 billion and applying *all* of the savings towards extending the program. But the legislation doesn't do that. Instead it applies about half of the so-called $500 billion in cuts to the expanded health care program, thereby increasing the deficit by over $100 billion. [57] Worse, the legislation cuts benefits from senior citizens who are depending on Medicare at the time in their life when they need it most. So much for the progressives helping those who cannot help themselves.

Nor does the health care legislation include the $250 billion "doctor fix" needed to maintain payments to doctors at their already low levels. The progressive liberals took this out of the health care bill so it would show a net reduction in the deficit when scored by the CBO. In total, former CBO director Douglas Holtz-Eakin said if all the gimmicks and budgetary games were stripped out of the bill, the health care "legislation will raise not lower, federal deficits by $562 billion!"[58]

This is but the tip of the deceit iceberg. The entire bill is lies and misdirection designed to deceive the American people. This massive corruption and abuse of power was never intended by the Founding Fathers. *Corruption is, however, an inevitable consequence of Rousseau's model of governance.*

The Founders intended the Constitutional dilution of power within the higher levels of government, and the protection of private property rights to minimize corruption and protect the liberty of individuals. Without strong limitations on federal power, individuals are powerless to oppose any infringement on their rights due to government control over the fruits of their labor or their ability to live their lives without government interference. Consequently, they lose their liberty and often their lives.

Nowhere is this more apparent than in the old Soviet Union, where all property and means of living belonged to the state. No one could speak out against the government for fear of their family's eviction or that the local communist commissar would take away their job. If their offense was sufficiently serious, they could suddenly disappear or be subjected to a kangaroo court and sent to Siberia.

The *radical* progressive liberals claim they are Americans. To the extent they were born and live in America they are Americans. However, to the extent their ideology is diametrically opposed to the Constitutional Republican form of government established by our Founders they are un-American. At best they generally believe the Constitution has outlived its usefulness. At worst, many actually despise the Constitution and the Founders.

Most Americans reading this book probably bristle at this because they accept in varying degrees the Rousseau ideology. Yet, that proves the point. The Rousseau ideology has so penetrated every aspect of our society that most Americans cannot see they have been indoctrinated. They don't see it because they have never been taught the true foundational basis of the freedoms and prosperity we all enjoy but are rapidly losing.

The transition from the Locke to Rousseau model did not occur in a vacuum or overnight. It has been underway for over a hundred years. It is hard to believe that there are Americans who would deliberately seek to destroy what the Founders created, but that is exactly what has, and still is happening.

Except perhaps Ronald Reagan, most Presidents since the mid-twentieth century have succumbed to Rousseau philosophy. President Obama is merely the last and most obvious supporter of the Rousseau model. That is why the January 25, 2010 Gallup Poll found Obama is the most divisive first-year president in United States history. Eighty-two percent of the Democrats (who are either liberal or progressive liberal) approve of Obama, while his approval rating by Republican's is only 18 percent.[59] Given that many of the Republican 18 percent are also liberal; this poll is both stunning and very revealing. It clearly shows the root cause of the deep division between Americans. It also shows the level of penetration that the Rousseau ideology has made with at least half of the American people.

Make no mistake: the United States Constitution is the exact opposite of Rousseau socialism/fascism. The two cannot coexist. Ultimately the Locke basis of the Constitution will prevail, or the Constitution will become a meaningless document under evolving Rousseau legislation and case law. The division in America and the abuse of government power will only continue to worsen as long as the progressive liberals stay in power.

To understand this requires an understanding of what the Founders intended with Constitutional law, and how we got in the mess we are in today. Most importantly, we need to understand how the Constitutional provisions within current laws can be used to purge the legal system of its Rousseau cancer that threatens every man, woman and child in the United States.

3

The Constitution And
The Rule Of Law

"When all government, domestic and foreign, in little as in great things, shall be drawn to Washington as the center of all power, it will render powerless the checks provided of one government on another and will become as venal and oppressive as the government from which we separated." [60]

— Thomas Jefferson

AFTER EXPERIENCING THE OPPRESSION that comes from an unaccountable, all powerful king, the Founders wanted nothing to do with a strong central government. Consequently, the Articles of Confederation, the first constitution of the United States, created a very weak central government. The Articles were ratified in 1781 but it was soon apparent that they were too weak to establish an effective unified government and pay the war debt. This was underscored by the threat of internal conflict both within and between the states, especially after Shays' Rebellion threatened to topple the state government of Massachusetts.

After a couple of false starts, delegates met in Philadelphia in May, 1787 to amend the Articles. That proved impossible, so they secretly hammered out a new constitution which gave the needed power to the central government. By 1789 the new Constitution created a *federal* government in which the central government was stronger than with the Articles. Even so, it was still deliberately weakened by the tripart division of power between the legislative, executive, and judicial branches. The powers given the federal government were extremely limited to a few well defined areas. In all other areas the states and the people were sovereign.

Most people are shocked to realize that the Founders deliberately made the federal government weak and inefficient. The stronger and more efficient the federal government, the less liberty and power the people have over the government. This is completely contrary to the modern day understanding that we must make the federal government *more* efficient. It is highly likely this misperception has been deliberately engrafted into the nation's psyche to advance Rousseau's model, in which the state controls the people rather than the people controlling the state.

Most of the delegates argued the central government's power was severely limited by the tripart system and further weakened by dividing the legislative branch into two parts. In defense of the federal concept and limited powers, James Madison wrote in the *Federalist Papers 45*,

The powers delegated by the proposed Constitution to the federal government are few and defined. Those which are to remain in the State governments are numerous and indefinite. The former will be exercised principally on external objects, as war, peace, negotiation, and foreign commerce; with which last the power of taxation will, for the most part, be connected. The powers reserved to the several States will extend to all the objects which, in the ordinary course of affairs, concern the lives, liberties, and properties of the people, and the internal order, improvement, and prosperity of the State.

There were others at the time who believed the new Constitution gave too much power to the central government. In arguing against a strong federal government, an unknown author in *Anti Federalist Papers 46* says of the enumerated powers of Article 1:

My object is to consider that undefined, unbounded and immense power which is comprised in the following clause - "And to make all laws which shall be necessary and proper for carrying into execution the foregoing powers, and all other powers vested by this constitution in the government of the United States; or in any department or offices thereof." Under such a clause as this, can anything be said to be reserved and kept back from Congress?

Madison and the other federalist writers ultimately prevailed over the anti federalists and the Constitution was ratified in 1789. What did this new Constitution create? Historian Forrest McDonald, using the ideas of James Madison from *Federalist Papers 39*, describes the change this way:

The constitutional reallocation of powers created a new form of government, unprecedented under the sun. Every previous national authority either had been centralized or else had been a confederation of sovereign states. The new American system was neither one nor the other; it was a mixture of both.[61]

So profound and untested was this new form of government that upon leaving the close of the Constitutional Convention, it is recorded that Benjamin Franklin was asked a question by a lady, "Well, Doctor, what have we got—a republic or a monarchy?" Franklin responded, "A republic, if you can keep it."

Franklin's answer was profound. The new Republic depended on a common understanding and importance of the separation of powers and Natural rights. In *Federalist Paper 51*, Madison argued that the three branches of government have as little in common or in contact as possible, thereby being as independent of each other as possible.

The Founders knew the evils of a powerful central government. While serving as ambassador to France in 1787, Jefferson wrote to those who argued for a strong central government, "With all the defect of our constitution, whether general or particular, the comparison of our governments with those of Europe is like a comparison of heaven and hell."[62]

The separation of powers worked well for the first 150 years or so. Then as Rousseau ideology deliberately began to be introduced into every aspect of our society, the three tripart branches began to have a common goal of incorporating the Rousseau model into law. The Founders warned that the unscrupulous would gradually try to change the culture as to unite the goals of the legislative, executive and judicial branches. Thomas Jefferson wrote in 1821,

> When all government, domestic and foreign, in little as in great things, shall be drawn to Washington as the center of all power, it will render powerless the checks provided of one government on another and will become as venal and oppressive as the government from which we separated.[63]

Today we are witnessing the reality of Jefferson's warning. It turns out the Anti Federalists were right. Devious minds have all but broken down the protections granted by the tripart system and have allowed limitless expansion of Congressional powers. As a consequence, American families and lives are being severely harmed, even destroyed as the Rule of Law as intended by the Constitution has been changed before our eyes by Rousseau ideologues in every segment of our society.

The United States Supreme Court, corrupted with the deadly Rousseau ideology, proclaimed that the Constitution is a "living" document that "evolves" with changing circumstances. However, if that were true, the Founders would have made it much easier to change the Constitution. Instead, they made it extremely difficult so that it would not be easily changed. They tried to prevent evil men from ever gaining the ability to alter it by incorporating numerous checks and balances to ensure only principled men and women into these positions. However, as the Rousseau ideology permeated all levels of government, the ideology broke down the checks and balances. In doing so the immutable law as intended by the Founders in the Constitution cannot even be recognized today.

Purpose of the Law

Following the second French Revolution in 1848, France was plummeting headlong into complete Rousseau-based socialism under the leadership of Louis Blanc, a Jacobin socialist. French economist, author and statesman Frédéric Bastiat (1801-1850) was elected to the French Legislative Assembly in 1849. Bastiat was a strong supporter of private property rights, limited government and free markets. To expose the fatal flaws in the emerging Rousseau model of French government, Legislator Bastiat wrote a pamphlet in 1850 called *The Law*.

Like John Locke, Sir William Blackstone, James Madison and Thomas Jefferson before him, Bastiat asserts that since life, liberty and property (pursuit of happiness) are natural rights, any law that man makes *must* serve that purpose. Even as far back as 1850, Bastiat recognized the evil of socialism. Socialists, he said,

> Desire to set themselves above mankind in order to arrange, organize, and regulate it *according to their fancy*... They think only of subjecting mankind to the philanthropic tyranny of their own social inventions. *Like Rousseau, they desire to force mankind docilely to bear this yoke of the public welfare that they have dreamed up in their own imaginations.*[64] (Italics added)

Bastiat said this in 1850. It is shocking how similar the progressive socialists are today to Bastiat's description. He then goes on to define logically the true purpose of the law:

> What, then, is law? It is the collective organization of the individual right to lawful defense. Each of us has a natural right—from God— to defend his person, his liberty, and his property. These are the three basic requirements of life, and the preservation of any one of them is completely dependent upon the preservation of the other two.... If every person has the right to defend—even by force—his person, his liberty, and his property, then it follows that a group of

men have the right to organize and support a common force [i.e. government] to protect these rights constantly. Thus the principle of collective right—its reason for existing, its lawfulness—is based on individual right….

In saying the above, Bastiat defines the basis of Natural law or God's law. It rests on the Ten Commandments that forbid anyone from stealing or coveting anything that belongs to someone else. All individuals have a "natural right" to defend themselves against those who attempt to take what belongs to the owner. This includes the liberty for the owner to use whatever belongs to them as well as the property itself—as long as that use does not cause harm to another person or their property.

Without this natural right of property, a person, by definition, cannot have liberty or even life. How can a person have freedom of speech, for instance, if the person or government he would speak against can deny him housing, employment or even food for his family? Such a person is a slave to whoever controls these fundamentals of life, liberty and property. Bastiat then expands on this definition of government:

Since an individual cannot lawfully use force against the person, liberty, or property of another individual, then the common force [i.e. government]—for the same reason—cannot lawfully be used to destroy the person, liberty, or property of individuals or groups…. Who will dare to say that force has been given to us to destroy the equal rights of our brothers?[65]

If the Rule of Law was designed to protect life, liberty and property, as Bastiat claims, then "everyone would understand that he possessed all the privileges as well as all the responsibilities of his existence. No one would have any argument with government, provided that his person was respected, his labor was free [not forced], and the fruits of his labor were protected against all unjust attack."[66] Rather than the deep division that exists in America today, the division would evaporate because everyone would have *equal opportunity* to achieve the same goals and there would be no political incentive to either fight for what someone else has, or fight to defend what is yours.

Positive rights, on the other hand, create the deep division we see today because it is the government, specifically politicians and bureaucrats, who hands out favors or punishments. Therefore, there is a strong motivation of those who covet power or wealth to use or corrupt the government to gain that power or wealth over others.

Our Founding Fathers understood this weakness in human nature. It explains why they based the Constitution and the Rule of Law on natural rights. James Madison wrote long before Bastiat penned *The Law* that, "Government is instituted to protect property of every sort; as well as that which lies in the various rights of individuals.... this being the end of government, that alone is a just government, which impartially secures, to every man, whatever is his own."[67] Without the protection of the law, property rights are meaningless and become a victim of the unscrupulous who desire to take the benefits of someone else's property for their own use. But the right to use property is not limitless as some believe.

Law Limits the Use of Property

The Locke-Bastiat vision does not permit anarchy or might makes right, as some would have Americans believe. The Rule of Law must include regulations to *limit* what a person or company can do with their property that would cause harm to others. The law is the application of the golden rule—"Do unto others as you would have them do unto you." A person is free to live his life and use his property as long as it does not truly harm others or their property.

For instance, if a neighbor dumped his trash on a person's land, or cut his neighbor's trees, or built part of his house on his neighbor's land is considered a harm and would not be permitted under Bastiat's definition.

Also, if a person used their land in a way that harmed his neighbor or his neighbor's property, the Rule of Law would not allow that use. For instance, converting a home to a high-traffic business in a purely residential area is a harm or nuisance because it lowers the property value of the residential homes around it and may create a health or traffic hazard. Most city zoning ordinances codify these principles so that people do not have to clog up the courts with lawsuits.

On the other hand, if a neighbor built a home on his own land in a residential area that happened to block a beautiful view from another person's bay window, it would not be a legal harm and the new neighbor would be free to build his home. Certainly, it would harm the view and might even reduce the property value of the person who built first. However, the person never had a right to the view in the first place. If he wanted that right, he should have bought the land to keep it from being developed.

Rousseau socialists would demand they have a right to the view and would pass a law preventing the neighbor from building his home, or force him to build a smaller home. This concept is already happening as more and more laws and ordinances include "viewsheds" in determining whether a person can build a home on his or her own land. Unless checked, Rousseau socialism inevitably devolves into the philosophy of "what is mine is mine, and what is yours is also mine."

These are simple examples using physical property. However, the concept of property rights extends into all other areas of our life and economy as well. For instance, land, contracts and money are all forms of property. The Rule of Law simply states that no one should be allowed to use their property, including contracts, in a way that harms someone else or their property. That includes safety and health issues as well.

The British Petroleum (BP) oil catastrophe in the Gulf of Mexico in the spring of 2010 will probably turn out to be a classic case of a violation of private property rights. All property owners, even fishermen along to Gulf Coast have property rights that BP may have violated.

Although no cause of the failure has been defined as of this writing, if it turns out BP was negligent BP would have violated the property rights of the owners and fishermen all along the Gulf Coast. The tragic despoiling of the beaches is an obvious violation of property rights. Less understood, the property right of safety and protection from harm was also violated. The government has an obligation to protect these property owners by the actions of other property owners, in this case BP. The federal government would therefore be guilty of not protecting the victims' property rights.

This oil spill is an ecological and economic disaster of monumental proportions. The first response by the federal government should be to concentrate on stopping the spill and preventing the oil from doing more damage. The next step should be to determine how the regulatory system failed and then fixing it. This assumes, of course, that there was a failure, and the disaster was not created by, say, sabotage.

However, the Obama administration seems to be following the classic progressive liberal kneejerk reaction of blaming President Bush,[68] banning all off-shore drilling and suing BP.[69] Such a policy will slow down determining the cause, failing to find the appropriate solution by putting BP on the defensive, creating more economic damage, and potentially make the oil shortage worse.

2008 Financial Collapse

At the risk of oversimplification, the 2008 financial collapse was created by a series of violations of property rights and the Rule of Law. It started with the Community Reinvestment Act of 1977 (CRA). A classic piece of legislation born of the Rousseau progressive liberalism, the act was passed to address perceived discrimination in loans made to individuals and businesses from low and moderate-income neighborhoods.

While noble in its intent, it set the stage for the worst economic crisis since the Great Depression. It removed the protection historically provided for banks to base their loans on risk. Instead, the law forced them to enter into high-risk sub-prime loans (contracts) that carried a high liability for the bank's stockholders and depositors. The law violated stockholder's and depositor's real property rights to expect a reasonably safe investment.

The CRA provided the framework for newly formed community action groups like the Association of Community Organizations for Reform Now (ACORN) to flourish. These action groups lobbied congress for even more power to force banks into making bad risk sub-prime loans. According to the February 2010 U.S. House of Representatives' "Committee on Oversight and Government Reform Report," ACORN has hundreds of militant affiliates acting in concert to intimidate all opposition. It is also joined at the hip with SEIU (Service Employees International Union) in a way that "constitutes criminal activities." SEIU even gave ACORN $5.6 million.[70]

ACORN's "'Muscle for the Money' involves using non-profit corporations for electioneering activities and an SEIU strategy to threaten corporations and banks into brokering deals for ACORN's financial benefit,...receiving $40 million in fees" from a host of banks.[71] Barack Obama played a role in this kind of activity early in his career by legally representing ACORN and training members what to do.

In spite of the criminal and borderline criminal activities of ACORN, the CRA in itself did not cause the 2008 financial collapse. At least three other key violations of property rights occurred that opened the door to the collapse.

Following the Great Depression, congress passed the Banking Act of 1933 (called the Glass-Steagall Act of 1933). This act limited banks from engaging in investment banking or affiliating itself with an investment bank. Alternatively, it also prevented investment banks from engaging in commercial banking, or an investing bank director from serving as a director in a commercial bank. Both played key roles in precipitating the Great Depression. By also creating the Federal Deposit Insurance Corporation, the Act stopped the speculation and the bank runs that created the Great Depression. In short, the Glass-Steagall Act protected investors and depositors (property owners) from wild speculation.[72]

The Financial Services Modernization Act of 1999 (FSMA), repealed the regulatory protections of the Glass-Steagall Act, unleashing opportunists of all ilk to start milking the system and massively increasing the sub-prime mortgage market. Regular banks were merged with investment banks and became monoliths "too big to fail." Although Republicans sponsored the bill, President Clinton and key Democrats promoted it.[73] FSMA passed with nearly unanimous votes so both parties were to blame. Ironically, one of the few no votes was cast by Senator John McCain, who lost the 2008 election by being stereotyped with arch-villain George W. Bush who was widely accused of causing the collapse (American International Group).

Even the FSMA would not have caused the financial collapse by itself. The following year, the Commodity Futures Modernization Act of 2000 was passed with strong Democrat support. This act allowed credit derivatives or credit default swaps. Essentially they are side bets on the performance of the US mortgage markets and the solvency of some of the biggest financial institutions in the world. It is a form of legalized gambling that allows a person to wager on financial outcomes without actually having to buy the stocks and the bonds and the mortgages. Just as before the Great Depression, wild speculation was undermining the system.

Strongly supported by Congressman Barney Frank (D-MA) and Senator Chris Dodd, (D-CT), the act caused further corruption of Freddie Mac and Fanny Mae. Both Frank and Dodd adamantly defended these institutions when they were failing, claiming them to be healthy right up until collapse of the two institutions. They then stonewalled every effort by Republicans, including 2008 presidential candidate John McCain, from taking corrective action until it was too late.

There is one more big factor that led to the 2008 financial collapse; the AIG (American International Group, Inc.) Insurance Company. AIG insured the credit default swaps guaranteeing the value of the swaps in case of default, allowing huge profits for AIG and the speculators. The problem; AIG did not have to put up any capital to back up its swap guarantees as long as it maintained a triple-A credit rating. In other words, there was nothing to back up its default guarantees. AIG was not regulated so there was nothing to protect the homeowner, the bank depositors, stockholders, or investment firms. In other words, there was no property right that protected all these people and institutions from the unscrupulous actions of AIG and the big investment firms. When AIG lost its triple-A rating, the fraud was exposed and the entire financial crises collapsed like dominos.[74]   As this book went to press, the Senate had just passed the 1,500 page financial reform bill (S. 3217) on May 21, 2010. In promoting the bill President Obama used the opportunity to demonize Wall Street specifically and capitalism in general. Certainly, Wall Street needs to be regulated, but Congress specifically, and the federal regulatory system in general are equally guilty. That is no surprise. The demonization is purely political, designed to bolster Obama's flagging popularity, win votes for progressive liberals in November, force Republicans to vote no, and justify politicized regulations on the financial industry. An additional fallout is that it creates class warfare; something that progressive liberals do at every opportunity.

The bill creates a $50 billion fund to bail out financial institutions "too big to fail" when these institutions make bad decisions that would cause their failure if they were not bailed out. All this fund does is encourage big institutions to take big risks because they know they will be bailed out if their bad decisions blow up in their face. It favors the big firms at the expense of the smaller institutions. Although the $50 billion is to come out of the banking system, not the taxpayer, the taxpayer ultimately picks up the tab in higher fees.

The proposed legislation does not break up the "too big to fail" institutions into smaller firms. Small firms can be allowed to fail when they make bad decision, without causing a catastrophic failure of the entire financial system. So while demonizing the financial sector publically, President Obama and Congress are actually protecting the big institutions from the consequences of future bad decisions. [75] Senator Judd Gregg (R-NH) warned that the consumer protection agency created by the bill is "going to become an agency that defines lending on social justice purposes instead of safety and soundness purposes."[76] In other words, it promotes the same failed policy that the Community Reinvestment Act of 1977 that provided the first domino of the 2008 financial collapse.

Although much needed new regulations are in the legislation that controls the derivatives market, they are apparently written in a way that favors foreign markets. If correct, it provides incentives for financial institutions to move from New York City overseas. While there is little question that stronger regulations are needed that improve transparency, the way they are written seems to be tilted in favor of a few big institutions.[77] At the same time the loose wording about transparency could allow the federal government the right to access everyone's financial records. This will become clearer with time.

Fifth, the absence of *any* regulation of Fanny Mae and Freddy Mac is a glaring omission designed to protect the two institutions that played key roles in the 2008 financial collapse. Senator Gregg calls the omission of Fanny and Freddy "almost malfeasance of a criminal level."[78] As such, it will greatly increase the chance for another financial collapse. It is less clear (at this writing) how the new regulations will affect insurers like AIG, whose lack of capitalization was the final straw in the 2008 financial collapse.[79] However, unless the proposed legislation forces these insurers to become capitalized, more serious problems are inevitable.

Sixth, the consumer protection section of the bill would create a huge new federal bureaucracy at a time when the federal government should be contracting, not expanding.

Finally, the U.S. Securities and Exchange Commission (SEC) charged Goldman Sachs of fraud. Candidate Obama received one million dollars in campaign contributions from Goldman Sachs during his campaign and has hired numerous former Goldman Sachs employees into the White House. There is nothing wrong with the contributions, nor the hiring of so many high ranking Goldman employees to the White House. However, Minnesota political science advisor Prof. Lawrence Jacobs observed, "Almost everything the White House has done has been haunted by the personnel and money of Goldman" and triggered "suspicion that the White House was pulling its punches of deference to Goldman and its war chest."[80] This is not limited to the Obama administration. There has been a revolving door between Goldman and the White House for two decades. Just what the SEC charges will eventually reveal may actually involve several administrations.

This only touches on the machinations and deals being made within Wall Street and Congress. There are admittedly gaping holes in this analysis. Nonetheless, it is now clear that the big winners under the Obama administration are the "poor," unions, and big banks. The big losers are small business and the middle/upper income classes. They are being fleeced in order to redistribute their income to the winners, just as candidate Obama promised before the 2008 elections. That is social justice in action.

The point is that the fundamental premise behind the Rule of Law and private property rights was shattered by crooks, an incredibly corrupt Congress and a mix of greed and Rousseau socialism. The final insult is Congress. Although Congress accepts none of the responsibility for precipitating the crisis, it was the corruption of both parties that allowed the financial crisis to happen. *It would not, could not have happened without Congress.* The critical importance of this will become clear in a future chapter.

Plundering America by Law

When the Rule of Law is not used to protect individual life, liberty and property, Bastiat claims it becomes perverted, "used by the unscrupulous who wish, without risk, to exploit the person, liberty and property of others." In the process, the law converts *"plunder into a right, in order to protect plunder. And it [converts] lawful defense* [of life, liberty, and property] *into a crime, in order to punish lawful defense*…and *treats the victim—when he defends himself—as a criminal."*[81] (Italics added)

Rousseau bases his socialistic model upon the right of the government to force a person to adhere to the general will, which of course is defined by the elite and power brokers of society. The government becomes superior to the individual in all matters and ceases to be "of the people, by the people and for the people." If the government passes a law that harms the owners, then the owners automatically become criminals if they attempt to protect their property, or use it in a way that may be lawful and proper for other citizens. The law becomes arbitrary and capricious in its application.

Tragically, this is just the beginning of the vicious cycle of plunder. This plundering is not limited to progressive liberals. When unjustly plundered, people fight back. "Thus," explains Bastiat, "when plunder is organized by law for the profit of those who make the law, all the plundered classes try somehow to enter…into the making of laws."[82] In other words, once the law allows anyone to plunder once they are in power, then plundering becomes universal. Thousands and thousands of lobbyists assault congressional offices every day to lobby for laws that will benefit them at the expense of others.

When everyone wants to share in the plunder, the democratic process devolves into a madness whereby "men seek to balance their conflicting interests by universal plunder… As soon as the plundered classes gain political power, they…do not abolish legal plunder. Instead they emulate their evil predecessors by participating in this legal plunder, even though it is against their own interests."[83]

Hence, nothing really changes when the Republicans gain control from the Democrats or the Democrats from the Republicans. It creates partisan politics where the interests of the party come before the interests of the people. What is different in 2010 is that the Congress and White House are now controlled by radical progressive liberals for the first time in American history. For the first time Americans are finally seeing the incredibly dangerous goals of the Rousseau progressive agenda that has been attacking the U.S. Constitution for a 100 years.

Bastiat explains this degeneration further. As various factions grasp political power to plunder for themselves, the law becomes vicious and destructive:

As long as it is admitted that the law may be diverted from its true purpose—that it may violate property instead of protecting it—then everyone will want to participate in making the law, either to protect himself against plunder or to use it for plunder. *Political questions will always be prejudicial, dominant, and all absorbing. There will be fighting at the door of the Legislative Place, and the struggle within will be no less furious…* Is there any need to offer proof that *this odious perversion of the law is a perpetual source of hatred and discord; that it tends to destroy society itself?* [84] (Italics added)

This then, is the ultimate damnation of Rousseau progressive liberalism. Bastiat's conclusion cannot be denied in American politics today. It is right in front of our faces in the deep political divisions and vitriolic hatred that now characterize the American culture in the twenty-first century. Vicious political, racial and economic infighting is tearing America asunder. Polls have found that President Obama is the most divisive president in United States history.[85] Rather than bringing equality, the "social justice" demanded by Rousseau progressive liberals in general and the Obama administration and congressional leadership in particular, will inevitably paralyze and destroy America.

It is already happening. An April 22, 2010 Fox News Poll found that 57 percent of Americans is the biggest threat to the future compared to only 26 percent who believed big business was the greatest threat.[86] An April 18, 2010 Pew Research Center Poll found that nearly 80 percent of Americans were frustrated or angry with the federal government.[87]

Americans are seeing that the federal government is threatening financial solvency through reckless borrowing and increasingly denying personal liberty. At the same time, a smaller minority want the federal government to give them even more of what belongs to "others." This dog-eat-dog democracy is a direct result of the social justice philosophy of progressivism. Our founding fathers understood this unfortunate truth. That is why James Madison wrote in the *Federalist Papers 10*:

Hence it is that such democracies have ever been spectacles of turbulence and contention; have ever been found incompatible with personal securities or the right of property; and have in general been as short in their lives as they have been violent in their deaths. (Italics added)

Madison clearly identifies why Rousseau's model cannot work. It factionalizes an otherwise united people into special interest groups, each fighting to either take another's rights or property (including money) for their own purpose, or defending their own rights or property from the other group. Instead of unifying the whole, as Rousseau postulates, his model invariably creates hostility and division within the whole, ultimately tearing itself apart— just as is happening in the United States at the start of the twenty-first century.

A pure democracy is nothing more than two wolves and a lamb voting on what to have for dinner. Almost all politicians and national leaders have told Americans so many times that the U.S. is a democracy that they now believe it and are acting like a democracy. However, we are not a democracy; we were created to be a self-governing Constitutional *republic*. Because America is acting like a democracy based on Rousseau ideology, it is devouring itself through plundering. And, Americans are paying high taxes to do it to themselves!

4

The High Cost of
Rousseau Socialism

Our analysis strongly suggests that the U.S. government is, indeed, bankrupt, insofar as it will be unable to pay its creditors, who, in this context, are current and future generations to whom it has explicitly or implicitly promised future net payments of various kinds.[88]

— Federal Reserve Bank of St. Louis

ROUSSEAU SOCIALISM OF THE PROGRESSIVE LIBERALS IS NOT CHEAP. For the past fifty years or more, historical records show there has been a systematic effort to pass a host of Rousseau socialist laws that increase the regulatory burden to staggering levels. The IRS reports that tax collections went up from $187 billion in 1969, at the beginning of President Johnson's Great Society Program, to $1.25 trillion in 2001 and $2.5 trillion in 2008, the last year records are available. Most of the increase was due to burgeoning social and environmental programs, as well as the wars in Afghanistan and Iraq.

In 1900, before socialism began seriously to creep into the federal budget, Americans paid a total effective tax rate of only 5.7 percent. By 2000, the total effective tax rate for the 50th percentile of taxpayers surged to 33.3 percent.[89]

Although it dropped to 30.0 percent by 2005[90] because of the Bush tax cuts, those cuts will be allowed to expire at the start of 2011. Nearly a third of our salary and our lives go to feeding the Rousseau socialist behemoth that was created in the twentieth century. In 2002 alone, $2.7 trillion was budgeted for mandatory social programs—not touchable by Congress.[91]

Another way of looking at the impact of Rousseau socialism is the cost of regulation. Regulations cost $869 billion just to administer in 2002.[92] That means every family of four pays nearly $12,000 a year to maintain the regulatory structure in the U.S. Not only is this an incredibly enormous drain on the family budget, it is a huge drain on the nation's economy. Direct and indirect costs of regulation add up to slightly less than 40 percent of a family's gross income.

However, that is not the end of it. There is also a lost opportunity cost; businesses never created or products never developed because regulation hinders their creation or stifles the creativity of individuals. As discussed in Chapter 3, regulations are needed, and many of them do provide a very positive benefit to society. However, those based on "positive" rights rarely accomplish their goals and generally cost more than they save. The net result of Rousseau socialism is a huge drag on the economy that is much bigger than most people imagine.

Importance of Legally Protected Property Rights

Although regulations are very expensive, few people understand that there is another cost that dwarfs those mentioned above. In his compelling book *The Mystery of Capital*, Hernando de Soto accurately identifies formal private property rights as the key to reducing poverty and producing wealth. Legal title to use property represents equity. In turn, this equity can become collateral to create the capital needed to start, expand or buy into a business which then yields income and wealth. The amount of equity can be stunning, even in the United States. The average net worth of home-owning Americans is $132,100 verses $4,200 for American renters—30 times less!

True, other factors also play into these numbers, but property remains the key factor in creating wealth.[93]

The developing nations of the world perhaps provide the most striking example of how socialism destroys the wealth-building capability of property. In these nations, the simple act of legally transferring the title to property is very costly. It can take years, even decades, because of a sea of bureaucratic corruption and socialist regulations. Few people in these nations have the time or resources to own property legally. This "extralegal" property therefore has no legal asset value. De Soto calls this dead capital.

De Soto has shown that the total value of this kind of extralegal property within developing nations and former communist countries is at least *$9.3 trillion*! This is ninety-three times as much as all development assistance to the developing nations from all advanced countries during the past thirty years.[94] Incredibly, there would be *no need for development assistance* if these poverty-stricken people could have access to the asset value of their property that is presently dead capital.

Tragically, the United Nations and the international community are presently putting together a series of international treaties in the name of "sustainable development." Sustainable development is based on Rousseau ideology that ostensibly will get them out of poverty while living sustainably with the environment. However, the entire plan is structured around the Rousseau model of government control of property rights. In doing so, it systematically prevents citizens in the third world nations from ever attaining the formal property rights that will actually give them wealth and liberty. To be blunt; rather than decreasing poverty, sustainable development is a model for *increasing* poverty.

When strangling socialist regulations encumber property rights, there is little to no equity, and therefore little to no capital with which to create wealth. Without wealth, a nation cannot protect the environment. A family whose primary focus is to put food on the table is not going to be interested in protecting the environment. The contrast between the United States, Europe and the Third World is striking. The U.S. has some of the best defined property rights in the world and its citizens have an average income of almost $47,000. In contrast, the average income for socialist Europeans is only $34,000 and that for Third World Nations is slightly more than $1,000.

Although Rousseau progressive liberals would vehemently say they do not go far enough, the U.S. has one of the best environmental records in the world. So do the socialist Europeans. Both pay a very heavy price. Even so, these developed nations impose their very expensive and counter productive altruistic values on the people of the Third World nations. At the same time the first world nations do not provide them with the fundamental tools to create the wealth to pay for it. Paul Driessen calls it eco-imperialism in his book of the same name.[95]

Creating Third-World Conditions

Even more important, a planned society ignores the basis of the entire national economy—natural resources. The planner assigns a cog (a citizen) to develop a resource somehow, but does not provide an incentive to develop it cost effectively or efficiently. Nothing epitomizes this principle more than the former Soviet Union whose central planners could never provide the vision and the will to develop its vast natural resources. The nation was doomed to failure. Yet, our Rousseau progressive liberals are determined to recreate the same Soviet model.

Although the development of natural resources (agriculture, mining, oil, forestry and others) makes up only a small portion of the gross domestic product, *nothing* else in the economic structure can exist without them. They are the foundation of our entire economy. All the modern conveniences Americans take for granted, including computers and synthetic clothing, find their origin *in* the ground or *on* the ground. There are no exceptions. Everything we possess and use originally comes from natural resources. Even stock market speculation ultimately depends on natural resources to create real value.

The myriad of environmental laws, for instance, are building the same cumbersome bureaucracy that prevents third-world nations from building wealth. The Endangered Species Act, wetlands regulations, the Clean Water Initiative and a host of other environmental laws have one thing in common: Government control of the property rights for developing natural resources. Every environmental law currently on the books is based on the Rousseau model. These laws strip or plunder the value of property and resources from property owners. It is harming, even destroying the economic foundation of cities, counties and rural communities as the government transfers tens of billions, perhaps hundreds of billions of dollars of property value to itself via regulation.

The plundering of rural America has gotten so bad that a *Wall Street Journal* (*WSJ*) editorial on July 26, 2001, called it "rural cleansing." The *WSJ* claimed that this is the intent of the environmentalists: "The goal of many environmental groups…is no longer to protect nature. It is to expunge humans from the countryside" by suing or lobbying the "government into declaring rural areas off-limits to people who live and work there." This can be done outright or by having "restrictions placed on the land that either render it unusable or persuade owners to leave of their own accord."[96]

Worse, progressive environmental legal firms like the Sierra Club Legal Defense Fund use the Equal Access to Justice Act (EAJA) to bring billions of dollars into their coffers in lawsuits against federal agencies. For instance, recent studies by Wyoming attorney Karen Budd-Falen found that the Western Regions of the U.S. Forest Service alone paid out over $1 *billion* in EAJA funds between 2003 and 2005.[97] These progressive environmental organizations get paid by the taxpayer for destroying the lives of rural citizens trying to make a living. Although the progressives will probably not allow it to pass, a new bill, H.R. 4717, the Open EAJA Act of 2010 has been introduced to stop this abuse.

Anti-property rights activists use Rousseau's "perceived good result" or the "public good" to attack the basis for constitutional property rights. Since the 1970s, activist courts have been systematically ruling that the use of private property and "the rights of the individual" endanger the rights of all the people. On the other hand, why should the last owners of wetlands, endangered species habitat, beautiful scenery or many other environmental and social benefits, have to shoulder the entire cost of protection or provision when the problem was created by the activities of thousands of other people before them? Most Americans would say that they should not. Yet, that is exactly what is happening to tens of thousands of Americans.

The assault on rural America and its natural resource industries is not only threatening rural citizens, it is also threatening the American middle class which makes up urban America. Increasingly, manufacturers purchase basic raw materials abroad. In turn, jobs associated with their production also shift overseas. Multinational corporations become "transnational" and consider themselves above the law—bound only by laws they heavily influence in the Third World nations to which they move. They no longer consider themselves "American."

The shift of U.S. manufacturing overseas is eliminating the U.S. middle class. Economic analyst and investment manager, John Mauldin, warns that the jobless recovery is due to a major restructuring underway—the permanent relocation of workers from some industries to others—in the U.S. economy.[98] Increases in productivity played a large part in the jobless economic recovery of 2004. Contrary to the belief of many, free trade is not the enemy they decry. In the early 1990s trade exports supported 7 million jobs in the U.S. That increased to 20 million jobs by 2004.[99]

Thomas Sowell, on the other hand, found that increases in productivity should work to *keep* jobs in America. "An international study found the average productivity of the Indian economy to be 15% of that of American workers. In other words, if you paid the average Indian worker one-fifth of what you paid the average American worker, it would cost you more to get the job done in India," said Sowell.[100] Increases in productivity therefore should not translate into American jobs going to Third World nations. Yet, they are. The enormous burden of regulations more than tips the balance in favor of moving off shore. It is not free trade that's the problem, as liberals often claim. Rather, it is the massive burden of regulations and controlled trade created by the progressive liberals that are responsible. Ironically, the global financial cartel calls this "free trade."

The High Cost of Rousseau Socialism

Unneeded regulations have increased the cost of labor and business in relation to overseas competition. This forces economic restructuring and the corresponding loss of jobs to third-world nations; whose citizens are locked into low paying jobs due to a lack of formal property rights. As Hernando de Soto notes, if the Third World nations had formal property rights, they would build their own wealth, the average income for their citizens would increase, and the transnational corporations would no longer have an economic benefit to relocate from the U.S. to the developing nations. Increasing wealth of present-day Third World nations would in turn provide improving export markets to U.S. products.

There's more. The increasingly borderless world pits the U.S. economy against other nations in an open game of manufacturing warfare. At the same time, the U.S. finances the twin demons of federal spending and trade deficits through debt. In turn, the federal debt competes directly with the private sector for money that might otherwise go into capital expansion and job creation in urban America. The huge trade deficits move this same capital—and the manufacturing it creates—overseas.

The consequence of what has happened the past 70 years is shocking. The official national debt has increased from $3 million in 1913 (the year the Federal Reserve was created), to $250 billion in 1950, to less than $3 trillion in 1980,[101] to $13 trillion in 2010.

Congress just raised the limit of our national debt by $1.9 *trillion* to $14.3 *trillion* which we will reach after the 2010 elections.[102] The 2009 Gross Domestic Product was $14.3 *trillion*, which is down slightly from 2008.[103] At this rate our national debt will exceed our GDP sometime in 2011. This will give the U.S a debt to equity ratio of over 100 percent. In the business world, anything over 70 percent represents very serious trouble for the company.

Even that is not a complete picture. When unfunded liabilities are included, such as future Social Security and Medicaid payments, the debt jumps to $107 *trillion*. That equals more than $347,000 dollars per citizen.[104] For a family of four that is almost $1.4 *million* per family! To say that we are living beyond our means is the understatement of the twenty-first century.

There is no way an average family could pay that debt even if every cent of their income went to pay off the debt over several generations.

The United States government cannot pay it off either. The Federal Reserve Bank of St. Louis gave this gut-wrenching conclusion in 2006:

> Our analysis strongly suggests that the U.S. government is, indeed, bankrupt, insofar as it will be unable to pay its creditors, who, in this context, are current and future generations to whom it has explicitly or implicitly promised future net payments of various kinds.[105]

The Federal Reserve Bank of St. Louis wrote this in 2006. The amount added since then is staggering. President Bush added more to the debt than any president before him. In his first term alone, Bush added $1.9 *trillion*. In Obama's *first year*, he added $1.6 *trillion*.[106] The expected increase in debt for 2010 is another $1.4 *trillion* and for 2011, $1.6 *trillion*. Projections put Obama's total debt increase during his first term at $4-6 *trillion*[107] with future obligations of $10 trillion in ten years.

The 2011 budget does not even include the expected long-term deficits if health care and cap and trade (global warming) legislation passes. In a devious slight of hand, Obama's 2011 budget includes increased short-term revenues as if health care is really going to be deficit neutral, and cap and trade legislation is already passed, signed and bringing in short-term revenue. Otherwise, the 2011 would have been over $2 *trillion* dollars!

President Obama created a Debt Commission in April, 2010 to recommend how to reduce the deficit and National Debt. However, the commission is loaded with progressives who are adverse to cutting federal programs and expenses. It is generally assumed that the commission will most likely recommend sweeping increases in taxes that could increase everyone's tax load by as much as 10-20 percent. Most analysts believe President Obama created the commission to hide behind when he calls for increasing taxes in December 2010, breaking his campaign promise for no new taxes for those making less than $250,000 a year.[108]

The Debt Commissions tax recommendation will probably be a VAT tax (Value added tax). As the name implies, a VAT tax taxes ever step of production so the tax is cumulative. Everyone pays it, including the poor. Europe heavily depends on the VAT tax which adds huge revenues to their bloated governments, but stifles their productivity.[109]

What add insult to injury is the huge salary and benefit discrepancy between federal employees and private sector employees who pay for the bloated federal salaries. The average annual wage for a private sector employee in 2008 was $50,028 compared to $79,197 for a civilian federal employee. When employer-paid benefits are added it gets worse.[110] Wages and benefits for private sector employees averaged $59,909 in 2008 while that of federal civilian employees averaged *more than twice* that; $119,982. The federal government and many progressive state governments like California are bloated, overpaid and on a spending binge they refuse to reign in. They are literally out of control. This must change if America is to survive as a free nation.

Most analysts blame political cowardice and irresponsibility for the shameful mess we are in. Most of it is due to the cumulative effects of the positive rights socialist programs passed by Rousseau progressive liberals over the decades. It cannot be sustained. There are only two ways the national debt can be paid; by default or inflation. Historically, bad debt like this has been paid by deliberately inflating the dollar—which in effect is a huge hidden tax.

Few people understand that the purchasing power of $1 in 1900 is now worth about 3 cents.[111] In other words, the bonds and other securities sold, to say China for example, at 2010 dollars will be paid back in much cheaper inflated dollars. China takes a hit, as do all American's who have to buy much more expensive products. Worse, monetary actions taken by the Obama administration have caused many analysts to predict hyperinflation which would likely make the U.S. dollar worthless.

The alternative to inflation, or a long-term result of hyperinflation, would be to default on the debt and the collapse of US dollar. The dollar would become essentially worthless. What is concerning more and more analysts and citizens is that the monetary policies of the past two presidents (actually all of them for the past 100 years; even Ronald Reagan), seem to actually be designed to collapse the U.S. dollar.

Fortunately, a March 23, 2010 Fox Opinion Poll found that 79 percent of the American people believe the economy could collapse. It is fortunate only because we can't start solving the problem until the American people realize there is one. They now do, and at least have an inkling of what the problem is. Two-thirds of all Americans think the federal government is too big and is restricting personal freedoms. The same percentage also does not believe the Obama administration has a good plan for solving our financial crisis.[112]

Ironically, while only 24 percent of Americans believe the Democrats have clear plans to solve the financial crisis, only 16 percent think the Republicans have a good plan.[113] The key to the problem is progressive liberalism in both parties. Yet, the poll results clearly show that the American people still do not understand this. What is worse, time may be running out. The leadership of the progressive liberals has been deliberately planning for decades to collapse the American system.

Collapsing the System

While such a pessimistic conclusion is not certain, there is evidence to support those concerns. Saul Alinsky's 1971 *Rules for Radicals* is generally accepted as the blueprint progressive liberals use to radically change American culture[114] to a positive rights ideology. The twelve civilization destroying rules call for lying, intimidation, ridicule, threats, blackmail, and even mild violent action.[115] Alinsky advocated that the end result justifies using any means. He once said, "The first step in community organization is community disorganization.

Alinsky called for creating a mass army to intimidate the government and society into capitulating to their demands.[116] "The only place you really have consensus is where you have totalitarianism," claimed Alinsky.[117] In other words, he advocates a totalitarian government. Is Alinsky's belief so farfetched? Obama's manufacturing Czar, Ron Bloom proclaimed that "We know that the free market is nonsense…. We know this is largely about power, that it's an adults only, no limit game. We kind of agree with Mao [Zedong] that political power comes largely from the barrel of a gun."[118]

Community and union organizing use this strategy in their effort. Groups like environmental organizations, the Association of Community Organizations for Reform Now (ACORN) and the Service Employees International Union (SEIU) have been *extremely* successful in their attacks on American institutions.[119] Both ACORN and SEIU have used intimidating, but legal protests of banking institutions to force them to grant what have become toxic mortgages to people who could not afford them. When they were only partially successful they turned to protesting the homes of senior banking officials. They were highly successful when terrorized family members demanded their spouses give in to the demands of ACORN or SEIU.

These intimidating practices are still used. On May 16, 2010 fourteen busloads carrying 500 plus angry SEIU union members descended on the home of Greg Baer, the deputy general counsel for corporate law at Bank of America. Located in a normally quiet neighborhood the mob hurled angry epithets. The only family member home was the Baer's terrified 14 year old son who locked himself in the bathroom. Nina Easton, a neighbor across the street said:

> …this event would accurately be called a "protest" if it were taking place at, say, a bank or the U.S. Capitol. But when hundreds of loud and angry strangers are descending on your family, your children, and your home, a more apt description of this assemblage would be "mob." Intimidation was the whole point of this exercise, and it worked-even on the police. A trio of officers who belatedly answered our calls confessed a fear that arrests might "incite" these trespassers. [120]

This was not a media event. No media were notified. It was designed specifically to create terror, so SEIU did not want the media to record it. Nina just happened to be the Washington Bureau Chief at *Fortune* magazine and was able to get the event video taped. The video showed an angry, barely constrained mob trespassing on the Baer property right up to their front door. The police refused to intervene for fear of further inciting the trespassers to violence. That left the SEIU mob free to terrorize other homes before they quit for the day. The police did nothing to protect its citizens.

In his early life, President Obama has actually represented ACORN and helped train activists as well. Likewise, he has always been united with SEIU in their goals.[121] He proved his faithfulness to unions when he gave unions' preferential treatment over investors when bailing out General Motors and Chrysler.

When Tea Party protests in Town Hall meetings became embarrassing to President Obama, Health and Human Services Secretary Kathleen Sebelius called SEIU to solicit their help to neutralize accusations and perceived distortions from opponents of ObamaCare. The next day the White House issued a "battle plan" to Senate Democrats to quell the protests by "punch[ing] back twice as hard."[122] Just as *Rules for Radicals* advises, SEIU sent large numbers of counter-demonstrators to intimidate and speak in favor of ObamaCare at several Town Hall meetings. At a St. Louis Town Hall meeting, four SEIU members surrounded and physically attacked ObamaCare protester Kenneth Gladney.[123] Video of the attack showed Gladney's SEIU attackers (wearing SEIU shirts) violently kicking him in the head and back. Even though the attack was violent and Gladney was only a 130 pound diabetic, the SEIU thugs were never prosecuted.[124]

To his credit, Alinsky claimed he never wanted to create demagogues and hated the fascist model that his *Rules for Radicals* inevitably created.[125] He believed that when a disenfranchised group achieved the power it wanted it should be willing to share that power within the existing structure. In fact, in his twisted way, Alinsky believed he was actually following the Founding Fathers.[126] He was very discouraged when some of his groups became demagogues and racial bigots in their own right.

Enter Richard Cloward and Frances Piven. Radical socialists at Columbia University, professors Richard Cloward and his wife Frances Piven wrote a 1966 article titled "The Weight of the Poor: A Strategy to End Poverty" in *The Nation*.[127] Now known as the Cloward-Piven Strategy, the strategy took off like wildfire among the progressive liberals. Using Alinsky as their inspiration, the Cloward-Piven strategy "seeks to hasten the fall of capitalism by overloading the government bureaucracy with a flood of impossible demands, thus pushing society into crisis and economic collapse." [128] The strategy calls for creating a massive movement so that the rest of society fears them.

Cloward-Piven initially wanted to collapse the welfare system by overwhelming welfare rolls. The result would be "a profound financial and political crisis" that would unleash "powerful forces…for major economic reform at the national level." They would do this by the "collapse of current financing arrangements," thereby creating a "climate of militancy" and fear.[129] The strategy did this by:

> Carefully orchestrated media campaigns, carried out by friendly, leftwing journalists, would float the idea of "a federal program of income redistribution," in the form of a guaranteed living income for all – working and non-working people alike. Local officials would clutch at this idea like drowning men to a lifeline. They would apply pressure on Washington to implement it. With every major city erupting into chaos, Washington would have to act.[130]

The strategy was extremely successful right from the start. Cloward and Piven recruited an organizer named George Wiley to lead their movement. In 1967, he created the National Welfare Rights Organization (NWRO). His very militant followers invaded welfare offices around the United States, sometimes violently. Social workers were always intimidated. Other tactics involved signing up people who were eligible, but not on welfare. They intentionally wanted to overload the system.[131] One of their early targets was New York City. *The New York Times* commented on September 27, 1970,

There have been sit-ins in legislative chambers, including a United States Senate committee hearing, mass demonstrations of several thousand welfare recipients, school boycotts, picket lines, mounted police, tear gas, arrests - and, on occasion, rock-throwing, smashed glass doors, overturned desks, scattered papers and ripped-out phones.[132]

The protests were so successful that one out of two residents was on welfare by the early 1970s. Just as planned, New York City was overwhelmed and was forced to declare bankruptcy in 1975. New York City Mayor Rudy Giuliani attempted to expose them in the late 1990s and again in 2009-2010 when ACORN became front-page news. He accused them of deliberate economic sabotage. Not surprisingly, the mainstream media turned a deaf ear.[133]

The strategy has proved to be so successful that Cloward and Piven began to use the strategy on other fronts as well. In 1982 they, along with their supporters, branched into voting rights movement. The Association of Community Organizations for Reform Now (ACORN) grew out of George Wiley's NWRO. ACORN was created by Wade Rathke, who was a NWRO organizer and a protégé of Wiley. Rathke also organized the militant Students for a Democratic Society (SDS) during the same period. ACORN has morphed into hundreds of front groups, all of which have used the same militant/violent tactics as NWRO did in New York City.[134] When ACORN had to close its doors in early 2010 in many cities because of the 2009 video scandal, it merely moved its activities into these other front groups.

In summary, debt and money speculation now sustains the U.S. economy. The foundation of that money—natural resources and manufacturing—is rapidly shifting from the U.S. to third-world nations where it is controlled by transnational corporations and global financial institutions. The U.S. produces very little to support the middle class. Both rural residents and urbanites are being hurt. Urbanites just don't realize it yet.

At the same time hundreds of highly militant, sometimes violent organizations like ACORN and SEIU purpose to collapse the financial and social system of America. They intend to institute an entirely different system of government, most closely resembling fascism and communism. They are being protected by Rousseau progressive liberals in Congress, the White House the courts and the media.

How could this happen? Why aren't Americans being told? Something is terribly wrong. Part II of this book defines how powerful global institutions have systematically corrupted the Locke-based United States Constitution in order to create the Rousseau-based all-powerful federal government; all without Americans understanding what was happening.

Part II

How Did
It Happen?

5

The Global Agenda

...the powers of financial capitalism had another far-reaching aim, nothing less than to create a world system of financial control in private hands able to dominate the political system of each country and the economy of the world as a whole.[135]

— Carroll Quigley, *Tragedy and Hope*

AS AMERICA SLIPS FURTHER AND FURTHER from the rock solid principles of freedom enshrined in the Locke model of life, liberty, and property, it is moving toward Rousseau socialism where the state controls everything. Over time, men have perverted the purpose of the law—to protect the god-given unalienable rights of individual people—into an instrument of plunder—of what rightfully belongs to the individual. This perversion of the law has turned otherwise law-abiding citizens into criminals if they attempt to defend their constitutional unalienable rights. Class warfare and a host of factions have been created and are tearing the heart out of America.

How did this happen? More importantly, what can be done to reverse it? Part II details how it happened with numerous examples illustrating its tragic effect on American lives and communities. Part III will provide a solution. Many people reading Part II will have difficulty believing that the deliberate efforts of a few very powerful men and their families could gradually manipulate and generally control the culture and the lives of all Americans. Yet, it is a historical fact based on volumes of information of which the following provides but a brief summary.

Global Financial Imperialism

There are those who, through manipulation, coercion or blackmail, have sought to establish global control through a number of U.S. and international institutions. They may be progressive liberals or they may be capitalists, albeit a form a capitalism that drives a stake through the heart of free market enterprise. There is strong evidence that they have systematically used Rousseau progressive liberalism to dumb down the American people to make them more receptive to central control—with this cartel at the helm of power. Ironically, it is the intellectual elite of America, especially in higher education, who have fallen into this trap the easiest. Vladimir Lenin called them useful idiots.

Professor Carroll Quigley, a Professor of History at Harvard and Georgetown University, was an insider with these power brokers and wrote a detailed book about their agenda in a thirteen-hundred-page magnum opus he titled *Tragedy & Hope, A History of the World in Our Time* in 1966. Quigley is considered by many authorities to be the quintessential historian of the twentieth century. He admitted that a global network or cartel existed, which he studied in depth:

> *There does exist*, and has existed for a generation, an *international Anglophile network* which operates, to some extent, in the way the radical Right believes the Communists act. In fact, this network, which we may identify as the *Round Table Groups*, has no aversion to cooperating with the Communists, or any other groups, and frequently does so. I know of the operations of this network because *I have studied it for twenty years and was permitted for two years, in the early 1960's, to examine its papers and secret records.* I have no aversion to it or to most of its aims and have, for much of my life, been close to it and so many of its instruments.[136] (Italics added)

Quigley was included in the inner circle of this elite group. He even agreed with their goals and was given access to their secret records. This isn't speculation or some kind of conspiracy theory, it is first-hand knowledge. As a Harvard and Georgetown University history professor, his credentials cannot be questioned, although his sanity could be questioned. Just what does this group of high rollers plan for the world? Quigley also answers that question:

> ...the powers of financial capitalism had another far-reaching aim, nothing less than to *create a world system of financial control in private hands able to dominate the political system of each country and the economy of the world as a whole*. This system was to be *controlled in a feudalist fashion by the central banks of the world acting in concert* by secret agreements arrived at in frequent private meetings and conferences. The apex of the system was to be the *Bank for International Settlements in Basel, Switzerland*, a private bank owned and controlled by the world's central banks which were themselves private corporations. *Each central bank... sought to dominate its government* by its ability to control Treasury loans, to manipulate foreign exchanges, to influence the level of the economic activity in the country, and to influence cooperative politicians by subsequent economic rewards in the business world.[137] (Italics added)

Quigley details the financial and political exploits of this small cartel of globalists to manipulate national and global events to their own advantage. He claims this cartel even controls the Federal Reserve, the privately controlled central bank in the United States. It is nothing less than nouveau financial imperialism and has very little to do with true capitalism. In a second book entitled, *The Anglo-American Establishment,* Quigley goes on to say, "this group is...one of the most important historical facts of the twentieth century."[138] The actions of this group have benefited only themselves, not the world's citizens, and certainly not American citizens. Quigley notes that the efforts of the group have "been a disaster to our way of life."[139] Yet, very few people are even aware this group exists, let alone the huge negative impact this cartel has on their lives.

By the beginning of the twenty-first century, everything Quigley said the global cartel planned to do has almost been accomplished. The Bank for International Settlements (BIS) was working closely with the UN to restructure the global financial architecture so the BIS could control the world at the international level.[140] Their goals include dividing the world into economic regions patterned after the European Union. This effort has been underway since the mid-1990s and formalized at the 2002 International Conference on Financing for Development in Monterrey Mexico.[141] While many are far from being politically viable, they include:

1. European Union—Europe; the admitted template for all the other regions.

2. Russian Federation—The old Soviet Union minus the East Bloc European nations. Formed in August, 2000.

3. ASEAN (Association of Southeast Asian Nations)—Southeast Asian nations plus China, Japan and South Korea as adjunct members. ASEAN members signed Declaration of ASEAN Concord II on October 6, 2003, which unites them into European Union like economic and military cooperation zone. Inclusion of China and Japan has been delayed primarily because Japan insists that the United States has some type of associative status. China refuses to allow this. There is also the Shanghai Cooperation Organization (SCO) linking China with Russia, Kazakhstan, Kyrgyzstan, Tajikistan and Uzbekistan. Neither will probably survive as they presently exist, but be called by a different name without the links to the Russian Federation.

4. AOSIS (Alliance of Small Island States)—The South Pacific Islands, most likely to eventually be led by Australia under a different name.

5. African Union—Formalized in August, 2002. However, this is likely to fail, resulting in two, possibly three economic regions making up Africa.

6. Arab League—While not yet designed to be an economic region, it is being actively discussed.

7. Free Trade Area of the Americas (FTAA)—Includes North and South America but has never been formalized.

    7a. North American Union—officially called the Security and Prosperity Partnership (SPP), it extended NAFTA into Mexico. The efforts were temporarily suspended following an uproar when investigators found long-term plans that were striking similar to the structure of the European Union.

    7b. Union of South American Nations—created in 2008, it is patterned after the European Union.

    7c. Central America Free Trade Agreement. Authorized in 2005, but will go nowhere.

The restructuring of the world would also include establishing a global tax to fund the UN and implementing a common accounting system for keeping the books of all nations and businesses. The books would then be open to the BIS and UN for oversight purposes. The only major failure of the United Nations International Conference on Financing for Development meeting came when President G. W. Bush refused to support the idea of a global tax. Instead he said the U.S. would provide an additional $5 billion to poor nations.

Joan Veon, a financial advisor who has attended hundreds of UN, BIS, World Bank, IMF and other meetings recently observed, "While the BIS has always been the focal point of central bank activity globally, it now is finalizing the structure Dr. Quigley wrote about. Over the years it has expanded to the point that *every aspect* of banking, finance, insurance, deposit insurance, and regulation now constitute its core workings." (Italics added)

Quigley's story gets even more bizarre. He wrote in a second book entitled, *The Anglo-American Establishment,* which was not published until after his death in 1977, "I have been told that the story I relate here would be better left untold, since it would provide ammunition for the enemies of what I admire. I do not share this view. The last thing I should wish is that anything I write could be used by the Anglophobes and isolationists of the *Chicago Tribune*. But I feel that the truth has a right to be told…"[142] He goes on to say, "It is not easy for an outsider to write the history of a secret group of this kind, but…it should be done, for this group *is…one of the most important historical facts of the twentieth century.*" (Italics added) He admits "In this group were persons whose lives have been a disaster to our way of life."[143] The front cover of the book shows the U.S. flag upside down—a sign of distress. It also shows the U.S. flag inside the British flag.

Quigley shares in *The Anglo-American Establishment* that the members of the organization call it "the Group," or "the Band, or simply "US."[144] Ironically, it was the various members of the Group that helped finance the writing of *The Anglo-American Establishment*, "…it would have been very difficult to write this book if I had not received a certain amount of assistance of a personal nature from persons close to the Group. For obvious reasons, I cannot reveal the names of such persons…"[145] Former Hoover Institute Research Fellow Antony Sutton, who has studied this agenda all of his life, agrees with Quigley. However, he claims the American players are called "the Order" because the majority of the players are members of the Order of the Skull and Bones of Yale University.[146]

While Quigley could not name the specific funders for the writing of his books, he does define the major families involved, "The French economy was dominated by three powers (Rothschild, Mirabaud, and Schneider); the German economy was dominated by two (I. G. Farben and Vereinigte Stahl Werke); the United States was dominated by two (Morgan and Rockefeller). Other countries, like Italy or Britain, were dominated by somewhat larger numbers."[147] The Group is principally made up of a powerful axis of financial and industrial people and families of Europe and the "Eastern Establishment"[148] of the United States. It all started with the banking influence on the industrial revolution and railroads. Says Quigley:

Rothschild interests came to dominate many of the railroads of Europe, while Morgan dominated at least 26,000 miles of American railroads. Such bankers went further than this. In return for flotations of securities of industry, they took seats on the boards of directors of industrial firms, as they had already done on commercial banks, savings banks, insurance firms, and finance companies. From these lesser institutions they funneled capital to enterprises which yielded control and away from those who resisted. *These firms were controlled through interlocking directorships, holding companies, and lesser banks.*[149] (Italics added)

In time they brought into their financial network the provincial banking centers, organized as commercial banks and savings banks, as well as insurance companies, to form all of these into single financial system on an international scale which manipulated the quantity and flow of money so that they were able to *influence, if not control, governments on one side and industries on the other.*[150] (Italics added)

The Eastern Establishment, Quigley affirms, "reflects one of the most powerful influences in the twentieth-century American and world history."[151] The who's who and the machinations of this group is fascinating, but beyond the scope of this book. As such, however, Quigley found that "The influence of these business leaders was so great that the Morgan and Rockefeller groups acting together, or even Morgan acting alone could have wrecked the economic system of the country merely by throwing securities on the stock market for sale.... Morgan came very close to it in precipitating the 'panic of 1907,' but they did not hesitate to wreck individual corporations, at the expense of the holders of common stocks, by driving them into bankruptcy."[152] As powerful as they are, however, they are not invincible:

In no country was the power of these great complexes paramount and exclusive, and in *no country were these powers able to control the situation to such a degree that they were able to prevent their own decline under the impact of world political and economic conditions,* but their ability to dominate their spheres is undeniable. In France, Rothschild and Schneider were not able to weather the assault of Hitler… in the United States, *Morgan was unable to prevent the economic swing from financial to monopoly capitalism, and yielded quite gracefully to the rising power of du Pont* [and Rockefeller]….But all these shifts of power within the individual economic systems indicate merely that individuals or groups are unable to maintain their positions in the complex flux of modern life, and *do not indicate any decentralization of control.*[153] (Italics added)

This admission by Quigley refutes the myth that the financial elites "control" the world in general and the United States specifically. They do not. If that were the case we would have a despotic world government already. But the cartel does wield incredible influence, made all the more powerful by progressive liberals whose emotional ideology make them amazingly easy to manipulate.

Even though the political and economic fortunes of individual families or groups wax and wane, the power of the Group or financial cartel continues to increase. While the BIS is the center of their power, the greatest financial power block today is Great Britain and the United States. It is known as the Anglo-American Establishment or Anglo-American Faction. Although England no longer has the global economic power it once had, its dominance as a global financial center in spite of the introduction of the much-glamorized euro is still all powerful.

Out of 48 international central banks, the Bank of England handles roughly 33 percent of foreign exchange turnover, or $1.4 trillion per day in early 2010.[154] London's slice of currency trading was equal to that of its three nearest rivals with the United States taking 16 percent, or $675 billion per day, Japan 9 percent and Singapore 6 percent.[155] Together, the U.S. and United Kingdom handle nearly half of all monetary exchanges in the world. Link that with the raw economic power of the U.S., and the Anglo-American axis is very powerful. Ironically, the British Empire is not dead. It has been transformed into financial imperialism .

Tongue-in-cheek, Quigley summarizes the reality and power of this open conspiracy:

The two ends of this English-speaking axis have sometimes been called, perhaps facetiously, the *English and American Establishments*. There is, however, a *considerable degree of truth behind the joke*, a truth which reflects a very real power structure. It is this power structure which the *Radical Right in the United States has been attacking for years in the belief that they are attacking the Communists*. This is particularly true when these attacks are directed, as they so frequently are at 'Harvard Socialism,' or at 'Left-wing newspapers' like *The New York Times* and the *Washington Post*, or at foundations and their dependent establishments, such as the Institute of International Education.[156] (Italics added)

In one sweeping statement Quigley implicates some of the faculty of Harvard and the left-wing newspapers like the *New York Times* and *Washington Post* as being part of this power structure. It is no small wonder publication of Quigley's book *Tragedy and Hope* ceased in 1968. It was even pulled from the bookshelves and library stacks after people had already purchased nine thousand copies.[157] Author Ted Flynn in *The Hope of the Wicked* explains why: "Quigley's book *Tragedy and Hope* was intended for an elite readership composed of scholars and network insiders. But unexpectedly it began to be quoted in the journals of the John Birch Society, which correctly had perceived that his work provided a valuable insight to the inner workings of a hidden power structure. That exposure triggered a large demand for the book by people who were opposed to the network...."[158]

In a personal letter by Quigley dated December 9, 1975, Quigley acknowledged the book "has brought me headaches as it apparently says something which powerful people do not want known."[159] In another letter Quigley said, "I am now quite sure that *Tragedy and Hope* was suppressed."[160]

Institutions Implementing the Agenda Today

How the cartel has extended its power over the economy and politics of the United States is far too extensive for this book. However, the short

83

version of this incredible story must be discussed. The power of The Anglo-American axis was the direct result of the early twentieth century Rousseau progressive liberals who were able to elect President Theodore Roosevelt and President Woodrow Wilson in 1901 and 1912 respectively. Although one was a Republican and the other a Democrat, both were self-proclaimed progressives of the day.

These progressive liberals were able to ram through the Sixteenth Amendment establishing the federal income tax, the Seventeenth Amendment transferring the election of Senators from the state legislators to the people, and the creation of the Federal Reserve (the U.S. private central bank), all in 1913.[161] These actions gave the cartel the ability to exert tremendous influence over national and global events. Quigley explains,

> In the 1920's, they (the cartel) were determined to use the financial power of Britain and the United States to force all the major countries of the world to go on the gold standard and to operate it through central banks [primarily the Bank of England and the U.S Federal Reserve] free from all political control, with all questions of international finance to be settled by agreements by such central banks without interference from governments.[162]

They not only succeeded, but Quigley even explains in great detail that it was the early actions by the cartel through the Federal Reserve that directly led to the Great Depression of the late 1920s and 1930s.[163]

The cartel itself arose from the fortunes of Cecil Rhodes and the Rothschild's. They implemented its agenda through what they called their roundtables. Quigley confirmed that the Council on Foreign Relations (CFR) in New York was "a front for J. P. Morgan and Company in association with the very small American Round Table Group."[164] Quigley explains;

> The Round Table Groups were semi-secret discussion and lobbying groups organized...on behalf of Lord Milner, the dominant Trustee of the Rhodes Trust... The original purpose of these groups was to seek

to federate the English-speaking world along lines laid down by Cecil Rhodes…and the money for the organizational work came originally from the Rhodes trust. By 1915 Round Table Groups existed in seven countries, including England…[and] the United States… Since 1925 there have been substantial contributions from wealthy individuals and from foundations and firms associated with the international banking fraternity, especially the Carnegie United Kingdom Trust, and other organizations associated with J. P. Morgan, the Rockefeller and Whitney families, and the associates of Lazard Brothers and of Morgan, Grenfell, and Company.

Edward Mandell House created the CFR in 1921. Colonel House is commonly referred to as President Woodrow Wilson's "alter ego" because he all but ruled the Wilson administration and policy. He was the driving force behind the creation of the Federal Reserve System (the privately controlled central bank) and the Sixteenth Amendment to the Constitution instituting the income tax. Milner's U.S. Roundtable was at the heart of the CFR, which in turn, drove U.S. policy using the membership of CFR as a cover.[166]

While the New York-based CFR has a membership of only a few thousand members, these members hold the pinnacles of power in American government, finance, media and other key American institutions. Since the council's founding in 1921, 21 Secretaries of Defense or War, 19 Secretaries of The Treasury, 17 Secretaries of State, And 15 CIA Directors have hailed from the Council on Foreign Relations.[167] While President Obama is not a member of the CFR, 10 of the 14 cabinet members are.[168] Many of 84 mainstream media have directors or senior executives who are also members of the CFR. Membership also includes 200 of the who's who of corporations.

A Few of the More Recognizable CFR Corporate and Media Members

Sample of 200 Corporations in 2009		Sample of CFR 250+ Members in the Media or Directors1	
AARP	Morgan Stanley	The American	New York Times (19)
Airbus N. America	New York Life	Spectator (3)2	Newsweek (7)
American Express	Nike	Associated Press (1)	Parade (2)
Aramco	NYSE	The Atlantic	Reuters (1)
Bank of America/	Occidental Petroleum	Monthly (3)	San Francisco
Merrill Lynch	PepsiCo	Business Week (2)	Chronicle (1)
Barclays	Pfizer	ABC (7)	Sports Illustrated (3)
BASF	Pillsbury	Chicago Tribune (1)	The Progressive (2)
Bloomberg	Pricewaterhouse	Christian Science	Time Magazine (10)
Boeing	Prudential	Monitor(4)	Turner Broadcasting
Chevron	Raytheon	CBS (12)	(1)
Chrysler	Rockefeller Group	CNN (8)	Times Mirror (6)
Citi Bank	International	Dow Jones (15)	The Los Angeles
De Beers	Rothschild North	Fortune Magazine (4)	Times (6)
Deutsche Bank	America	Gannett (3)	U.S. News and World
Exxon	Shell Oil	Harper's Magazine (2)	Report (7)
FedEx	Sony	Harvard Business	Viacom (1)
Ford Motor	Soros Fund	Review(1)	Washington Post (14)
GE	Standard & Poors	The Nation (2)	Washington Times (1)
Goldman Sachs	The Nasdaq	Money Magazine (3)	Washington Week in
Google	Reuters	National	Review (3)
Hitachi	Time Warner	Empowerment TV(1)	Weekly Standard (1)
IBM	Toyota	National Review (6)	Wired Magazine (1)
JP Morgan Chase	U.S. Chamber of	NBC (2)	
Lazard	Commerce	New Republic (6)	
Marathon Oil	United Technologies	Newsday (1)	
Merck	Visa	New York Daily	
Mitsubishi	Volkswagen of	News (1)	
Moody's Investors	America		
	Warburg Pincus		
	Xerox		

1   Number of senior officers and directors of the media is from 1997. More recent information is not available.
2   Number in parentheses indicate the number of executives or directors in the media organization.

Not all members of the CFR are part of some elaborate conspiracy. There are dozens of non-conspiratorial reasons for joining the CFR. Most are members for perfectly legitimate reasons. It is the Roundtable core that sets the direction and policy of the CFR. However, it is easily seen how unwary corporations and media, many of whom are progressive liberals or use the CFR for business reasons, can easily be manipulated into following the lead of the core Roundtable.

It is no accident that every major change in U.S. policy is first floated in articles published in *Foreign Affairs*, the quarterly magazine of the CFR. It is simply not healthy to have so many key government, corporate, and media members belonging to a single organization whose expressed purpose has been to create a world government. To put this into perspective, there would be screams of protest if these same companies and individuals belonged to the John Birch Society or The National Rifle Association.

Since the creation of the Round Table Groups and the Institutes of International Affairs (including the CFR), the globalists have created three other organizations for different purposes; the Bilderbergs, (economic), the Club of Rome (occult environmental), and the Trilateral Commission (political). There is one person who has been either responsible for their creation or a guiding influence in their goals; David Rockefeller.[169] Rockefeller was Chairman of the CFR from 1970 to 1985, and remains Honorary Chairman today. He helped create the Club of Rome in 1968 and the Trilateral Commission in 1973. To a large extent, the Club of Rome created the global template for the modern pantheistic environmental movement and what is now known as "sustainable development."[170] More on this in a later chapter. It should surprise no one that Al Gore is a current member of the Club of Rome.[171]

It has met annually in different areas since then. The shared goal of these secret organizations is shocking. Daniel Estulin, author of the hot-selling book *The True Story of the Bilderberg Group*, told the European Parliament on June 1, 2010;

These people want an empire.... The idea behind each and every Bilderberg meeting is to create what they themselves call the aristocracy of purpose between European and North American elites on the best way to manage the planet. In other words, the creation of a global network of giant cartels, more powerful than any nation on Earth, destined to control the necessities of life of the rest of humanity, obviously from their vantage point, for our own good and in our benefit – the great unwashed as they call us.... They are destroying the world economy on purpose.[172]

This can only be described as evil, yet explains almost all major legislation passed in recent history. Yet, it wasn't long ago that anyone who mentioned the Bilderbergs was labeled a conspiracy nut by the progressive press.

The first Bilderberg meeting was held at the Hotel de Bilderberg, near Arnhem in The Netherlands, from 29 May to 31 May 1954. David Rockefeller has attended nearly all the Bilderberg meetings throughout its existence and has been on its steering committee.[173] The relentless exposés by people like Alex Jones and Jim Tucker have finally exposed the Bilderbergs. Jones and Tucker hound them at every Bilderberg meeting.

It should be headline news. It is not; at least not in America. The typical reaction by the progressive mainstream press is "so what? The Bilderbergs is just a group of like-minded contemporaries. Jones and Tucker are crackpots." The next chapter will explain why the media hide the truth.

There are those analysts who believe that the influence of the Trilateral Commission (TLC) is even greater than that of the Bilderbergs and CFR. The TLC was created in 1973 by David Rockefeller and Zbigniew Brzezinski (President Carter's National Security Advisor). The original stated purpose of the Trilateral Commission was to create a "New International Economic Order." That's very similar to the goal of the CFR. Twelve members of the Obama administration are TLC members including Timothy Geithner as Secretary of Treasury, National Security advisor Gen. James L. Jones (now resigned), the Assistant National Security Advisor Thomas Donilon and Director of National Intelligence, Admiral Dennis C. Blair. In other words, the entire U.S. intelligence apparatus is staffed with TLC members![174]

Since its inception, six TLC members has served as World Bank presidents out of eight total, including the current president, **Robert Zoelick. Also,** eight out of ten U.S. Trade Representatives were TLC members; President and/or Vice-President of every elected administration (except for Obama/Biden); seven out of twelve Secretaries of State; nine out of twelve Secretaries of Defense. Lest you become too comfortable realizing that neither President Obama or Vice

President Biden are members, Zbigniew Brzezinski was candidate Obama's foreign policy advisor during his 2008 campaign.[175]

Patrick Wood, editor of *August Review* provides this warning; "in 1972, Brzezinski wrote that, 'nation-state as a fundamental unit of man's organized life has ceased to be the principal creative force: International banks and multinational corporations are acting and planning in terms that are far in advance of the political concepts of the nation-state.'" That, of course, is right out of Carroll Quigley's *Tragedy and Hope* and shows how the global cartel was implementing their agenda. Senator Barry Goldwater (R-AZ) also warned in his 1979 book *With No Apologies,*

> The Trilateral Commission is international and is intended to be the vehicle for multinational consolidation of the commercial and banking interests by seizing control of the political government of the United States. The [TLC] represents a skillful, coordinated effort to seize control and consolidate the four centers of power- political, monetary, intellectual and ecclesiastical.[176]

One of the primary goals of the Round Table group controlling the CFR is to manipulate American politics so that voters elect people having a globalist mentality and give them key positions of power. It really doesn't matter which party is in office, the agenda always stays the same. Quigley proudly defines this horrifying, manipulative agenda:

> The chief problem of American political life for a long time has been how to make the two Congressional parties more national and international. The argument that the two parties should represent opposed ideals and policies, one, perhaps, of the Right and the other of the Left, is a foolish idea acceptable only to doctrinaire and academic thinkers. Instead, the two parties should be almost identical, so that the American people can "throw the rascals out" at any election *without leading to any profound or extensive shifts in policy.*[177]

It is no wonder that it doesn't matter which party controls the White House or Congress. The cartel's agenda keeps spinning along using the Rousseau progressive liberals in both parties. These progressives may not even understand that they are being used by the cartel as "useful idiots" as Vladimir Lenin once called them. Their ideology makes them wide open for manipulation.

The September 2, 1961, issue of the *Christian Science Monitor* described the CFR as "probably one of the most influential, semipublic organizations in the field of foreign policy.... It has staffed almost every key position of every administration since FDR." The November 21, 1971, issue of the *New York Times* stated, "For the last three decades American foreign policy has remained largely in the hands of men—the overwhelming majority of them Council members (CFR).... One of the most remarkable aspects of this remarkable organization...is how little is known about it outside a narrow circle of East Coast insiders."

One of the major goals of the cartel was to eventually control U.S. policy through massive planning by "experts" and "technocrats." Quigley explains,

It is increasingly clear that, in the twentieth century, the expert will replace the industrial tycoon in control of the economic system even as he will replace the democratic voter in control of the political system. This is because *planning* will inevitably replace laissez faire in the relationships between [government and business]. This planning may not be single or unified, but it will be *planning*, in which the main framework and operational forces of the [economic] system *will be established and limited by the experts on the governmental side*; then the experts...on the economic side will do their *planning within these established limitations.*[178]

The massive planning structure that drives environmental law and urban planning today shows how successful the cartel has been since 1966 when Quigley wrote these words. It is the "experts" and "technocrats" that have created the alleged need for planning and environmental laws. These in turn have given the cartel very strong influence over the U.S. economy that is gradually choking innovation, property rights and the free market system. The final step was to be the ratification of the United Nations Convention on Biological Diversity, which would have given them the ability to abolish private property rights once and for all. Global warming fear mongering would provide the emotion needed to pass cap and trade legislation (as well as treaties at the international level) now in the U.S. Senate. Cap and trade legislation will give them final control over the United States economy. Both will be discussed in a later chapter.

If you have any doubt about this cartel's power, ask yourself, why did Goldman Sachs and the major banks get bailed out by TARP, while the small businesses in the United States, which create 70 percent of all jobs got nothing? And why weren't the banking institutions "too big to fail" broken up like they were prior to 1999? Again, the finger points back to a corrupt Congress who did not correct the problems it created. Why? *It was these very banking institutions, with the help of a corrupt Congress that caused the failure in the first place. With the exception of the auto industry, which was bailed out to save the unions, not the companies, it was the cartel's banks and investment firms that were bailed out with U.S. taxpayer money. The cartel loses nothing, the American people lose everything.*

It Is No Coincidence

The attack on the Constitution of the United States and the protections it offers to its citizens is not a coincidence. As urbanites lost touch with the importance of natural resources, they became vulnerable to propaganda from special interest groups seeking to create a controlled society; all funded by the cartel. Taking a step into the arena of speculation for a moment, it only makes sense that if a group of imaginary financiers wanted to influence or control the economy and culture of the nation, all they would have to do is give billions of dollars to specific special interest groups that would energize their efforts.

ACORN and its myriad of spin-offs are in the news lately as one of these special interest groups that is funded to do community organizing to create a society based on Rousseau's positive rights. Obama's 2011 budget includes over *$4 billion* for groups like ACORN. Almost every environmental group follows the same script and uses the Rousseau model to restrict the use of private property. Billions of dollars in funding is enabling these groups to heavily influence public education. Through education, they could influence politics, the media, and the judiciary.

Unfortunately, this is not speculation. The federal government and special interest groups spend billions of dollars annually funding this agenda. A 1956 Congressional investigation lead by Congressman Carroll Reece found that, "In the aggregate, the officers of [private] foundations wield a staggering sum of influence and direction upon research, education and propaganda in the United States."[179] The Congressional report confirms that these family foundations "exercise a very extensive, practical control over most research in the social sciences, much of our educational process, and a good part of government administration in these and related fields." Since they have "practical control" over "government administration," an increasing amount of the funding for this agenda also comes from tax dollars of the American people.[180]

How could these financial overlords enact such a diabolical plan without the American people knowing it is happening? Those promoting the Rousseau model in America have used a little known strategy called the Hegelian dialectic that incrementally moves American education, culture and economy from Locke's model to that of Rousseau over the past one-hundred years. Although few people have even heard of, let alone understand the Hegelian dialectic, Lenin, Stalin and their successors used the technique extensively to expand communism in the twentieth century. It has especially dominated the U.S. political process since the 1960s.

Georg Hegel (1770-1831), another of Rousseau's disciples, developed the Hegelian dialectic. Hegel found that he could manipulate people into accepting any goal desired by artificially creating outrageous solutions to manufactured crises. It works like this: The status-quo suddenly becomes deficient in some way. The status quo could be labor relations, environmental, health care, perceived discrimination, anything. There is usually some truth in the observation, but the use of alarmist propaganda blows the problem out of proportion until it becomes a crisis. The deceivers then offer an outrageous solution that they know no one will accept. Suddenly, someone offers a compromise which the people gladly accept because it is better than the outrageous solution. What the people do not know is that the compromise is the original goal of the dialectic. The Hegelian dialectic is truly insidious.

Larger goals may require several small steps. Step by treacherous step, the compromise solution of the Hegelian dialectic has incrementally brought America closer to the Rousseau model of governance. Each step has taken America further from Locke's model upon which the U.S. Constitution rests. The evolution from Locke's model to that of Rousseau supposedly benefits everyone, when in fact, it is merely a slow poison that gives the elites more power. It incrementally strips citizens of their individual freedoms and individual ability to create wealth.

Government intrusion into the right to own and use property under the Trojan horse of the "public good" is beginning to cause great harm to Americans. Citizens can blindly continue to convert to the Jean Jacques Rousseau model of governance by the whim of corrupt politicians and bureaucrats, or they can return to the model of John Locke where the government *protects* private property by law. It is clear from a myriad of examples that the Rousseau model leads to staggering corruption in government and a decline in the human condition, while the Locke model yields freedom, prosperity and environmental protection. Which one would you choose?

The Rousseau model causes government regulators having a normal morality to destroy the lives of people in the process of "just doing their job." It does not have to be that way. Part III of this book will show how the law still incorporates Constitutional principles which allow local communities to level the playing field to protect the lives of its property owners and resource users.

It is a shock to some that the so-called radical right in America has been correct all along. The John Birch Society was demonized and discredited, not because they were baseless conspiracy theorists, but because they were too close to the truth. There *is* a real global agenda, and its existence cannot be denied. From the vantage point of nearly forty years of additional history since Quigley wrote his book, the economy of the world *is* almost controlled in a feudalistic fashion by this powerful group of people. They are using the Rousseau model of governance to do it. How the Group (the financial cartel) did it is fascinating.

6

Co-Opting of
American Institutions

The purpose therefore of civics and social studies is not to teach history as it happened, but rather to indoctrinate the student to become a global citizen. Today, Rousseau indoctrination is so entrenched in journalism schools that direct control by the cartel is not even necessary.

TO ACHIEVE THEIR AGENDA OF GLOBAL DOMINATION, the global cartel had to change the education of American children. By doing so, Americans within two to three generations would no longer understand the foundation principles of unalienable rights and freedom upon which the Constitution of the United States rests. They also had to gain control over the money supply of the United States. Concurrently, they had to load the judicial system with judges who would be ideologically sympathetic to their goals of government control and who would be willing to change the law from the bench. Finally, they had to dominate property rights to impede the ability of ordinary citizens to protect their freedoms and create wealth. They did this by incrementally shifting the form of government from that based on the John Locke model to one based on the writings of Jean Jacques Rousseau.

The Corruption of Education

As stated by historian Carroll Quigley, their efforts have been a disaster to the American way of life.[181] Our public education system originally taught constitutional principles and even used the Bible as a textbook. It now has been totally corrupted. Public education in America has evolved into a system of mind control based on the psycho manipulation principles of Burrhus Frederic Skinner, Benjamin Bloom and Alfred C. Kinsey.[182]

Mastery Learning, Outcome-based Education, Quality Learning, Total Quality School Restructuring, Performance- or Achievement-based Education and Goals 2000 depend on psycho manipulation to achieve certain social goals.[183] In this approach, feelings are more important than knowledge. Worse, Goals 2000 directly links to the highly occult United Nations *World Core Curriculum*, supposedly written by the Tibetan Ascended Master Djwhal Khul.[184]

In 1965, the U.S. Department of Health, Education and Welfare funded a report entitled, "The Behavioral Science Teacher Education Program" (BSTEP). Published in 1970, BSTEP laid out the goal of this education process. BSTEP claimed, "We are getting closer to developing effective methods for shaping the future and are advancing in fundamental social and individual evolution." This evolution was to be done by "technological-scientific elite" planners and "long-range planning;"

Most people will tend to be hedonistic, and a dominant elite will provide bread and circuses to keep social dissension and disruption at a minimum. *A small elite will carry society's burdens.* The resulting impersonal manipulation of most people's lifestyles will be softened by provisions for pleasure-seeking and guaranteed physical necessities.[185]…The *controlling elite will engage in power plays largely without the involvement of most of the people.* The society will be a leisurely one. *People will study, play, and travel; some will be in various stages of the drug-induced experiences.*[186] Each individual will be saturated with ideas and information. Some will be self-selected; other kinds *will be imposed overtly by those who assume responsibility for others' actions. Relatively few individuals will be able to maintain control over their opinions. Most will be pawns of competing opinion molders.*[187] (Italics added for emphasis)

Historian Carroll Quigley called this the "managerial society," within which *there will be a "scientific and rational utilization of resources, in both time and space, to achieve consciously envisioned future goals."*[188] Forty-five years later this precisely describes what is happening in America today. The Skinner-Kinsey-Bloom psycho models have worked exceptionally well to achieve the cartels "consciously envisioned future goals."

Not only did the U.S. Health, Education, and Welfare fund BSTEP, but so did the American Academy of Arts and Sciences—Commission of the Year 2000; American Academy of Political and Social Science; United Nations Future-Planning Operation in Geneva, Switzerland, World Future Society of Washington, D.C., General Electric Company, The Air Force and Rand Corporation, The Hudson Institute, Ford Foundation's *Resources for the Future and Les Futuribles,* University of Illinois, Southern Illinois University, Stanford University, Syracuse University, and IBM.[189]

As BSTEP evolved in 1967, the National Education Association (NEA) declared war on the American people. NEA's executive secretary arrogantly, but accurately proclaimed: "NEA will become a political power second to no other special interest group... NEA will organize this profession from top to bottom into logical operational units that can move swiftly and effectively and with power unmatched by any other organized group in the nation."[190] The NEA is coming closer and closer to that goal, and along with the SEIU (Service Employees International Union) is now the most powerful and largest labor union within the Democratic Party.

Since its inception in Philadelphia in 1857, the NEA has helped in every way possible the globalization and psycho manipulation coup d'état of U.S. public education. Largely funded by the Rockefeller Foundation and Carnegie Corporation,[191] the NEA's goal was always to establish a national, then a global system of education. This was reaffirmed in the NEA's 1976 U.S. Bicentennial entitled *A Declaration of Interdependence: Education for a Global Community*: "We are committed to the idea of Education for Global Community. You are invited to help turn the commitment into action and mobilizing world education for development of a world community."

Charlotte Iserbyt, former Senior Policy Advisor of the Office of Educational Research and Improvement in the U.S. Department of Education, details in her book *The Deliberate Dumbing Down of America* how education in America became co-opted and corrupted. While at the Department of Education, Iserbyt found that Skinner, Bloom and Kinsey changed "education from a general, liberal arts education which benefitted *man as a whole* to a narrow training which would be based on behavioral psychologists' determination of what changes in 'thoughts, feelings, and actions' would be desirable and, perhaps, necessary for the benefit of *society as a whole*."[192] (Italics original)

Iserbyt found "tons of materials containing irrefutable proof…of deliberate, malicious intent to achieve behavioral changes in students/parents/ society which have nothing to do with commonly understood educational objectives."[193] She provides numerous documents detailing how "An alien collectivist (socialist) philosophy, much of which came from Europe, crashed onto the shores of our nation, bringing with it radical changes in economics, politics, and education, funded—surprisingly enough—by several wealthy American families and their tax-exempt foundations." She concludes, "Only a dumbed down population, with no memory of America's roots as a prideful nation, could be expected to willingly succumb to the global workforce training planned by the Carnegie Corporation and the John D. Rockefellers, I and II, in the early twentieth century which is being implemented by the United States Congress [today]."[194]

The power of these foundations created by the wealthy elite is staggering. Alarmed by this increasing power, the U.S. Congress launched several thorough investigations during the first half of the twentieth century. U.S. Representative Carroll Reece (R-TN) led the last one in 1953. The *Findings and Concluding Observations* of The Reece Committee state that foundations: "exercise extensive, practical control over most research in the social sciences, much of our educational process, and a good part of government administration."

All this is a matter of history. Nonetheless, foundations and elite influence have become so powerful that during the last half of the twentieth century they have thwarted every effort to expose this agenda by demonizing both the data and the people who attempted to expose it.

In 1994 Congress signed into law H.R. 1804, Goals 2000 Act,[195] H.R. 2884, the School-to-Work Opportunities Act[196] and H.R. 6, Elementary and Secondary Education Acts.[197] In 1995, they passed companion legislation H.R. 1617, The CAREERS Act.[198] All passed with strong Republican support.

Space does not permit an in-depth review of the mind-bending results of these bills. To provide a flavor of just how they revolutionized education in American, H.R. 6 states:

(1)(A) The Secretary [of Education] is authorized to carry out a program to enhance the third and sixth National Education Goals [of Goals 2000] by *educating* students about the history and principles of the United States, including the Bill of Rights….[199] (Italics added)

Simply translated, the federal government will now define the "history and principles of the United States, including the Bill of Rights..." Specifically H.R. 6 stated that federal control would be administered through a non-governmental organization(NGO) called the Center for Civic Education:

(B) Such programs shall be known as *"We the People: The citizen and the Constitution."* (2) The programs shall (A) continue and expand the educational activities of "We the People: The Citizen and the Constitution" program administered by the Center for Civic Education..."[200]

In other words, a *single* NGO now controls the entire curricula of the U.S. Constitution, the Bill of Rights and civics—by law! Allen Quist, three-term Minnesota legislator serving on the House Education Committee and currently a professor of political science at Bethany Lutheran College, warns:

This single organization would dictate what was true and what was important in these academic areas. There would be no review of its dictates by Congress. There would be no review of its dictates by American citizens. Our schools would have nothing to say about what this one group determined was true and important regarding civics and government. One organization (NGO) would determine the new National Curriculum in these areas, and no one else would have anything to say about it.[201]

H.R. 6 also required the federal government to award a grant or enter into a contract with the Center for Civic Education to carry out the program. There was no competition, no scrutiny by the voters of America. This was not a partisan effort by the Clinton administration to slip one over on the voters. H.R. 6 passed overwhelmingly by Republicans. Worse, similar language authorizing and funding the Center for Civic Education to continue its control of the federal curriculum was in President Bush's "No Child Left Behind" education bill in 2002.

Within a few months of the passage of H.R. 6, the Center for Civic Education released the federal standards for civics and government. They were obviously ready *before* the law even passed. Remember, H.R. 6 mandates that the standards be based on the textbook, *We the People: The Citizen and the Constitution* written by the Center for Civic Education. Page 207 of this book states:

> As fundamental and lasting as its guarantees have been, *the Bill of Rights is a document of the eighteenth century, reflecting the issues and concerns of the age in which it was written.* (Italics added)

When written in this way it does not take a rocket scientist to realize that a student who has little, if any, knowledge of the importance of the Bill of Rights will assume it is no longer relevant to today's society. The twist and distortion is obvious. *We the People* does not mention national sovereignty once in the book. It does, however, extensively promote the concept of the global village and world citizenship in Lesson 37 for high school students.

In fact, many reading this book today may agree with it because of the indoctrination they already received while they were in school. Lesson 40 on page 214 even encourages the student to challenge the foundational principles of the U.S. Constitution that have made the United States the greatest nation in the world:

> The Founders, themselves, were vigorous critics of the wisdom they inherited and the principles in which they believed. They were articulate, opinionated individuals who loved to examine ideas, to analyze, argue and debate them. They expected no less of future generations. They would expect no less of you.

We the People provides only one side of the information needed to challenge the foundational principles of the United States. It fails to mention even one of the hundreds of reasons expounded on by our Founders for writing the Constitution the way they did. They did not want the form of government Rousseau progressive liberals now say we should have because our Founders experienced or saw first-hand its oppressive results. Yet, *We the People* makes no mention of that.

We the People leads the student to believe the U.S. Constitution is a relic and there are no unalienable rights. Therefore, the only rights Americans should have are "positive rights" defined by the federal government. How can a student possibly analyze and debate the foundational principles when they receive no information on why they might be critically important?

It should therefore be no surprise that the National Standards for Civics and Government written by the Center for Civic Education is biased. For example, they include:

References to the environment	17
References to multiculturalism	42
References to the First Amendment	81
References to the Second Amendment [202]	0

Regardless of the reader's position on gun control, the Second Amendment is one of the Bill of Rights and a discussion of the reasons it was included should be included in any textbook discussing the Bill of Rights. This glaring omission distorts any historical discussion of the founding documents of the United States and predisposes the student to anti-gun literature. Why is the Second Amendment not included? The reason is that the federal curriculum is not about education, it is about politics. More specifically, political science professor Allen Quist states: "The purpose of the Federal Curriculum is to indoctrinate, not to inform."[203]

Quist conducted a thorough study of the new *National Standards for Civics and Government*. He found that the curriculum is not organized as informational subjects, but as themes designed to form attitudes that influence future behavior. He found that the principle themes of the federal curriculum center on:

1. Undermining national sovereignty
2. Redefining natural rights.
3. Minimizing natural law [as used by Thomas Jefferson in the Declaration of Independence]
4. Promoting environmentalism.
5. Requiring multiculturalism.
6. Restructuring government.
7. Redefining education as job skills.

In summary, Eagle Forum's president, Phyllis Schlafly, warned that these laws were intended to restructure the public schools by:

*   Bypassing all elected officials on school boards and in state legislatures by making federal funds flow to the Governor and his appointees on workforce development boards.
*   Using a computer database, a.k.a. "a labor market information system," into which school personnel would scan all information about every

schoolchild and his family, identified by the child's social security number: academic, medical, mental, psychological, behavioral, and interrogations by counselors. The computerized data would be available to the school, the government, and future employers.

• Using "national standards" and "national testing" to cement national control of tests, assessments, school honors and rewards, financial aid, and the Certificate of Initial Mastery (CIM), which is designed to replace the high school diploma.[204]

Now incorporated into the National Curriculum Standards for Social Studies, these anti-American, anti-freedom concepts form the basis for all national education tests. Every student must learn this material lest the national tests show the schools are performing poorly and they lose their federal funding.

In early 2010 alone, the Texas State Board of Education is under fire for removing from its textbooks any mention of the heavy Christian influence in the formation of the United States.[205] Additionally, the curriculum almost eliminated any mention of Christopher Columbus. The history was eventually restored, but not without a knockdown drag out fight with the progressive liberals.[206] Texas is unique in that it is large enough that textbook publishers write their books to meet Texas standards.

Texas is reacting to this by refusing to accept a $700 million grant in federal stimulus money to participate in Obama's $4.3 billion Race to the Top program. One teacher with decades of experience said the standards are being written by "liberal policy wonks," "elitist professors," and people who do not hold the values that most Americans hold. Tragically, with the exception of Alaska, all other states seem to be jumping at taking the grant. "This is nothing less than a federal takeover of the public education system."[207]

Even more alarming, the North Carolina Department of Public Instruction was attempting to remove all United States history prior to the presidency of Rutherford B. Hayes in 1877. In one fell swoop, all mention of our Founders, the history of the U.S. Constitution, the Civil War and Abraham Lincoln would disappear from textbooks.[208]

What is still unknown is the impact of the Education Affordability Reconciliation Act of 2010 that was packaged with the health care bill and signed into law on March 23, 2010. This act essentially socializes all student loans by the federal government taking full control over all new loans. Little to no attention was paid to the education bill, so little is known about it. At best it represents the nationalization of another segment of our economy—something that characterizes a socialist, fascist and communist forms of government.

Perhaps of more concern is how this will affect loans to students in private, especially private Christian schools. It is hard to imagine the federal government not discriminating against private conservative and Christian schools by denying their students federal loans. It would not be long before those colleges would have to close their doors, which would leave all higher education to the progressive ideology. Time will tell.

Once a revisionist curriculum indoctrinates a full generation, its propaganda becomes truth. The general population will believe that socialism and world citizenship is the only truth, and will resist all efforts to expose how they have been dumbed down. It is happening before our eyes.

The Corruption of the Media

As discussed in Chapters 1-4, the mainstream media immediately label anyone who even tries to raise the alarm of this horrendous agenda as an incompetent nut, a conspiracy theorist, or a right-wing extremist in order to discredit their message. This cartel heavily influenced, some say controlled, the news itself as early as 1917. On February 9 of that year Representative Oscar Callaway from Texas took the floor of the U.S. Congress and reported that, "In March, 1915, the J. P. Morgan interests …and their subsidiary organizations, got together 12 men high up in the newspaper world and employed them to select the most influential newspapers in the United

States and sufficient number of them to control generally the policy of the daily press of the United States...."[209]

Historian Carroll Quigley in his book *Tragedy and Hope* confirmed that this cartel still influenced the press in the 1960s by exerting "much of its influence through five American newspapers (*The New York Times*, New York *Herald Tribune*, *Christian Science Monitor*, the *Washington Post*, and the lamented *Boston Evening Transcript*.)"[210] Today, Rousseau indoctrination is so entrenched in journalism schools that direct control by the cartel is not even necessary. Bernard Goldberg, former correspondent for *CBS* news, shares in his explosive book *Bias* that, "TV journalists simply don't know what to think about certain issues until the *New York Times* and the *Washington Post* tell them what to think."[211]

Goldberg claims that the biggest problem in today's media lies in their ultra-liberal mentality (now called progressive liberals). Media personalities blindly accept Rousseau-oriented socialism as truth. It is how they *think*. It is their worldview. "That's one of the biggest problems in big-time journalism," claims Goldberg, "...its elites are hopelessly out of touch with everyday Americans." They do not just disagree with conservatives, "they see them as morally deficient." The media elites do not see their views as liberal, but "as simply *the correct way to look at things.*"[212] (Italics added) They believe, claims Goldberg, "They're simply reasonable views, shared by all the reasonable people the media elites mingle with at all their reasonable dinner parties in Manhattan and Georgetown."[213]

The American public agrees with Goldberg. A CNN/Opinion Research Corporation Poll on October 16, 2009 showed that 70 percent of Americans believe that the media is out of touch with Americans.[214] A 1996 Roper Poll of 139 Washington bureau chiefs and congressional correspondents provide context as to just how skewed the mainstream media truly is. The poll found that while only 43 percent of the general American population voted for Bill Clinton in 1992, twice as many journalists, 89 percent, did so. Likewise, only 7 percent of the journalists voted for George H. W. Bush compared to 37 percent of the general voters.[215] Although Americans voted in the majority for the 1994 Contract with America, which called for a smaller, more conservative government, 59 percent of the media called it a "an election year campaign ploy" while only 3 percent thought it was a "serious reform proposal."[216]

Bob Kohn, author of *Journalistic Fraud: How The New York Times Distorts the News and Why It Can No Longer Be Trusted*, details that the *Times* manipulates one of the six key components of a news article: the "who," "what," "why," "when," "where" or "how" of the news.[217] This manipulation is so refined that the reader is convinced black is white and white is black.

In spite of efforts to control the news through the mainstream media for decades, the truth is finally getting to those who use the alternative media. These are independent internet news sites and Fox News. Although the mainstream media considers Fox "far right wing," many conservatives still see a slight liberal bias in some of its reporting. Nonetheless, Fox News has shot through the ratings ceiling because of their "fair and balanced" reporting. On any given day or hour Fox has more than twice the viewers than CNN, Headline News or CNBC. CNN's viewership plummeted 30 percent between the third quarter of 2008 and 2009. The top show for ten years running is The O'Reilly Factor on Fox. Close behind is Hannity, Glenn Beck, Greta van Susteren, and Special Report with Bret Baier.[218]

Of that lineup, the progressive liberals literally hate Glenn Beck with such passion they almost become spastic with rage on a daily basis. They call him a hate monger, fear monger, a liar, plus a lot of things that can't be printed. Beck uses actual video, audio, or written quotes in context to back up his allegations. Like Rush Limbaugh, another hated commentator, he couches all this in humor. Beck's (and Limbaugh's) allegations are based in fact rather than the vitriolic tirades of the progressive liberals.

Beck believes he is being attacked because of the truth he shares with the audience. His message is simple. The progressive liberals are restructuring this nation and destroying its Constitutional protections. Well known writer/ speaker Robert Ringer notes:

Beck's show is so good that I'm convinced if a person doesn't watch it on a regular basis, it's almost impossible for him to understand the true causes of the moral and economic collapse of the United States – or even that it *is* collapsing – because no one else on TV covers most of the stories he dissects in impeccable detail.[219]

We have a choice. We either allow them to do it and watch the destruction of America, or we expose the progressive liberals, vote them out of office and get back to Constitutional principles. Beck's message is resonating with the American people and his ratings are skyrocketing. His viewership is four times that of CNN and of MSNBC for the 5 o'clock Eastern Time slot. He is even exceeding The O'Reilly Factor with some of his specials.

Editor and CEO of Internet media giant *WorldNetDaily*, Joseph Farah says the real failing of the mainstream media is that it is "not tough enough on the government."[220] Farah reminds us that, "*the central role of a free press is to serve as a watchdog on government.*"[221] (Italics added) In contrast, the 1996 Roper poll showed newspaper editors believe their No. 1 goal is to be a "news explainer." This is far and above any other goal they listed. "In other words," explains Farah, "newspaper editors don't think their job is to report the news. They believe their job is to explain it to their stupid readers."[222] Worse, many responded that they believe it was their job to be "opinion leaders and agenda setters."[223]

The mainstream print media's market share is plummeting.[224] Several have gone out of business. Progressive liberals try to blame it on people opting to go to the internet, rather than read a newspaper or magazine. That is partially true. However, even their websites suffer. A 2007 poll by the very liberal Pew Research Center found that 64 percent of the American people believed mainstream internet media were biased and 59 percent believed they were inaccurate. Fifty-three percent believe the mainstream internet press was too critical of America.[225] In spite of this the progressive liberals just don't get it. They are so blinded by their ideology they are convinced more than ever the American people are too stupid to understand their enlightened wisdom and are now blatantly, in-your-face biased.

Because they have been so successful, progressive liberals trash the alternative media. The attack is a double-edged sword, however. Al Gore tried to demonize the alternative media by implying they are merely toadies of the Republican Party. In a December 2, 2002 interview with the *New York Observer* Gore cried, "Fox News Network, *The Washington Times*, Rush Limbaugh—there's a bunch of them, and some of them are financed by wealthy ultra-conservative billionaires who make political deals with Republican administrations and the rest of the media..."[226]

The Obama administration did the same thing in October of 2009. Like Gore had done seven years earlier, Obama White House Communications Director Anita Dunn claimed Fox News was "a wing of the Republican Party."[227] Obama refused to appear on Fox News September 20, 2009, when he made appearances on every other network. On October 18 Rahm Emanuel, President Barack Obama's chief of staff, said, "It is not a news organization so much as it has a perspective."[228] Dunn fired off that Fox is "opinion journalism masquerading as news." The attack did not work.

Such baseless attacks have been used by progressive liberals for decades to discredit or even destroy all opposition. The truth is that the liberal Pew Research Center found that of the five major cable news networks, Fox was by far the most balanced. Pew found that 40 percent of Fox's news stories the last six weeks of the 2008 election were negative for *both* Obama and McCain. That compares to CNN's 39 percent negative reporting for Obama compared to a whopping 61 percent for McCain, and an incredible 14 percent and 73 percent negative reporting respectively by MSNBC. The mainstream media totally lost any semblance of true journalism in the 2008 election reporting. They literally became propaganda outlets for Obama specifically, and progressive Democrats in general.

Dunn, in contrast has praised Chinese dictator Mao Zedong as one of "her favorite political philosophers" whom she "turn[s] to most to basically deliver a simple point..."[229] The same is true of Obama's Manufacturing Czar Ron Bloom.[230] Mao is one of Dunn's and Bloom's most favorite political mentors? Mao is reported to have killed up to 60 million Chinese citizens during his reign of terror. He was ruthless in how he treated his enemies and used an iron fist to control the economy and the Chinese press. Because of Beck's and the alternative media's relentless exposure of the statement, Dunn had to step down from her position earlier than intended in November 2009.[231]

Green Czar Van Jones is another Beck/alternative media casualty of the Obama administration. Jones, a self-proclaimed radical communist had been helping Obama shape his green agenda, especially on global warming and cap and trade, when Glenn Beck played numerous video clips of Jones ranting about his communist ideas. The mainstream media attempted to ignore the growing outrage by Americans until Jones was forced to resign. Then they savagely accused Beck and the alternative media of a "vicious smear campaign" based on "lies and deceptions."[232]

When Glenn Beck played the tapes of these statements by Dunn, Bloom and Jones in context, the progressive liberal press went ballistic, accusing Beck of every nasty thing they could think of. What did Beck do? He played the accusations by the mainstream media and then played the tapes of Dunn, Bloom and Jones again. There was no contest. Beck was right on target. The mainstream media came off as idiots. The fact that anyone still watches them is a sad commentary of just how indoctrinated our society has become.

Beck has become a force the militant liberal progressives cannot silence. Writer/Speaker Robert Ringer notes, "Beck has become so good at exposing the truth, so well-respected and so powerful that the Forces of Darkness in the White House and Congress view him as a major threat to their aspirations to eliminate the Constitution, the rule of law and individual sovereignty in the United States." [233]

Is radical socialism the advice Obama is getting from his advisors? Is exposing the real philosophy of the Obama administration why it has waged all-out war against Fox? It would seem so. Yet, the mainstream media have attempted to cover up the blatant, in your face socialist, fascist, even communist beliefs of some of Obama's Czars. As discussed in Chapter 2, Dr. Rossiter, an experienced forty-year psychiatrist, warned that the progressive socialist media will never hold the increasingly socialist government responsible for the problems socialism creates. It is always an individual, usually a Republican, who is at fault. Or, it is because government does not spend enough money. Or, there are too many Constitutional restrictions hindering the effective implementation of an obvious (to them) social solution.

Unless you understand the psychological filter that warps a progressive liberal's thinking, it defies understanding why the Rousseau oriented press is so blind to their pro-government bias. One of the fatal flaws of progressive socialism is the belief that government bureaucrats have no self-interest and therefore can be trusted to define and administer Rousseau's "general will." Yet, it is not only the individual, nor the landowner, nor the corporate executive who has self-interest; it is part of human nature. All of us have self-interest. Self-interest is often worse in government because there are fewer controls to curb the desire of petty bureaucrats to build empires or act as tyrants.

Business at least has the leash of having to make profits to pay for empire building. If they act as tyrants they are not in business for long. Not so the socialist bureaucrats. They just cry that disaster is inevitable if Congress does not fund their programs to protect those who are suffering from their own mistakes. Congress responds by merely levying more taxes, the Federal Reserve just prints more money, further plundering the people. And, it's almost impossible to fire bureaucrats if they are ever caught abusing their responsibilities.

7

Environmentalism: The Key to Controlling Property Rights

The changes required by Agenda 21 and Sustainable America meant a complete shift from the constitutional basis of "life, liberty and the pursuit of happiness" to one of protecting nature at all costs

BY THE LAST HALF OF THE TWENTIETH CENTURY the global financial cartel was gradually exerting more and more influence over the federal government, education and finance. Two major roadblocks remained that prevented them from shifting the Locke form of constitutional and limited government to Rousseau's state-controlled socialist government.

The first roadblock involved the millennia-old tactic of creating a fear of war as a mechanism to focus a population's efforts in a direction that benefited the nation's power structure. The threat of war originates from real or contrived animosities between two nations. Kings and tyrants over the millennia have used this time-tested strategy to refocus their nation's population from internal problems to an external threat. However, if a peaceful world government were instituted, the threat of war would evaporate as an instrument that could distract the population's attention. A substitute was required.

The second problem was the Constitutional protection of private property. As discussed in Part I, private property is essential to the creation of liberty and wealth. It was therefore an obstacle to the Rousseau model of state control over the people and their resources.

To address these problems, America's shadow government gathered a group of like-minded specialists in Iron Mountain, New York in 1963. Dubbed the Special Study Group, experts in the fields of social science, history, economics, international law, cultural anthropology, psychology, psychiatry, mathematics, astronomy and others were tasked with the responsibility of developing an alternative mechanism to replace the threat of war to focus the minds and will of the masses. The Special Study Group discussed dozens of alternatives as possibilities, including such things as the plight of the poor (welfare), UFOs, space exploration and many more.

After meeting in different places for more than three years, this group wrote a confidential report that leaked out and was published in 1967. This was exactly the same time period historian Carroll Quigley and the BSTEP education program said that planning technocrats would begin to assume dominance in U.S. society.

Called the Report from Iron Mountain, this amoral report first defines how to use war or the threat of war to control the masses. War to them was essential to the survival of civilization: "War is not...an instrument of policy utilized by nations to extend their expressed political values or their economic interests. On the contrary, it is itself the *principle basis of organization on which all modern societies are constructed.*"[234] (Italics added) War acts as brake, throttle, and rudder to the nation's economy; "[M]ilitary spending can be said to furnish the only balance wheel with sufficient inertia to stabilize the advance to [those] economies. The fact that war is 'wasteful' is what enables it to serve this function. And the faster the economy advances, the heavier this balance wheel must be."[235]

Not only does war act as a balance wheel, it "served as the last great safeguard against the elimination of necessary social classes." The report reaffirms that:

The arbitrary nature of war expenditures and of other military activities makes them *ideally suited to control* these essential *class relationships*.... Until [a substitute] is developed, continuance of the war system must be assured, if for no other reason, among others, than to *preserve whatever quality and degree of poverty a society requires as an incentive*, as well as to maintain the stability of its internal organization of power.[236] (Italics added)

This cold, calculating group not only believes that peace destabilizes nations, but that there must be a *class system* where the *poor are kept in poverty* for the good of the nation (and one would assume, for the global financial elite)! According to this philosophy, the American people are merely pawns to be kept dumbed-down, loyal and in bondage—like serfs to the lords of the realm during the medieval days. Although these monsters promote welfare, they never intend to help the poor. They merely want to enslave them. Once a social welfare program is in place, these elite employ class warfare to maintain well defined classes by manipulating them to distrust or even hate each other—poor against rich, blacks against whites, male against female. The mechanism for doing this is explained in detail in Dr. Rossiter's book, *The Liberal Mind; The Psychological Causes of Political Madness.*[237]

Of all the strategies developed by the Special Study Group, exploiting pollution and protecting the environment seemed the most viable—even if "such a threat [had] to be invented."[238] It would also serve the dual purpose of allowing the federal government to control property rights ostensibly to protect the environment. In any event, the Report from Iron Mountain estimated it would be "sufficiently menacing before environmental pollution, however severe, will be sufficiently menacing, on a global scale, to offer a possible basis for a solution."[239]

When the report leaked to the public in 1967, it created shock waves across the country. Not surprisingly, the major media immediately denied its authenticity. Such denial calmed the storm until Dr. Harland Cleveland admitted the authenticity of the Report in 1999.[240] Cleveland is a Princeton University graduate and a Rhodes Scholar. He served as Assistant Secretary of State for International Organization Affairs in the administration of President John F. Kennedy, and in 1965 was appointed by President Lyndon B. Johnson to be the U.S. Ambassador to NATO. In 2002, he was the senior advisor on the State Department Policy Planning Division. He is a who's who in globalist circles and would have had insider knowledge of the Report from Iron Mountain.

Even as the public memory of the Report from Iron Mountain faded, the focus of the nation quickly turned to the environment. Congress passed the National Environmental Policy Act in 1969 and the Clean Air Act in 1970, the same year it created the Environmental Protection Agency (EPA). The Clean Water Act passed in 1972 with a stronger version in 1977, and the Endangered Species Act passed in 1973—along with dozens of other environmental laws following Rousseau's statist philosophies. Just as predicted by Carroll Quigley and planned by the BSTEP education program, every one of these laws put the future of America into the hands of planning technocrats. Quigley's "managerial society"[241] was born.

As happened in education, the big foundations began to pour hundreds of millions of dollars annually into environmental activism to achieve the progressive concept of environmental justice. This has created one of the most powerful political forces in the twentieth century alongside the National Education Association (NEA), SEIU and ACORN. Federal agencies also began to fund environmental organizations through a host of federal projects. By the mid-1990s (two and a half generations after the Report from Iron Mountain was written), the Boston Globe estimated the combined revenue for environmental groups was $4 *billion* annually, dwarfing any organized opposition.[242] Today, federal spending on global warming alone is to $4-5 billion a year. Meanwhile the well-oiled propaganda machine ensured that the public's perception was that environmentalists were underpaid souls defending the environment and the common person.

Not all of this was bad. America's rivers and air are much cleaner today than in the early 1970s. People do need to protect the environment. The question is how best to do it. Rousseau's model of state control and forced compliance formed the basis of nearly all federal environmental laws passed since 1967. If instead of using the Rousseau model, Congress used the Locke model, the same results may have been legally attainable without the loss of private property rights and usurpation of local and state sovereignty by the federal government.[a]

The Birth of Sustainable Development

It was clear right from the start that there was a deliberate effort by the elite to shift control of property rights from the individual to the state or federal government. A year after the Report from Iron Mountain was published; David Rockefeller co-founded the Club of Rome,[243] which helped put into action the goals of the Iron Mountain Report at the international level. The Club of Rome published *Limits to Growth* in 1972, which called for severe limits on human population and the control of all development in the world to achieve "sustainable development." Sustainable development was eventually formalized into a United Nations global action plan called *Agenda 21*, which President Bush committed the U.S. to at the 1992 Earth Summit in Rio de Janeiro.

Continuing this blizzard of progressive activity following the 1967 Report from Iron Mountain, David Rockefeller co-founded the Trilateral Commission in 1973. At the same time Laurence Rockefeller commissioned and led the study entitled *Use of Land: A Citizen's Policy Guide to Urban Growth* that was published in 1973. The nationally based *Use of Land* was a companion to the Club of Rome's internationally based *Limits of Growth*. The *Use of Land* was edited by William Reilly, who would later be appointed by George G. W. Bush as the Administrator of Environmental Protection Agency in 1989. A third effort was made by Nelson Rockefeller, New York's Governor, to create the Adirondack Park Agency, which was patterned exactly after the *Use of Land*.

---

a   To understand better the Locke approach to sustainable development and a point by point comparison to *Agenda 21* read the *Freedom 21; Promoting Sustainability through Political and Economic Freedom*. http://www.freedom21agenda.org/Freedom21Agenda.pdf

Although utterly evil, the Rockefeller brother's effort to destroy the Constitutional basis of property rights was brilliant. The thrust of the *Use of Land* report supported the premise that development rights of private property should be at the discretion of the government for the "good of society;"

> "Landowners expect to be able to develop their property as they choose, even at the expense of scenic, ecological, and cultural assets treasured by the public....[However], with private property rights go obligations that *society can define and property owners should respect*."[244] (Italics added)

This verbiage could leap right from the pages of Rousseau's description of the general will in his *Social Contract*, Book 1. The paragraph first states the expectation of Constitutional property rights, and then subverts those rights to Rousseau's model. Society (i.e. the elite), not the individual should define the property rights permitted the individual. Environmental protection would occur "not by purchase but through the police power of the federal government." The book then goes on to say,

> It is time that the U.S. Supreme Court re-examine its precedents that seem to require a balancing of public benefit against value loss in every case and declare that, when the protection of natural, cultural, or aesthetic resources or the assurance of orderly development are involved, a mere loss in land value is no justification for invalidating the regulation of land use.[245]

Think about this for a moment. *Use of Land* recommends that the Supreme Court throw away 200 years of Constitutional law to justify constantly changing regulatory law. The new interpretation of the Constitution would not only apply to cases of harm and nuisance based on Locke's Constitutional limitation of property rights, but also for the whim of some arbitrary natural, cultural, or even aesthetic reason. The *Use of Land* literally advocates reversing the Constitution through successive Supreme Court decisions.

What is especially shocking, the book's recommendations are precisely what the Supreme Court has done since the book was published. Page after page of the *Use of Land* describes what has happened to create the Rousseau model of state control today.

Concurrent to the study and writing of *Use of Land*, Laurence Rockefeller teamed up with his brother, New York Governor Nelson Rockefeller, to launch a study in 1968 that led to the creation of the Adirondack Park Agency (APA) in upstate New York three years later.

The Adirondack Park Template

Laurence Rockefeller provided foundation funding to a dozen activist environmental organizations which joined to form the Adirondack Council in Upstate New York. In turn, the Council demanded state control over land-use in the Adirondacks. At the same time, Governor Nelson Rockefeller provided the political hammer to force the APA bill through the legislature. To cap it off, the progressive *New York Times* promoted blatantly false propaganda to a largely ignorant, but politically powerful urban majority in New York City. The *Times* falsely asserted that unless the APA Act passed immediately, development would overrun the Adirondacks. Although over 80 percent of the Adirondack citizens were against the bill, the cartel's machine prevailed and the APA Act passed in 1971.

This "unless we do it now the world is going to end" Hegelian Dialectic is standard operating procedure for the Cartel specifically, and progressive liberals in general. Two recent successes are TARP in 2008 and the Stimulus Bill in 2009.

The APA perfectly reflects the *Use of Land* and Rousseau model of state control of private property. It controls all land-use activity on private property within the blue line of the park boundary. It dictates the number of acres required per home (up to forty acres per home), all new home construction or renovations, and a host of regulations that have stifled most development. Except in the exempted cities and communities, driving through the Adirondacks today is like driving through a 1960s landscape. Urban New

Yorkers who want a bucolic experience may love the effect in order to sooth their hyper-stressed nerves, but the APA has locked the Adirondack citizens into a Rousseau socialist time warp that has denied them the rights enjoyed by other American citizens.

The Adirondack citizens are now experiencing the kind of socialist bureaucracy Hernando de Soto found in third world impoverished nations in his book *The Mystery of Capital*. The lack of private property rights traps people into poverty. The APA has subjected Adirondack residents to layers and layers of bureaucratic red tape that require citizens to plow their way through a maze of constantly changing regulations to get a permit of any kind. Just as in third world nations, this bureaucracy can cost tens of thousands of dollars and take many years to get a simple permit that might take a few days or weeks anywhere else in America at a nominal cost. That is, if the citizen is lucky enough to get a permit at all.

By 1976, New York State conducted a $350,000 study to determine the impact of the APA on property value. The state, however, could not complete the study. Aghast, New York Senate Minority Whip Ronald Stafford expounded, "a study instigated to discover whether Adirondackers can sell their land at fair values can't be completed because *no one can sell their land at all*."[246] (Italics added) Not all people are penalized by the Rousseau-oriented APA. One of the evils of the Rousseau model is that it opens the door to corruption because so much power is placed in a few bureaucratic hands. The Adirondacks provide a classic example. Adirondackers found that environmentalists and power brokers seemingly got permits in a matter of days to build trophy homes anywhere they wanted, even if it meant building roads across wetlands.[247]

The raw ugly power of the APA used on the citizens of the Adirondacks would shock most Americans. The blatant abuse and horror by the APA, and the citizen's unsuccessful efforts to defend themselves makes for gut-wrenching reading. *The Adirondack Rebellion*, authored by Anthony D'Elia, details D'Elia's effort to fight the cartel's political machine. His effort eventually bankrupted him and he died prematurely a broken man.

Intoxicated by the successful effort to control land development in the Adirondacks, the APA model became the template for what is now called sustainable development and environmental justice across America and around the world. Without knowing it, residents of the New Jersey Pinelands had the APA template applied with the creation of the New Jersey Pinelands Commission in 1978. Likewise, residents of the Columbia River Gorge in Oregon had the APA model forced on them with the creation of the Columbia River Gorge National Scenic Area in 1986.

The federal government then attempted a two pronged effort in the 1990s to advance the APA model on a regional scale. The Northeast had the Northern Forest Lands encompassing 20 million acres almost forced on them by the Northern Forest Lands Council. At the same time, the federal government attempted to swallow up the entire Interior Columbia River basin with the proposed Interior Columbia Basin Ecosystem Management Project (ICBEMP) during the Clinton Administration. ICBEMP is the biggest effort to date, encompassing most of Washington, Oregon and Idaho as well as portions of Montana and Utah. Both the Northern Forest Lands Council and ICBEMP were eventually rejected by the people, but neither has been fully deactivated. They live on like latent cancer cells waiting for the moment they can once again metastasize.

Smart Growth

Smart growth is another means of attempting to control property rights in urban areas. Like the Adirondack Park Agency, smart growth had its origins with the *Use of Land*. Not surprisingly, the same foundations promoting the education and environmental agendas are funding the smart growth agenda.

While smart growth…well seems so smart, it has a fundamental flaw. In order for the Rousseau concept to work, government bureaucrats must control property rights. There is simply no other way to implement smart growth. The government must have the ability to tell landowners what they can and cannot do. Otherwise, urban sprawl results.

Smart growth seeks to preserve land in a natural or agricultural state by encouraging individuals to live in denser communities that take up smaller amounts of land per housing unit. Such communities also encourage residents to rely more on walking or public transit than on cars for mobility. Retail and other commercial facilities are also more closely mixed with residential units to foster easy access to jobs and shopping.

Smart growth is supposed to solve urban problems from air pollution and traffic congestion to providing access to single-family dwellings for the poor. Smart growth not only does none of these things, it actually accelerates the ills it is supposed to cure. Increased numbers of people bring increased congestion. The transient nature of the apartment dwellers can lead to crime or a reduction in property values.[248] As a rule, more dense areas cost more to build, tend to have higher taxes, higher levels of pollution, and a higher cost of living. As a result the poor in any community are hit the hardest.

Again using the Adirondack model, it attempts to force people into higher density urban areas, while depopulating rural areas by demanding multi-acre lot sizes. No matter how they cut it, urban planning and smart growth is a bald-faced fraud that is creating a nightmare for people across America. It is artificially driving up the equity value for existing homeowners while denying access to the poor and lower middle class.

Land-use zoning has a devastating impact on the cost of land. The Harvard Institute of Economic Research showed that zoning dramatically increases the cost of land in urban areas. The study found that when regulatory zoning does not artificially drive up the price of land, the cost of an extra quarter-acre in a single lot is very similar to a separate and independent buildable quarter-acre lot. This condition exists in urban Kansas City.[249]

However, in San Francisco, Los Angeles, Anaheim, San Diego, New York City, Seattle and others cities like them, the difference between the cost of an extra quarter-acre in a lot, and a separate buildable quarter-acre lot is in the hundreds of thousands of dollars. "In these areas," claims the Harvard study, "only a small percentage of the value of the lot comes from an intrinsically high land price; the rest is due to restrictions on construction."

Although many other variables were tested, land-use regulation was the only one correlated with the huge cost increases. [250]

In another in-depth study by Randal O'Tool published in *The Planning Penalty* found that in 2005, smart growth and other land-use restrictions cost U.S. homebuyers at least $275 billion. Almost all of the more than 124 metropolitan areas having affordability problems in 2005 were caused by comprehensive planning and smart growth. Most enlightening, the report found that, "more than 30 percent of the total value of homes in this country is attributable to prices inflated by planning-induced housing shortages." [251] This contributed to the wild increases and speculation in housing prices from 2000-2006, which inevitably led to the housing crash in 2007-2008, and the financial crash of 2008-2009.

The comprehensive planning/smart growth model is taught in college planning programs today. It is vigorously advanced by the American Planning Association (APA) and International Council on Local Environmental Initiatives (ICLEI). This attack on property rights is spreading like wildfire across America. In just one example the Town of Falmouth, Maine, a bedroom community of Portland Maine, has adopted the smart growth model. As expected, its taxes and cost of housing has risen sharply. Falmouth's planning manager, George Thebarge, gave very revealing instructions in 2002 to the newly formed citizen's Study Area Committee (SAC). SAC was charged with determining how property owners were going to be allowed to use their private property. In his opening comments Thebarge claimed, "There is no such thing as private property in Falmouth....Remember, a property owner's control of his property stops at his front door! How the rest of his property is used is up to you." [252] Unfortunately, that Rousseau mentality is not uncommon today, and is exactly opposite of the original intent of the Constitution.

Like the Adirondack example, this misguided Rousseau experiment in land control has spread despite overwhelming evidence that it does not work.[a] The persistence of these beliefs, despite all facts to the contrary, is a

---

a For a more thorough discussion on this subject, Review the hundreds of papers and links found on: http://www.americandreamcoalition.org.

tribute to the power of a small group of progressive elitists to make a ruinous idea fashionable in order to increase federal intervention and control.

Agenda 21

While all of this had been going on at the national level, the same effort had been underway at the international level. The effort by the United Nations to control land and property rights is long and complex.[a] As already noted, the concept of sustainable development had evolved into a forty chapter United Nations plan called *Agenda 21*.[253] It covered everything from human population, urban development, global warming, biodiversity destruction and much, much more. It is stunning in its magnitude. *Agenda 21* and its implementing treaties provide a web of interlocking international laws that regulate virtually every aspect of human interactions with the environment. *Agenda 21* was signed by President Bush Senior at the 1992 Earth Summit in Rio de Janeiro. Although most Americans have never heard of it, *Agenda 21* spells out UN requirements for sustainable development within every nation, including the United States. Progressives viciously attack anyone who even mentions *Agenda 21* as being a kook and ill-informed.

Key to this process is the Rousseau model of state-controlled property rights which had been the foundation of all United Nations treaties since its 1976 Habitat I conference in Vancouver, British Columbia:

Land...cannot be treated as an ordinary asset, controlled by individuals and subject to the pressures and inefficiencies of the market. Private land ownership is also a principal instrument of accumulation and concentration of wealth and therefore contributes to social injustice; if unchecked, it may become a major obstacle in the planning and implementation of development schemes. The provision of decent dwellings and healthy conditions for the people can only be achieved if land is used in the interests of society as a whole. Public control of land use is therefore indispensable.[254]

a   For a more thorough list of references and discussion of this effort go to our website at http://www.sovereignty.net/p/land/index.html

Agenda 21 was converted into United States policy in a 1996 policy document entitled *Sustainable America. Sustainable America* and a host of sub documents were written by the President's Council on Sustainable Development (PCSD). *Sustainable America* changed the mission statement for every land-based federal agency in the United States without a vote in Congress. No longer was a federal agency's mission to "serve the citizens." Under *Sustainable America,* the mission of federal agencies is to "control citizens" in order to protect the environment and ensure sustainable development. The changes required by *Agenda 21* and *Sustainable America* meant a complete shift from the constitutional basis of "life, liberty and the pursuit of happiness" to one of protecting nature at all costs.

In spite of these advances, *Agenda 21* and *Sustainable America* was never intended to have the force of law. That was to change with the acceptance by the United Nations of the Earth Charter at the 2002 World Summit on Sustainable Development in Johannesburg, South Africa. The Earth Charter was originally written for acceptance in the 1992 Earth Summit, but was refused because it was so blatantly pantheistic. Briefly, pantheism is the broad belief that nature (or earth) is god (or goddess) and that all of humanity must serve and protect mother earth. When it was rejected in 1992, the task to sanitize it for public consumption was given to Maurice Strong, founder of the Earth Council, and Mikhail Gorbachev, former president of the USSR and founder of Green Cross International. Both Strong and Gorbachev were also members of the Club of Rome. Steven Rockefeller (son of Nelson Rockefeller, governor of New York), was given the responsibility to write the various drafts.

According to Elaine Dewar's stunning revelations in her book *Cloak of Green,* Strong was the almost superhuman mastermind behind global environmentalism from the 1970s into the late 1990s. Strong was a close friend of the Rockefellers and was brilliant in implementing the Rockefeller agenda.[255] He was a member of the occult Club of Rome and was the Secretary General of the UN's first Earth Summit in Stockholm in 1972 and the second Earth Summit in Rio in 1992. In opening the 1992 session Strong said,

It is clear that current lifestyles and consumption patterns of the affluent middle class – Involving high meat intake, consumption of large amounts of frozen and convenience foods, use of fossil fuels, appliances, home and work-place air-conditioning, and suburban housing – are not sustainable. A shift is necessary toward lifestyles less geared to environmentally damaging consumption patterns.

In a nutshell this is what sustainable development intends to do. Also notice the class division in this statement. Other international documents clearly show that it is all right for the elite to have these modern conveniences and comforts. Steven Rockefeller, son of Nelson Rockefeller, provides the occult definition in his and John Elder's book *Spirit and Nature*:

Sustainable by definition, means not only indefinitely prolonged, but nourishing, as the earth is nourishing to life and the self-actualizing of persons and communities. The word development need not be restricted to economic activity, but can mean the evolution, unfolding growth and fulfillment of any and all aspects of life. Thus sustainable development may be defined as the *kind of human activity that nourishes and perpetuates the fulfillment of the whole community of life on earth.* [256] (Italics Added)

Steven Rockefeller currently chairs the Rockefeller Brothers Fund, one of numerous Rockefeller foundations which have funded many environmental organizations supporting sustainable development to the tune of tens of millions of dollars.

The sanitized version of the Earth Charter was taken to the 2002 World Summit on Sustainable Development in Johannesburg in what they called the "Ark of Hope." The Ark of Hope was patterned after the Biblical Ark of the Covenant, except it had dozens of occult symbols painted on its exterior. The Earth Charter was in the final consensus document. However, the Committee For A Constructive Tomorrow (CFACT), probably along with others, convinced the U.S. State Department Delegates that the Earth Charter was a very dangerous document. Hours before the Summit delegates were to accept the UN consensus document, the United States demanded that the Earth Charter be removed.

The removal of the Earth Charter proved to be a wrenching blow to the Cartel's agenda. In the wings, the Cartel had another treaty waiting called the Covenant on Environment and Development. This treaty was designed to put the force of international law behind the Earth Charter and *Agenda 21*, and lay the foundation for a world religion based on pantheism. The world came within hours of that reality.

8

Biodiversity and Global Warming

The United States was within one hour of ratifying a United Nations treaty that would have destroyed Constitutional property rights and divided America up into human occupation zones when it was stopped dead in its tracks.... Regardless of what the progressive media try to make you think, the scientific evidence for man-caused global warming is about as close to zero as is possible.

THE DISCUSSION IN CHAPTER 7 is but the very tip of the proverbial iceberg. Entire books can, and have been written on these subjects. Yet, thanks to the mainstream media's bias, these issues are never discussed, so most people have never heard of them. They even have a hard time believing them. Yet, the global agenda is being implemented. The deep divisions that presently exist in America are a direct result of this agenda. The jaws of this trap are about to close on America. While there are forty goals of *Agenda 21* currently being implemented, space and time allow only two to be *briefly* discussed in this book. These two goals almost had, or may yet have an incalculable devastating impact on American citizens. They are biodiversity and global warming. Both are enormous frauds, based in a little truth, and designed to justify global control over private property rights and the economy of the United States.

Biodiversity

Chapter 15 of *Agenda 21* calls for the conservation of biological diversity. It demands that the earth's biological diversity be protected by the ratification by each nation of the Convention on Biological Diversity (Biodiversity Treaty). In typical Hegelian dialectic, *Agenda 21* demands biodiversity must be protected to save the earth from certain collapse of her ecosystems. In classic Rousseau progressive and/or pantheistic logic, humanity is guilty of destroying ecosystems with development. Therefore, all development must be severely limited. Yet, as a research scientist who has conducted research into biological diversity, this author has found this belief is not based in scientific fact, but in religious belief or progressive nihilism; man is the cause of all evil. Biodiversity is important, but it is not as fragile as *Agenda 21* and the Biodiversity Treaty makes it out to be.

The need for the Biodiversity Treaty is predicated on a new science called Conservation Biology, which in turn is based in pantheistic ideas that "nature knows best" and *natural ecosystems* have to be managed, well, *naturally*. Artificial management (i.e. cattle ranching, forest management, agriculture, and other management manipulations) are generally destructive. The anti-human underpinning of conservation biology is revealed in the purpose of conservation biology:

> The society is a response...to the biological diversity crisis that will reach a crescendo in the first half of the twenty-first century. We assume implicitly that...the worst biological disaster in the last 65 million years can be averted.... We assume implicitly that environmental wounds inflicted by ignorant humans and destructive technologies can be treated by wiser humans and by wholesome technologies.[257]

Biodiversity and Global Warming

This wild-eyed purpose gives a flavor of the zeal of those who support *Agenda 21*. Such belief seems bizarre for the average American. Yet, it is fully entrenched in our universities today because foundations provided endowed chairs and millions of dollars of research money to entice universities. Land management federal agencies are full of graduates having this indoctrination.

Conservation biology provides the basis for how the Biodiversity Treaty was supposed to protect biodiversity.[a] If a person pictures the human body with its network of arteries and veins, you have a picture of what is called for in the treaty. Real zealots would even include a nervous system because they believe the earth (Gaia) is a living, sentient being. At any rate, the treaty calls for establishing a system of huge core wilderness areas called core reserves that are interconnected by wilderness corridors and all surrounded by buffer zones.

Five of us succeeded in temporarily stopping U.S. Senate ratification of the treaty in August of 1994.[258] It was brought up for another vote in the Senate on September 29, 1994. The ratification of the treaty was certain. In the meantime, however, the five of us had received the actual documentation[259] the day before the vote was scheduled. The document, called the UN Global Biodiversity Assessment (GBA), proved this treaty was literally going to destroy the integrity of the UnitedStates.

A full color map depicting what the treaty would do had been under construction for two years by this author. It was over-nighted (see black and white map) to the U.S. Senate

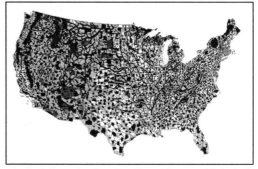

A depiction of what the Convention on Biological Diversity would have done over the next 50 years if it was fully implemented according to recommendations by the UN funded Global Biodiversity Assessment. The black areas are wilderness reserves and corridors and the gray areas buffer zones. The author used an earlier color version of this map to stop the ratification of the Convention on Biological Diversity in the U.S. Senate. (Used by permission from Environmental Perspectives Incorporated, Bangor Maine 207/945-9878)

---

a For more background information on the treaty go to http://freedom.org/reports/srbio.htm

along with the UN documentation. The map was blown up into a 4 x 6 foot poster and taken out on the Senate floor an hour before the cloture vote. It stopped the ratification dead in its tracks. The Senate never voted on it.[260] The United States was within one hour of ratifying a United Nations treaty that would have destroyed Constitutional property rights and divided America up into human occupation zones when it was stopped. The machinations and intrigue behind the Convention on Biological Diversity would make a best-selling novel.[261]

The Global Warming Fraud

The issue of global warming is yet another Hegelian Dialectic effort to use fear to motivate citizens and governments around the world to pass legislation that will destroy property rights and the very basis of the free market system. As a research scientist who led a multi-million dollar research effort on the subject in the 1990s, it quickly became obvious that there was little scientific evidence to back up the belief that man was causing global warming. Nonetheless, the United Nations made this a priority in Chapter 9 of *Agenda 21*.

Since *Agenda 21* was written and accepted, nearly 20 years of research has been conducted. According to the 2007 United Nations Intergovernmental Panel on Climate Change (IPCC), the world's alleged scientific authority, report shows there is now a 90 percent certainty that man is causing global warming. At least that is what the IPCC claims. However, since 2001 there have been several major errors in the proof presented by the IPCC. Those errors have developed into a cascade of outright fraud that has been exposed since October of 2009. This includes modifying data sources when one set of data no longer supports the man-caused theory; and using un-refereed magazine articles written by environmental activists. Perhaps the worst evidence of fraud is the elimination of major temperature data sources from northern or high elevation weather stations, which once removed from the last twenty years of earth's average temperature, show a warming that has nothing to do with global warming.

The man-caused theory of global warming is simply the largest fraud ever perpetrated on the people of the world. In spite of the overwhelming hard scientific evidence that man is not causing global warming, the progressive mainstream media has ignored the hard science and made light of the revelations of fraud. The media merely claim the fraud doesn't affect the IPCC's conclusions. As usual, the progressive media is wrong. They either cannot admit they are wrong, or they are desperate to keep the global warming agenda alive.

The first glaring error is known as the "hockey stick curve," so called because the data looked like a hockey stick lying down. The IPCC heralded the hockey stick as absolute proof man was causing global warming in the IPCC's 2001 report. By 2003 it was shown by two Canadian scientists; engineer Steven McIntyre and statistician Dr. Ross McKitrick; that the wrong statistical package was used to create the curve.[262] Without any retraction, the IPCC abandoned the hockey stick curve as their only 'proof' of man-caused warming as if it never existed.

When Steven McIntyre requested the hockey stick data to test its veracity, the principle author of the Hockey Stick Curve, Dr. Michael Mann at the University of Pennsylvania, refused him for four years. The data used by Mann was eventually used in another journal which required the data to be made available to other scientists, so it had to be given to McIntyre in 2009. What McIntyre found shocked him. Mann not only used the wrong statistical package, but eliminated most of the dataset after 1960! The tree ring data he'd used for the first thousand years no longer showed warming after 1960. So he discarded all the tree ring data not showing warming after 1960 and only used the 10 trees which did show warming.[263] This is data manipulation of the worst kind. When the data from all the trees was added back in, there was *no* upward trend of temperature in the last half of the twentieth century at all.[264] Yet, Mann continues to get millions of dollars from the federal government and National Science Foundation.[265]

The roof caved in on the man-caused theory in late November 2009, when thousands of emails in the computer of Britain's Climate Research Unit (CRU) were either hacked or leaked to the public. The CRU is one of four principle data repositories of temperature data in the world. The other three are the *National Oceanic and Atmospheric Administration* (*NOAA*), The National Atmospheric and Space Administration (NASA), and Japan's JMA (Japan Meteorological Agency). Of the four, the CRU and NOAA are the most important. The hacked emails are stunning to say the least. The general picture of the series of emails is one of collusion, exaggeration of warming data, manipulation of data, conspiracy, possible illegal destruction of data and violation of Britain's Freedom of Information Act, and organized resistance to anyone who defies them.[266]

Dr. Phil Jones, the Director of the CRU even admitted to using Michael Mann's approach to "hide the decline" of global temperature after 1960 in another paper.[267] Of the hundreds of damning CRU emails, the worst was an email from Director Jones to Michael Mann that said in part, "I think I'll delete the file rather than send [it] to anyone." The file he was referring to was the original un-manipulated raw temperature data from around the world; of which the CRU had *sole* possession. The CRU only gives cleaned or corrected data to scientists for their research work, which is not wrong if it is done correctly.

Steven McIntyre had been trying for years to get the raw data to test whether the corrected data the CRU gives to other scientists is accurate. With the new Freedom of Information Act, Jones had to give McIntyre the raw data. Rather than giving McIntyre the raw data, Jones deleted it, just as he claimed he would (or at least part of it). This is a potentially criminal act and Jones has been forced to step down. He may be facing criminal charges.

The deletion of raw data is *extremely* serious. Raw data is never deleted in science because it would prevent research results from ever being verified and duplicated by other scientists using the original data. This is at the core of the scientific method. This entire affair tends to discredit *every* research study that used the CRU summarized data. It may mean that there is no longer any original empirical scientific data that even suggests that man is responsible for the twentieth century warming. Even the computer models used to prove man-caused global warming are made invalid because they all use the corrected CRU data in their models.

Again, the mainstream media dismissed the emails and the deleted data, claiming the NOAA and NASA datasets still exist. But that is *very* misleading. NOAA and NASA have some of the original data, mostly for the United States, but the CRU had the *original* raw data for much of the rest of the world. It was that data which Jones deleted. The only global dataset NOAA and NASA has is from the CRU *after* it was allegedly "corrected."

Even if the mainstream media were correct there is ample reason to question the CRU data. The CRU has refused to adjust its data for what is known as the Heat Island Effect. This effect occurs when meteorological temperature measuring stations once in rural areas outside of the urban boundary are gradually surrounded by urban development. The asphalt roofs, streets and parking lots can increase ambient temperature by up to 12°F. It has nothing to do with global warming. Therefore, the strong warming shown for the last half of the twentieth century in the CRU/IPCC's reports may be largely caused by the Heat Island Effect.

The entire CRU/IPCC claim of excessive warming in the late twentieth century is made even more suspicious because the United States temperature data does not show the same large temperature increases. The U.S. dataset, the largest in the world, is allegedly corrected for the Heat Island Effect. Ironically, U.S. temperatures the last half of the twentieth century are *not any greater* than occurred in the 1920s-1940s.[268] Yet, even the U.S. data is suspect. Independent analyses show that there still may be Heat Island Effect in the U.S. data.[26]

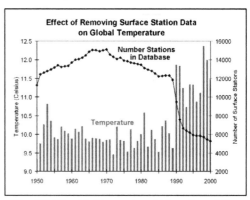

When NOAA's global temperature database dropped from around 11,500 stations to under 10,000 in the early 1990s (mostly from colder latitudes and elevations) the unmodified global temperature suddenly shot up from about 10°C to 11.5°C. However, after NOAA applied their "correction" algorithms, the data showed a smooth, but rapid increase in temperatures starting in the early 1980s through the mid 1990s, leading skeptical scientists, like Joe D'Aleo, first Director of Meteorology for the Weather Channel to accuse NOAA of cooking the books. Source: Source: Joe D'Aleo / Dr. Ross McKitrick. http://www.uoguelph.ca/~rmckitri/research/nvst.html

It gets worse. The NOAA data is now suspect. Very

suspect. Joseph D'Aleo, first Director of Meteorology at the cable TV Weather Channel, has strong evidence that NOAA cooked the books by systematically eliminating most of the temperature data after 1980 taken in northern and high elevation weather stations from the global temperature data base. This sleight of hand would automatically show a large increase in global temperature after 1980.[270]

Not only is the basic data for the man-caused warming theory likely corrupted, but the IPCC's own 2007 highly publicized claims that the world's glaciers are melting, and the Amazon forest is disappearing have been shown to be false. This fraud was exposed in a cascade of damning revelations in January and February 2010. The first to be exposed was the IPCC's claim that the Himalayan glaciers would be melted by 2035.[271] The scientist who made the claim in the IPCC's 2007 report, later admitted he knew the claim hadn't been verified. He included it to encourage policymakers and politicians to take action.[272]

Next the IPCC's claim that extreme weather would increase with global warming was shown to be false.[273] That revelation was followed by exposing the false claim that large tracts of the Amazon forest would disappear.[274] The IPCC's Amazon claim was based on an article not even related to global warming in an environmental magazine. Immediately following that revelation, the IPCC's claim that the Alps' glaciers were melting was shown to be based on anecdotal evidence by hikers published in a hiking magazine.[275] Well-known warming alarmists are now saying the IPCC has crossed into advocacy and they don't want anything to do with it. "By exaggerating the certainties, papering over the gaps, demonizing the skeptics and peddling tales of imminent catastrophe, they've discredited the entire climate-change movement."[276]

In any other scientific endeavor, a sequence of disastrous exposures of fraud would signal the death knell to the science. Not so global warming. Although the mainstream media is finally wavering – a little – politicians are not. President Obama proclaimed in his January 27 2010, State of the Union Address,

And, yes, it means passing a comprehensive energy and climate bill with incentives that will finally make clean energy the profitable kind of energy in America. I'm grateful to the House for passing such a bill last year. And this year – this year, I'm eager to help advance the bipartisan effort in the Senate. I know there have been questions about whether we can afford such changes in a tough economy. I know that there are those who disagree with the overwhelming scientific evidence on climate change.

Overwhelming evidence? Regardless of what the progressive media try to make you believe, the empirical scientific evidence for man-caused global warming is about as close to zero as is possible. The only real evidence of man-caused warming is the global warming models. Yet, every one of them is based on the assumption that warming is caused by increasing carbon dioxide creating high elevation clouds, which trap more heat. Study after study has shown that this cloud formation has not happened over the past 50 years, therefore disproving this assumption.[a] [277] (see graphs, below)

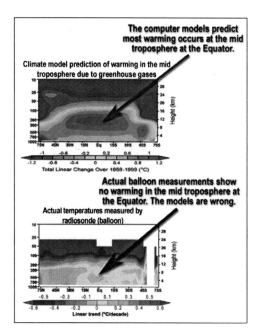

a For a more complete discussion on climate models and the real science go to www.nocapandtrade.us. The site has a wealth of written information as well as a series of short YouTube videos to help understand this confusing issue.

Although global warming alarmists continue to point to computer climate models as proof man is causing global warming, the models are based on incorrect assumptions. The top computer output shows most warming between 1959 and 2000 should have occurred in the tropical latitudes between 8-14 kilometers in elevation. Actual measurements for the same period show that the models are wrong. For an explanation, see http://www.youtube.com/watch?v=Z-9B42RasmQ

Over 31,000 scientists in the United States, 9,000 of whom are Ph.D.s, have signed a petition saying "There is no convincing scientific evidence that human release of carbon dioxide, methane, or other greenhouse gases is causing or will, in the foreseeable future, cause catastrophic heating of the Earth's atmosphere and disruption of the Earth's climate."[278]

So why are other scientists, politicians and others still clinging to the theory? Michael Madden, State Legislator in Wyoming has a good grasp of the reasons:

Liberal politicians are adherents [of global warming] because they thirst for unlimited tax revenue through cap and trade laws. For pseudo-scientists, the global warming scheme is a smooth path to lucrative government research grants and the resulting prestige. To green energy producers, it is a financial bonanza for startup companies since the federal government is the largest venture capitalist in this field. Global warming is the basis for green energy continually seeking special tax favors, carbon portfolios and other benefits from all levels of government. For undeveloped countries global warming is a justification for restitution payments from the U. S. taxpayers. To the hard left it provides an environmental basis for one-world government and complete control over the production and lives of the planet. To people like Al Gore, who refers to global warming as "settled science," it provided an effective vehicle for becoming a multimillionaire.[279]

Actually, Madden is slightly incorrect. Al Gore would likely become a billionaire, not a multimillionaire. Taking this a bit further, progressive liberals dominate the halls of Congress and state Legislators, even down to the local level. They also tend to be fearful of anything that may harm them, no matter how small the risk. They are easily convinced the sky is falling by the global cartel. Led by President Obama, most are willing to spend trillions of dollars "just in case" the claims about man caused warming are true. Yet, even after trillions of dollars are spent, undoubtedly destroying the U.S. economy in the process, the destructive effort *might* reduce global temperature by 0.06°C. The entire effort is insane.

There are a million risks that may happen that would be catastrophic—like an asteroid hitting the earth and causing an extinction event. The United States can't spend trillions of dollars on every low probability, high impact eventuality that may or may not happen. Yet, that is what the United Nations and the United States are bent on doing—while a billion people are living on the edge of starvation.

How did the science on global warming get so corrupted? Senator James Inhofe (R-OK) has determined that the world's governments have spent a whopping *$50 billion* on global warming research and promotion since 1995.[280] Dr. Arthur Robinson, sponsor of the Petition Project discussed above, warns that the federal government has built "a giant welfare program for Ph.D.s – now known as 'big-time science.' As this science welfare program has expanded, the conservative culture among American academic scientists has gradually been replaced by an ultraliberal, pro-big-government culture – in just the same way that large government welfare programs have induced this political change in many other national sectors."[281] In short, big money has bought the science it wanted to "prove" man caused the warming.

There is one bright spot in this horrendous agenda. China and India refused to accept the conditions mandated by the Copenhagen Agreement put forth at the UN's December 2009 Climate Change Conference in Copenhagen Denmark. The Agreement would have meant Third World nations could have never expanded their use of fossil fuel energy to expand their economies and get their people out of poverty. China and India demanded a minimum of $100 billion annually be given by the developed nations to Third World nations to get them to agree. The developed nations would not agree. These irreconcilable differences caused the collapse of Copenhagen Convention in December 2009. As if in answer to prayer, the failure of the much heralded meeting perhaps saved the world from creating a world government.

The Cost Of Global Warming Regulations
By 2035

- $2,872 *per family per year* in increased energy costs[a]

- $4,600 per family per year total increased taxes.[b]

- $662 billion a year loss of GDP or $6,790 per family of four [b]

- Each family of four's share of the debt accumulated by cap and trade would be equal to $114,915 [c]

- $5.7 Trillion in increased taxes[a]

- $9.4 Trillion total GDP cost thru 2030[d]

- $4.35 to $5.10/gallon gas price [b]

- Requires all homes to pass federal inspection for energy efficiency that will require thousands of dollars for compliance

- Up to 6 Million lost jobs (based on real Spanish experience)[c]

- 2.2 jobs lost for every green job created (based on real Spanish experience)[e]

- $750,000+ cost for every green job created [e]

- Trading of carbon credits on the derivatives market – the same one that caused the financial collapse in 2008

- Devastating to 3rd World Nations

a   David Kreutzer, Discounting and Climate Change Economics. The Heritage Foundation, WebMemo #2705, November 19, 2009. http://www.heritage.org/Research/EnergyandEnvironment/wm2705.cfm
b   CBO Grossly Underestimates Costs of Cap and Trade. The Heritage Foundation, The Foundry, June 22, 2009 http://blog.heritage.org/2009/06/22/cbo-grossly-underestimates-costs-of-cap-and-trade/
c   Nicolas Loris. Cap and Trade: A Comparison of Cost. The Heritage Foundation, WebMemo #2550. http://www.heritage.org/Research/EnergyandEnvironment/wm2550.cfm
d   Waxman-Markey's Effect on Gas Prices In Your State. Heritage Foundation, The Foundry, August 27, 2009. http://blog.heritage.org/2009/08/27/waxman-markeys-effect-on-gas-prices-in-your-state/
e   Gabriel Calzada Álvarez, et. al. Study of the Effects On Employment of Public Aid to Renewable Energy Sources. University of Rey Jan Carlos, Madrid Spain. March 2009. http://www.nocapandtrade.us/Spain-employment.pdf

Even though the international agenda is in disarray, the progressive liberals in the U.S. House of Representatives have already passed the mind bending 1500 page *American Clean Energy Security Act of 2009* (H.R. 2454) on June 26th, 2009. The US Senate is now considering this dangerous cap and trade legislation as the *Clean Energy Jobs and American Power Act*, S 1733. If passed or implemented in any form, this legislation will be the most punitive and expensive set of Rousseau regulations ever imposed on the citizens of America (See sidebar).

Cap and trade requires the government to reduce carbon emissions by progressively placing caps on how much carbon can be emitted. Both Congressional bills require that the U.S. reduce carbon emissions (mostly carbon dioxide) 17 percent by 2020, 42 percent by 2030 and 83 percent by 2050. At each step, the government will allocate carbon credits to different segments of our society, which decides who gets to emit how much of the remaining carbon allowances. Once allocated, these credits can be traded much like the stock market trades stock, including the derivatives market which was partly responsible for the 2008 financial crash.

If the legislation fails, President Obama has announced he will implement even *more* punitive EPA regulations.[282] Because progressive liberals were able to ram through health care legislation, they are emboldened to pass either S 1733 or implementing the new EPA regulations.

Rousseau progressive liberals trumpet that conversion to green energy will solve all our problems by creating jobs and providing reliable energy to replace fossil fuel energy. The problem is that this is another progressive boondoggle that will cost trillions of dollars. Green energy is a completely false expectation. Spain has been doing this for eleven years and they have found that each new green job cost $750,000 and they lost 2.2 jobs in the regular economy. Maybe the U.S. can do better, but not enough to make it a positive addition.[283] Not only is wind power 75 percent more expensive than coal generated electricity, solar power is 570 to 887 percent more expensive.[284]

Renewable energy has a niche in any energy strategy. However, to claim the US can increase its renewable energy from less than 4 percent to 17 percent by 2020 is not economically doable. It can only be done with enormous subsidies at taxpayers' expense. Wind and solar power have two fatal flaws. Wind farms cannot produce electricity when the wind is not blowing, and solar farms cannot produce power when the sun is not shining. On average the wind only blows 25 percent of the time. Although giant strides have been made in solar energy conversion technology, it is still very inefficient.[285]

The space required for either wind or solar is staggering. Physicist Howard Hayden at the University of Connecticut sums up the situation; "Imagine a one-mile swath of wind turbines extending from San Francisco to Los Angeles. That land area would be required to produce as much power around the clock as one large coal, natural gas, or nuclear power station that normally occupies about one square kilometer."[286]

Except for some *natural* warming in the twentieth century, there is nothing about the global warming scare that is true. Even so, most of the twentieth century warming occurred in the first half of the century, before the dramatic rise in carbon dioxide started. It is almost as if the progressive liberals in Congress in general and President Obama specifically want to set the United States on a course of economic destruction. It doesn't matter whether they push their Pollyanna cap and trade schemes because they are blinded by their Rousseau progressivism, or if they are doing it deliberately to crash the economy. If they really wanted to reduce the use of fossil fuel, why not just tax it directly? Why go through all the gyrations of cap and trade? One explanation of course is that they are trying to hide the fact that cap and trade is the largest tax increase in U.S. history by not calling it a tax. If the progressives are trying to hide the tax, it means they are deliberately deceiving the American people.

Cap and trade also allows the illusion that they are using the free market to trade carbon credits. Again that is false. Cap and trade will totally destroy the free market system.[287] Since carbon-based energy is directly tied to the economy, cap and trade allows the federal government to control the entire economic engine. Cap and trade also sets up an easily corruptible fascist system whereby the federal government decides who gets carbon credits and who does not. Europe has been trading carbon credits for years. Europol, the EU's "FBI," uncovered massive corruption throughout the entire European carbon trading system in 2009 involving 90 percent of all carbon trading.[288] As with all Rousseau schemes, perversion of the law from "equal opportunity" to "forced compliance" always creates an environment that is ripe for corruption. Incredible power in the hands of a few bureaucrats is exploited by the unscrupulous to get special favors.

Is a Carbon Currency in Our Future?

There is one more chilling possibility for the insistence on using a cap and trade system that most economists say cannot work. It wouldn't be worth mentioning if it didn't explain the otherwise unexplainable cap and trade insanity. There is a small, but growing suspicion that national currencies, including the U.S. dollar will be replaced with a single carbon currency, i.e. a global monetary system except it would not be based on money but on carbon credits. It is nothing less than a revolutionary new economic system based on energy consumption and production rather than price.[289]

Our current price-based economic system and its related currencies that have supported capitalism, socialism, fascism and communism, seems to be herded to the slaughterhouse. Greece, Ireland, Italy, Portugal, Spain and other European nations are in catastrophic financial trouble. By mid-May 2010, Moody's, Standard & Poor's and/or Fitch had downgraded the credit ratings of Greece, Portugal and Spain. On May 27, Greece's rating was dropped to junk status. There were riots in Greece resulting in three deaths. [290, 291, 292]

The United States is also *very* vulnerable. By May of 2010, many analysts were saying Greece's monetary system would totally collapse, despite hundreds of billions of dollars being pumped into Greece by the European Union and International Monetary Fund (IMF). Many Americans are outraged that the U.S. taxpayer is funding the IMF's contribution, adding addition debt when U.S. spending and debt is following right on the heels of Greece.

The European crisis may provide a domino effect that could (emphasize could, not would) ripple through Europe[293] and to the United States, causing a global monetary collapse. The spectacular stock market plunge on May 6, 2010 is a direct result of the market's nervousness about Greece and Europe.[294]

The global financial architecture developed over decades and formalized at the 2002 Monterrey Mexico International Conference on Finance for Development is set up for regional monetary control patterned after the European Union.[295, 296] The long-term goal is to establish regional currencies, then a global currency.[297] The Bank for International Settlements was given oversight through their Financial Stability Forum,[298] now called the Financial Stability Board.

Remember, Carroll Quigley said in *Tragedy and Hope* that, "The apex of the system was to be the Bank for International Settlements in Basel, Switzerland; a private bank owned and controlled by the world's central banks which were themselves private corporations."[299] (See Chapter 5) Financial consultant Joan Veon, who has attended hundreds of BIS, World Bank, IMF and UN meetings on the subject, now says "While the BIS has always been the focal point of central bank activity globally, it now is finalizing the structure Dr. Quigley wrote about."[300]

The entire purpose of the BIS' Financial Stability Board (FSB) is to stabilize the global financial architecture to prevent exactly what happened in the 2008-2009 financial collapse. Either the FSB is a total failure, or they let the financial collapse happen to allow the central banks more control. It is hard to understand how the repeal of the Glass-Steagall Act that allowed the merger of banks with investment firms, or the lack of capital backing of AIG's insurance of toxic mortgages could have been missed by the FSB. In fact, they couldn't. Joan Veon makes a very good case that the Fed (the unaccountable Central Bank of the U.S.), the BIS and the FSB used the crises to basically take control over the U.S. financial and regulatory structure,

Since most [people] are not acquainted with our financial and regulatory structure, they will not appreciate the incredible transfer of power being given to the Federal Reserve, a private corporation. Once Congress passes the necessary [financial reform] law, the Fed will be given massive powers over the entire financial and economic industry, the insurance industry, non-banking institutions as well as the mortgage industry.[301]

If Veon is only partially correct, it means Carroll Quigley's prediction of global financial control is almost complete with the passage of the current financial reform laws currently in the House and Senate. Virtually no one knows this.

It is beyond the scope of this book, but once carbon trading is instituted world-wide, it may not take much to switch to a carbon currency in order to make way for a new carbon-based world. Unfortunately for individual people living in this new system, it will also require authoritarian and centralized control over all aspects of life, from cradle to grave.[302]

The idea for a carbon currency has been around since the 1930s under the banner of Technocracy. Technocracy is a world run by scientists and experts. The concept may have been the basis of Carroll Quigley's "managerial society" within which he said there will be a "scientific and rational utilization of resources, in both time and space, to achieve consciously envisioned future goals."[303] Global analyst Patrick Wood explains;

What is Carbon Currency and how does it work? In a nutshell, Carbon Currency will be based on the regular allocation of available energy to the people of the world. If not used within a period of time, the Currency will expire (like monthly minutes on your cell phone plan) so that the same people can receive a new allocation based on new energy production quotas for the next period. Because the energy supply chain is already dominated by the global elite, setting energy production quotas will limit the amount of Carbon Currency in circulation at any one time. It will also naturally limit manufacturing, food production and people movement.[304]

A carbon currency must depend on a finite supply of fossil fuel so that it can be strictly "allocated" (i.e. controlled) by technocrats. Since the founding of Technocracy, every generation has been taught the "peak oil" theory; i.e.

the world only has "x" number of years before the earth's oil is depleted. There is a problem with this theory, however. More oil is discovered every year. In fact, enough oil and gas exist in shale oil formations in Colorado, Utah and Wyoming to last several hundred years with current technology and oil prices.[305]

The U.S. Bureau of Land Management estimates that "1.2–1.8 *trillion* barrels of oil is available in Wyoming's Green River Formation alone. A moderate estimate of 800 *billion* barrels of oil that would be recoverable from oil shale in the Green River Formation is *three* times greater than the proven oil reserves of Saudi Arabia"[306] That is about a 100 year supply of oil at present U.S. consumption rates—just from Wyoming.

It is already economically feasible to start producing this shale oil for oil and gas. However, Congress has been stalling for well over a decade and finally passed the mostly Rousseau-based Omnibus Public Land Management Act of 2009. This Act forever locked up much of this shale oil from being developed. The Heritage Foundation found that "331 million barrels of recoverable oil and 8.8 trillion cubic feet of natural gas would be taken out of exploration in Wyoming. The total amount of energy that would be restricted is equivalent to the amount of natural gas the entire U.S. produces in 15 years…. The bill could not only restrict conventional energy resources, but it could also restrict access to oil shale in parts of Colorado and Utah as well. [307]

Has Congress gone mad? Why did it do this? It is perhaps very revealing that at the same time Congress locked up most of this 100+ year supply of oil, Congressmen and Senators were wringing their hands pontificating to their constituents back home that we must break the dependence on foreign oil. Why? Congress was told that this bill would help make us energy free. Worse, they were told that the bill it would have a devastating impact on the future of energy in the United States. Senator Tom Coburn (R-OK), warned the bill would put 1.3 *trillion* barrels of shale oil, out of the total of about 2 trillion barrels, off limits to development. It also cuts off 9.3 *trillion* cubic feet of natural gas permanently.[308]

Passage of the Omnibus Public Land Management Act doesn't make any sense unless the progressive liberals in Congress are so blinded by their destructive ideology they cannot see the irrationality of the legislation. The only other explanation is they deliberately did it to make oil and natural gas artificially a finite energy source to justify a carbon currency. That seems very unlikely, however, because it would have somehow leaked and even the mainstream media could not cover it up.

On the other hand, evidence exists there is a guiding hand in the process. It is called smart grid technology. The *Technocracy Study Course*[309] initially written in 1932 details what is needed for Technocracy and a carbon currency to work:

- Register on a continuous 24 hour-per-day basis the total net conversion of energy.

- By means of the registration of energy converted and consumed, make possible a balanced load.

- Provide a continuous inventory of all production and consumption

- Provide a specific registration of the type, kind, etc., of all goods and services, where it is produced and where it is used

- Provide specific registration of the consumption of each individual, plus a record and description of the individual." [310]

The technology to implement this did not exist in 1932. It does now. Smart grid technology implements monitoring *and* control from production to consumption. It also allocates how much energy each home or business can use, even down to the appliance level. It is total control of energy use. Smart grid technology has not been developed because of demand or any perceived need. Private industry did not develop it. Rather, the entire idea was advanced by the Department of Energy (DOE) starting with President Bush.

President Obama has allocated $2.3 billion from the Stimulus money to jump start it.[311] The DOE's technology is spreading like wildfire across the world. Why? How? Patrick Wood provides this warning; "Smart Grid meets 100 percent of the Technocracy's original requirements.... If the Federal government had not been the initial and persistent driver, would Smart Grid exist at all? It is highly doubtful."[312]

These are just a few examples of the gross distortion and machinations of all the global environmental and financial crises that most Americans have accepted at face value. While America has a responsibility to protect the environment, the financial elite have squandered enormous sums of money to distort environmental problems into crises of global proportions—all to justify the need for global governance and government control of the lives of all people on earth.[a]

America, with its Locke form of government has been the major obstacle to this effort. This is changing, however. Through foundations, corrupt courts, and progressive politics, the powerful elite are systematically destroying the Locke-based foundation of the U.S. Constitution. They are implementing legalized plunder through the destructive application of "expert planning" and the public good doctrine inherent with the Rousseau model of governance. And because of our Rousseau-oriented education, press, and environmental propaganda machine, most Americans are totally ignorant of what these globalists are doing to our children's future.

There is hope, however. As will be explained in Part III, Americans can take back America for Americans. It is up to each individual American whether America returns to its Locke roots, or continues its progression into Rousseau socialism, fascism and global control. We are out of time. We must act this year. The choice is yours.

---

a   To better understand the Locke approach to sustainable development and a point by point comparison to Agenda 21 read the *Freedom 21; Promoting Sustainability Through Political and Economic Freedom.* http://www.freedom21agenda.org/Freedom21Agenda.pdf

PART III

Taking Back
America

9

Getting Back to
Constitutional Law

*The choice is simple. Americans can continue to suffer the
growing evil, or abolish those policies and actions that allow
plundering of the people.*

The Obligation to Reform Government

THE PREVIOUS SECTION OF THE BOOK reveals the historical
background defining how America got where it is today. After reading
these chapters there should be no doubt of the overwhelming importance
of stopping the global financial cartel from taking the final step to global
control. The America that was established by our Founding Fathers is as
much at war with this destructive progressive ideology as we were as a
nation against Nazi Germany in World War II. It is even more dangerous
because it is an internal war that we didn't even know we were in until very
recently. It is a war America is losing unless you make a stand to stop it.

This country no longer has a Republican form of government "instituted
among Men, deriving their just powers from the consent of the governed."
Instead, it has an intelligent, but poorly educated and indoctrinated population

that a very biased news media and powerful social-environmental lobby can easily manipulate. In turn, political and financial manipulation by the global financial cartel heavily influences public education, the judicial system, the media and environmental leaders.

To use an expression aptly coined by Vladimir Lenin to describe those who blindly parrot the party line, most of the education leaders, reporters (mainly editors), judges and environmental leaders are being used as 'useful idiots' that mindlessly advance the destructive global agenda. It is not that America does not have environmental and social problems. It does. The success of every great lie is that it contains some truth. One misconception is that most of those working to advance this agenda are doing so for malevolent reasons. Some do it because that is the way to get ahead, but most really believe what they advocate—in spite of overwhelming evidence that what they are doing has never worked, and is ultimately very destructive to the freedoms, wealth and sovereignty of individuals.

Thankfully, although each generation is progressively being dumbed-down, it does not mean Americans are unintelligent. Once they learn what is happening to them, these very same Americans have a long history of rising to the occasion and doing the right thing. The choice is simple. Americans can continue to suffer the growing evil, or abolish those policies and actions that allow plundering of the people. Our Founders wrote in the Declaration of Independence, "…That whenever any Form of Government becomes destructive of these ends, it is the *Right of the People to alter* or to abolish it, and to institute new Government, laying its foundation on such principles and organizing its powers in such form, as to them shall seem most likely to effect their Safety and Happiness."[313] (Italics added)

As the tyrannical nature of the federal government increased in the latter half of the twentieth century, many people began to advocate military revolution, ready to die for their freedom and beliefs. Others became "constitutionalists" who insisted that the United States must return to the original intention of the United States Constitution. Their goal is to roll back and constrain one-hundred years of legislation and case law that they believe has all but destroyed what was once a nation of the people, by the people, and for the people.

It is obvious, however, that the overwhelming majority of Americans have not understood the importance of the U.S. Constitution to their freedom or future—until now. Nor until 2008, did they even care. Never has life been as good as it was before 2008. Why spoil it? Nor, did the people even understand the issues. How could they? Progressive politicians and the group-think monopolistic mainstream media told them that everything was just fine.

The lock by the progressive mainstream media began to weaken with the growing importance of the conservative media in the late 1990s and 2000s. The economic collapse in 2008 shocked voters into reality and they voted for those promising change from the business-as-usual mentality that caused the collapse. The 2008 election of President Obama and a progressive liberal controlled Congress soon dashed that hope.

It did not take long before the very people Americans had hoped would save America revealed that the true agenda behind Obama's "change" was a major acceleration of the policies that had gotten the United States in the present mess in the first place. Worse, it soon became obvious that these progressives were going to implement their agenda despite overwhelming opposition from the American people—just like Frédéric Bastiat said the Rousseau socialists did in post-revolutionary France. If America is to remain a free nation dependent on Constitutional principles, this radical agenda must be exposed and its political power neutralized.

At the same time, the global cartel and Rousseau socialists have been working for a hundred years to achieve their goals. They will not willingly give up the reins of power. So far they have fought the battle by using the mainstream media to ignore or viciously attack anyone who opposes them. It is critical to understand that they never argue the facts with their opposition; rather they use tactics based on emotional demagoguery to destroy their opposition. The strategy has worked extremely well until now, but America is waking up and its people increasingly realize they have been duped by indoctrination for decades. As the grassroots efforts continue to grow, expect the politics of destruction to get ever more vicious. Sadly, it is the only defense the elite and mainstream media know how to use.

As people wake up and get fired-up they will want to know what they can do to stop this behemoth from taking total control of their lives. Violence of any form is not the answer. Violence only plays into the hands of a corrupt government because it provides them the public excuse to clamp down on all opposition. The demonization of the Tea Party Movement by linking them to terrorists may be a thinly disguised attempt to provoke confrontation. So far, the only hard evidence of violence has been on the part of the left. Yet, the mainstream media rarely, if ever mention the violence on the left, but consistently link tea party adherents to insurrection, sedation and other forms of terror.[314]

The media coverage of the immigration "rallies" in Phoenix and Washington D.C. following the passage of Arizona's Illegal Immigration law on April 24, 2010 provides a perfect example. Leftist rioters were throwing bricks and demeaning epithets at police, but were described by most, if not all, mainstream media as "mostly peaceful." Contrast those leftist actions with that with the April 15, 2010 tea party rally in Washington D.C., which were very orderly and disciplined, but which the mainstream media described as "growing ugly."

Even when footage of both were shown side by side, progressive commentators called the riots "mostly peaceful" while condemning the tea party.[315] The blatant bias of the left can only be described as bizarre. The mainstream media appear no longer to have a connection to reality. They have gone from "spin" to "propaganda."

Polls show that about 70 percent of the American people have seen through the progressive's shrill attack on the Arizona law and want their states to pass the same type of law.[316] Time will tell whether Middle America sees through the propaganda on almost every other issue pushed by the progressives. Evidence suggests that Americans are waking up and realizing they are being deliberately deceived. There is also a growing concern that it is only a matter of time before leftist extremists will use provocateurs within otherwise peaceful tea party protests to provoke a violent confrontation to discredit all opposition and invite repression of all dissent.

Violence is not the answer. A military revolution is even worse; to the point of being idiotic. In the 1700s, the British army and the colonists both were armed with the same weapons. While it is true that many militias have assault rifles and automatic weapons, they are no match to the sophisticated weapons that the police and military forces have today. A careful review of what happened in 2001 to the Taliban and Al Qaeda forces in Afghanistan and the Republican Guard in Iraq in 2003 should clearly illustrate that the use of force cannot take back the United States. Nor is force necessary.

Throw the Rascals Out

Ironically, the answer still lies in the Constitution, but perhaps in ways different than many strict constitutionalists believe. Certainly, those that want to reclaim their freedoms must do all they can to throw the progressive liberals out of office; starting in the 2010 election. This includes *any* Congressional, legislative, or local commissar who has voted the progressive liberal line *regardless* of their party affiliation. The 2009 off-year election of semi-conservative Republican Governors in New Jersey and Virginia, and the near election of a Tea Party conservative in the upstate New York House of Representatives race, tended to support the idea that a major November 2010 upset was in the wind. The election of Scott Brown to replace the progressive Ted Kennedy in Massachusetts merely confirms that.

Progressive liberals dismissed the Virginia and New Jersey gubernatorial elections as a minor setback and totally ignored the upstate New York's House of Representatives election. However, when conservative Scott Brown pulled ahead of the Democrat Martha Coakley in the polls a week before the Massachusetts election to replace Ted Kennedy's Senate position, the progressive liberals went into panic mode. Democrats outnumber Republicans by three to one in Massachusetts. The very progressive liberal Ted Kennedy was elected to the Senate for forty-six years. Everyone had forecast an easy win for Coakley. They could not believe that Kennedy's seat might be lost to conservative Scott Brown. The impossible happened though; Scott Brown won.

When Brown easily won over Coakley it should have sent a powerful message to the progressive liberals in Washington that they should move to the political center. It didn't. They threw Martha Coakley under the bus by blaming her poor campaigning for the election failure, not their radical progressive agenda. Progressive Democrats steadfastly denied it was their progressive liberal actions in the White House and Congress that the people were voting against. If conservatives can do this in the most progressive liberal state in the Union, it could portend a major blowout for conservative candidates in the November 2010 election.

The progressive Democrats unbelievable state of denial seems to many people to be delusional. It doesn't make any sense politically. Instead of moving toward the political center as such a historic defeat would call for, they are charging ahead as if they have won. Are they committing political suicide?

The seeming political schizophrenia by the progressive liberals only makes sense if they are following the Saul Alinsky formula for winning and radically transforming America. Alinsky coached that when you are surrounded and in trouble, put on the gas and attack the opposition. They have gradually come into power over the last few decades through the relentless attack against anyone who opposes them by demonization and false accusations. The end (victory) justifies the means even if it means lying, cheating, and conducting criminal activities. It has worked for ACORN and the SEIU for decades. It also worked in passing an extremely unpopular health care bill.

If the progressive liberals are truly using the Saul Alinsky strategy they will not give up and will intensify their attacks on anyone who opposes them. The much hated Glenn Beck warned that their first victims will be any Democrat in Congress who opposes them—even if it means destroying the traditional Democrat party in the process. It appears these progressives don't care, or may even desire the destruction of the party.

There will be an effort during 2010 to vote in universal voting registration whereby everyone who is on any government list is registered; sometimes in two or three locations. When that happens they can load the system with bogus voters and steal any election they desire. Another tool will be giving amnesty to illegal aliens, who will then be given voting rights. Yet another is giving voting rights to felons. All of these tricks will greatly favor Democrat candidates because they are falsely portrayed as the party of the little guy and those down and out. America must not allow these bills to pass.

Such a strategy by the progressives will only cause more people to join The Tea Party Movement. Tea Party leadership is already developing a strategy to replace progressive liberals of *both* parties with citizens desiring to uphold Constitutional principles. The danger that the Tea Party leadership may attempt to create a third party seems remote. Third parties have never worked in the past. Besides, if a party is formed, it quickly would become a target for the elite to put their people in to control it. The power in the Tea Party Movement is the thousands of like-minded groups at the local level. It is far easier to work effectively within the Republican Party to get them back to their original conservative Constitutional principles with bottom up control rather than the present top down. It is far more difficult for Constitutional Democrats to work within the Democrat Party because it has been totally hijacked by Rousseau progressive liberals.

However, the American people, even Republican leadership still do not get it. Almost no one realizes we are in a literal war to the death for the American mind over what model of governance we should have; Rousseau's progressive liberalism or Locke's Constitutional conservatism. Only one will survive. Republicans cannot take for granted that Scott Brown's Massachusetts victory gives them a shoe-in in the November 2010 elections. It does not. A January 22, 2010 poll by Fox News on Fox and Friends showed that as many people will vote for liberal Democrats as will vote for Republicans.

Many Republican politicians are closet progressives themselves, or have been intimidated to believe they must be partially liberal to stay in office. They still think it is politics as usual. It is not. We are witnessing a "paradigm" or fundamental shift in American politics as people begin to understand the dangerous progressive ideology that finally revealed itself in 2009. Yet, they still do not truly understand *why* we are in the mess we are in. A huge educational job lies ahead if the voters are to be educated as to *why* they are so upset. We must return to Constitutional principles as laid out by John Locke. The electorate is not yet aware why that is so critically important. Once the electorate is educated, even true Democrats (not progressives) have a chance to win in the November 2010 elections if they adopt Constitutional principles.

That raises another problem. Many neoconservatives and conservative Democrats will take on a more conservative image as they did in 1994 to win the 2010 election. They will not truly change their big government anti-Constitutional ideology. They will not understand why their beliefs are ultimately destructive. Once reelected it will be business as usual. Therefore, it is imperative that they be identified in the primary elections and exposed.

To do this, local activists can develop a list of pledge statements they can submit to candidates to force them to support Constitutional principles. Freedom 21[317] has put together such a list to which candidates must pledge agreement in order to get the organizations endorsement:

- I will vote *for* only that legislation which contains a citation to the specific authority granted in Article 1, Section 8 of the U.S. Constitution.
- I will vote *against* any legislation that infringes the individual right to keep and bear arms.
- I will vote *for* legislation that allows the use of domestic resources to achieve energy and food independence.
- I will vote *for* only that legislation which applies equally to the public, and to members of the judicial, legislative, and executive branches of the federal government.
- I will vote *against* any legislation that results in a federal takeover of any private corporation, institution, or entity.
- I will vote *against* any legislation that raises the pay of legislators in any year without a balanced budget

- I will vote *against* any legislation that authorizes the United Nations to impose a tax, levy, fee or royalty on the United States or any of its citizens.

- I will vote *against* any legislation that attempts to implement provisions of any treaty not approved by two-thirds vote of the Senate (as mandated by the Constitution in Article 2, Section 2).

Obviously, these principles apply best to Congressional candidates, but provide a template that is easily modified for other levels of government as well. If their past record does not support these principles, challenge them on it. Some candidates will have truly changed, but many who pledge to uphold these principles do so only to garner the conservative vote. Their commitment is only skin deep. If possible, vote for someone who clearly upholds these principles in their heart.

It is imperative to the future of America that candidates holding these Constitutional principles be elected to office. They should be heavily supported. Never will we have as good a chance to reform our political offices as we have now. If the elected offices are not taken back during the 2010 elections, it could very well be that the Constitution will be made a worthless piece of paper and it will be nearly impossible to recapture the freedoms the Founders wanted us to have.

Eventually, all future laws as well as the laws passed the last 100 years should go through the acid test of Constitutionality. In doing so, it must be understood that 100 years of systematic destruction of Constitutional governance cannot be undone over night. Our entire economy and culture is now built around the Rousseau socialist/fascist model of governance. The restoration of Constitutional governance must also be done with wisdom to minimize unnecessary turmoil. It will take time to undo the indoctrination and destructive laws done over the course of generations. The first step will be to reinstate local control of our public schools and demand textbooks be based on true facts rather than revisionist theory and history that is common in today's textbooks.

Equally important, the new Congress must uphold their Constitutional responsibility to impeach judges in the various courts if they stray from the Constitution. Under Article III of the Constitution, judges "hold their offices during good behavior." For the most part that means till death, resignation, or retirement, but judges who misbehave badly enough can be removed from office by impeachment, same as for the President and "all civil officers of the United States." To judge from the impeachment record, such misbehavior is rare. To date only 13 federal judges have had impeachment proceedings started against them in the House of Representatives; of the 11 tried by the Senate (the other two bailed first), only seven were convicted and removed from office.[318] While impeachment must never be taken lightly, it is imperative that the worst judicial offenders of Constitutional governance be quickly impeached.

The Rousseau mentality that pervades the bureaucratic culture of federal, state and local governments won't disappear overnight. Those who have forced to pay into social security, and whose retirement plan was built around it, cannot suddenly have it taken away. An increasing majority of today's bureaucrats believe it is their responsibility to control citizens in their jurisdictions rather than to serve them. The abuse of urbanites by smart growth laws and rural citizens by environmental laws are likely to continue for some time. There is hope. A process will be described in the next chapter using existing law that will often stop this bureaucratic tyranny in its tracks.

Never in recent history has there been a better opportunity to thwart the global agenda that the financial cartel is advancing. The goal should be; first to purge every progressive liberal from office, then to peacefully restore America's Constitutional Republic. This go-slow approach will stick in the throats of many conservatives who stand on an unyielding all-or-nothing principle. It will mean being flexible in applying the standards of Constitutional law. The rigid all-or-nothing approach to stopping this agenda in the past has yielded... *nothing*. If anything, it has propelled us ever deeper into Rousseau socialism and control by the planning elites.

The demands and clamor of constitutionalists to return instantly to the Constitutional form of governance has merely given Rousseau progressive socialists ammunition to paint "constitutionalists" as wide-eyed ideologues who are out of touch with reality, and who care nothing about the poor. However, if conservatives can take a longer, more flexible view of success, it is possible to avoid disaster. It starts with restoring the Tenth Amendment.

Restoring the Tenth Amendment

The Tenth Amendment to the Constitution of the United States affirms that, "The powers not delegated to the United States by the Constitution, nor prohibited by it to the States, are reserved to the States respectively, or to the people." In other words, state power trumps federal power except for the specific powers delegated to the federal government in the Constitution. Thomas Jefferson warned,

> When all government, domestic and foreign, in little as in great things, shall be drawn to Washington as the center of all power, it will render powerless the checks provided of one government on another and will become as venal and oppressive as the government from which we separated.[319]

Our Founders understood the dangers of a powerful central government. Therefore, they designed the structure of governance so that the powers delegated to the federal government are very few and well defined. The Tenth Amendment should guarantee that most government power resides with the individual states or its people. However, the usurpation of state powers by the federal government has all but eliminated the protection of the people by the Tenth Amendment.

The erosion of the Tenth Amendment started when the Seventeenth Amendment was ratified in 1913 after being promoted by the progressives of the era. This transferred the selection of a State's two Senators by each state's legislature, to popular election by the people of each state. The Constitution originally had Senators represent the state's interest, which would have all but prevented any legislation from passing that weakened the state's powers in relation to the federal government. With the ratification of the Seventeenth Amendment, however, Senators were elected by the people, who were heavily influenced by party propaganda.

An expansionist Congress and an activist Supreme Court wanting to *make* law rather than interpret it have assaulted the Tenth Amendment during much of the twentieth century. However, the Court has reversed itself in key decisions since the mid-1990s by finding many laws unconstitutional.

For instance, the U.S. Supreme Court declared the Gun-Free Zones Act of 1990 unconstitutional in the *United States v. Lopez* decision in 1995. Chief Justice Rehnquist said that the Act "would effectively obliterate the distinction between what is national and what is local and creates a completely centralized government." That is not all. "If Congress can," asserts Rehnquist, "…regulate activities that adversely affect the learning environment, then…it also can regulate the educational process directly… and mandate a federal curriculum for local elementary and secondary schools."[320] The decision not only reaffirmed the Tenth Amendment, but also stated the federal government cannot dictate school curricula.

If there was any doubt to the Court's intent in Lopez, *United States v. Antonio J. Morrison* on May 15, 2000, cast aside those doubts. In this case, the federal government attempted to expand gun control because a rapist used a gun to commit his crime. While not diminishing the horror of rape, the Court cited the Lopez decision, saying to have accepted the argument would have permitted Congress to:

> regulate not only all violent crime, but all activities that *might* lead to violent crime, regardless of how tenuously they relate to interstate commerce…. Under the[se] theories…, it is difficult to perceive any limitation on federal power.[321] (Italics added)

As with Lopez, the Court affirmed the police power of the Tenth Amendment, deferring to the sovereignty of the state.

The Brady Handgun Violence Prevention Act was also declared unconstitutional. In *Printz v. United States.* Justice Scalia stated in the majority opinion that:

> Congress *cannot compel the States to enact or enforce a federal regulatory program... The Federal Government may neither issue directives requiring the States to address particular problems, nor command the State's officers, or those of their political subdivisions, to administer or enforce a federal regulatory program...* [S]uch commands are fundamentally incompatible with our constitutional system of dual sovereignty.[322] (Italics added)

While the case specifically addresses the Brady Handgun Act, the principle follows through on a host of other federal mandates forcing the states or local government to carry them out. These decisions are encouraging. More recently four states have passed a "Firearms Freedom Act" and ten more states are considering it.[323] The Act openly challenges the authority of the federal government to regulate firearms that are made and sold within the state. Likewise, the federal Real ID Act of 2005 has been challenged in over 25 states.[324] As a consequence the federal government keeps postponing its implementation. Finally, 38 states have filed or pre-filed legislation to opt out of the federal health care legislation.[325]

A judicial system and a Congress that actually upholds the U.S. Constitution, as each judge or Congressman has sworn to do, is ultimately the only long-term solution to restoring the Constitutional foundation of the United States. In the meantime, activists and zealous bureaucrats seeking to impose Rousseau socialism on the American people are destroying individuals, families and entire communities. They are aided by an indoctrinated population that believes socialistic laws and regulations are the only solution for the nation's problems.

In addition to a number of other Supreme Court decisions, the Data Quality Act of 2001 has now gone into effect. This long overdue Act requires federal agencies to accurately report and use defensible science in making regulatory decisions. Most agencies screamed and attempted to worm their way out of the Act's requirements—to no avail. At a minimum, the Act requires federal agencies to disseminate accurately all information on their websites and literature. However, most attorneys believe that it also includes the science and information used in the rule-making process for creating regulations.

Since the Data Quality Act also includes rulemaking, federal agencies should no longer be able to use junk science or even pseudo science to administer harsh Rousseau oriented regulations. Citizens and companies can even take federal agencies to court if they attempt to use pseudoscience. This will go a long way in stopping the arbitrary and capricious administration of federal law. On the downside, opponents claim industry can use the Act to tie up the rulemaking process thereby allowing the companies to continue polluting and a variety of other alleged nefarious activities.[326] While this is definitely a deficiency, the danger of misusing junk science by federal agencies far outweighs the misuse of the Act by potential violators. The Act puts the onus of proof on the government, where it belongs.

The issuance of an Endangerment Finding of carbon dioxide by the EPA in 2009 based on provable junk science is a classic case of agency abuse of regulatory powers. The Endangerment Finding allows the EPA to unleash a torrent of new compliance regulations that allegedly stops global warming. The EPA regulations are far worse than the economically devastating cap and trade legislation proposed by Congress. The EPA even suppressed an internal report detailing the endangerment finding is not supported by science. Fortunately, three states and several private organizations have filed lawsuits to overturn the endangerment finding "on the grounds that EPA has ignored major scientific issues."[327]

Regardless of the Data Quality Act, however, local citizens have legal tools to defend themselves against federal intrusion into their schools and local economy. For instance, Section 319 of the Goals 2000: Educate America Act (HR 1804) clearly states, "The Congress agrees and reaffirms that the responsibility for control of education is reserved to the States and local school systems and other instrumentalities of the States…"

Although home schooling is under attack in many states, a close look at state law will affirm that the public schools have no legal authority to stop parents from home-schooling their kids. They do, however, have the legal ability and obligation to confront their own dumbed-down school system. There is a cost, however. Parents and citizens must convince their local school board to stop taking state and federal funds that come with a hangman's noose attached.

On the other hand, recent federal laws passed by Congress have empowered a *single* special interest, Non-governmental Organization (NGO) control to define the entire federal standards for civics and government! This one Rousseau-oriented NGO, The Center for Civic Education, is the federal government's *only* source to establish the federal standards for civics and government. Even if a local school district does not want to use this material, textbook writers are restructuring their textbooks to conform to progressive Rousseau revisionist history. Worse, national tests will also reflect this propaganda. In order for students to pass these tests, local school districts must teach this *extremely* biased curriculum—even in home schools.

Kelo vs City of New London

One of the biggest Supreme Court reversals of the Constitution's Fifth Amendment's protection against eminent domain takings by government is *Kelo vs City of New London*, Connecticut. In 1998, the drug company Pfizer built a new plant in New London, Connecticut. To take advantage of additional business and *taxes* the plant might bring in, the City of New London attempted to purchase 115 houses in a nearby area in order to sell it to commercial developers. Fifteen residents resisted, so the city used eminent domain to claim the land.[328] Petitioners brought this state-court action claiming that the taking of their properties would violate the "public use" restriction in the Fifth Amendment's Takings Clause.

The case should have been a no brainer. The Fifth Amendment states that, "No person shall be…deprived of life, liberty, or property, without due process of law; nor shall private property be taken for *public use*, without just compensation." In other words, government cannot use eminent domain unless the reason is for a public use such as roads, libraries, schools, and others. The legal precedents are well established, with the most famous the building of Rockefeller Center in New York City in the 1930s. Two property owners refused to sell their land for the development of Rockefeller Center. In spite of a multibillion dollar project in terms of today's dollars, Rockefeller could not force the owners to sell to him. Those two properties still stand today on either side of the main Rockefeller building.

However, over time, progressive judges began to allow cities to use eminent domain to condemn property for the city, which then gives or sells it for private development—in complete contempt for the Fifth Amendment. The abuse reached its peak in the *Kelo vs City of New London* Supreme Court case. In spite of a rich history of case law, along with the obvious intent of the Fifth Amendment, the Supreme Court ruled 5-4 in favor of the City of New London. The operative phrase in this case was "taken for public use."

In issuing the decision, the majority ruling basically upheld the "finding" that the neighborhood was "distressed" (which it was not) and ripe for urban renewal. Therefore the city had the right to implement a "carefully considered development plan, which was not adopted 'to benefit a particular class of identifiable individuals.'"[329] This blatantly ignores the fact that it *was* clearly done to benefit identifiable individuals. Furthermore, any simplistic reading of the Founders writings reveals that the intent of the Fifth Amendment was designed to protect citizens from *exactly this kind* of government abuse of power.

With the *Kelo vs City of New London* decision, no longer is it an unalienable right to own and use private property without the fear of the government taking it for any reason as long as it provides a public benefit. In their dissent, Supreme Court Justices Sandra Day O'Conner, Clarence Thomas, Anthony Scalia and Chief Justice William Rehnquist issued a scathing decent that the decision would create a reverse Robin Hood phenomenon—take from the poor and powerless and give to the rich and powerful. Justice O'Connor wrote:

[A] law that takes property from A. and gives it to B: It is against all reason and justice, for a people to entrust a Legislature with *such* powers; and, therefore, it cannot be presumed that they have done it…. To reason, as the Court does, that the incidental public benefits resulting from the subsequent ordinary use of private property render economic development takings "for public use" is to wash out any distinction between private and public use of property—and thereby effectively to delete the words "for public use" from the Takings Clause of the Fifth Amendment.[330]

Justice Thomas built upon O'Connor's dissent, "Today's decision is simply the latest in a string of our cases construing the Public Use Clause to be a virtual nullity, without the slightest nod to its original meaning."[331] Thomas even stated that the decision opens the door to using eminent domain to take property without *any* just compensation. Yet, a Rousseau oriented progressive Supreme Court has turned the Constitution on its head in this as well as many other cases. There is no longer protection for the citizen against a tyrannical government in these decisions. These cases have taken the United States from the John Locke model of government to the Jean Jacques Rousseau model.

It should now be obvious that it is imperative that the electorate elect only those candidates who pledge to follow the Constitution in the 2010 elections and begin to impeach federal judges who willfully make decisions in violation of the Constitution.

The *Kelo* decision suddenly drove home to urbanites the realization that they were vulnerable to the whims of government and the power brokers behind them. The abuse of another form of eminent domain—the power of regulation—is something that rural residents have been aware of for several decades. Urban Americans have heard rumblings from their rural brethren complaining about increasing land use regulations that made farming, ranching, forestry and mining economically infeasible. However, the mainstream progressive press often portrayed the grumblers as extremists or those in the pockets of big industry who put profits ahead of environmental protection. The complaints fell on deaf ears.

That is changing as urbanites are increasingly assaulted with smart growth regulations. There is a solution. Ironically, many of the laws that have caused great harm to Constitutional principles can be used to protect citizens from the heavy hand of government. They are not the total answer, but can provide a stop-gap measure until more permanent solutions are enacted! With a few major exceptions, recent federal, state and Supreme Court decisions have opened a door of opportunity that has not been open for many decades. Within every federal and most state environmental law are clauses that can be used to protect property owners from the abuse of Rousseau oriented laws and regulations.

10

Protecting Your Community

Where local government has forced the federal government to obey its own laws using the coordination process, it has worked to protect the local community

FORTUNATELY, LOCAL COMMUNITIES DO HAVE SOME CONTROL over most abusive federal environmental laws and some state laws. Congress has directed the federal agencies to coordinate with local government "because they recognize that local authority must be consulted and involved in the decision making process above and before the public input process."[332] Although few communities know about it, almost all federal environmental laws and many state laws require federal or state agencies to work with local government on a government-to-government basis. In other words, local governments have equal footing in the negotiating process.

For instance, the National Environmental Policy Act of 1969 (NEPA) requires every federal agency to comply with this law whenever they take any major federal action. Local communities have not recognized they could play a major role in the process to protect themselves. Instead, they have becomes victims. Radical environmentalists, however, quickly realized that by manipulating NEPA, the law gave them incredible power to trump property rights. They have used it mercilessly to deny people one of the fundamental civil rights given the American people in the Constitution.

Margaret Byfield, director of American Stewards of Liberty has studied how the environmentalists were so successful. She found that,

> To ensure the results the radicals wanted, the environmentalists picked their judges. They studied very carefully the jurisdictions in which they brought NEPA cases. The Ninth Circuit became the Promised Land for them because of the activist nature and environmentally biased judges. Once they secured a foothold with one victory, the decision became precedent for the next, and so on up the ladder of litigation experiences. They set their strategy and put it in motion decades ago.[333]

With their string of victories, radical environmentalists wound their way into the offices of the resource management agencies, talking to them daily, threatening them with litigation. It has become commonplace for management agency personnel to say, "if I did that the environmentalists would sue." So, their success in litigation has led to management through intimidation. Today, one would have difficulty finding agency personnel who even understood the purpose of NEPA, other than protection of the natural environment—the trees, the shrubs, the species—without any consideration of the human economy and human productivity.[334]

However, environmentalists can manipulate NEPA only as long as local governments remain in ignorance. NEPA gives local governments far more power than it does to environmentalists or other advocacy groups. NEPA sets the statutory coordination requirements in Title 42 §4331(a): "The Congress... declares that it is the continuing policy of the Federal Government, in *cooperation* with State and *local* governments, and other concerned public and private organizations..." (Italics added) Notice the sentence structure distinguishes the two groups. The first are units of government, the second are public and private entities, or non-governmental entities. Both federal and state non-environmental laws may also have this type of language local governments can use.

NEPA requires that the agencies coordinate with local governments. In section 4331(a), cited above, Congress set apart the relationship between the federal government and state and local governments from that of the public and private organizations. In §4331 (b), Congress directs the federal government to "*coordinate* federal plans, functions, programs and resources." This coordination is with the federal government and the government units identified in the previous section, not the public. The public, including environmental nongovernmental organizations, has no authority or standing to implement "plans, functions, programs and resources" in a manner binding on the citizens. State and local governments do. So by way of these sections of the statute, any agency carrying out an environmental study under NEPA has been directed by Congress to coordinate that study with local governments.[335]

Section 4331(b) of NEPA, cited above, continues by stating, "[to] preserve important historic, cultural, and natural aspects of our national heritage, and maintain, wherever possible, an environment which supports diversity and variety of *individual choice*..." According to attorney Fred Kelly Grant "Congress has directed the federal agencies to coordinate with local government because they recognize that local authority must be consulted and involved in the decision making process above and before the public input process."[336] Grant is one of the key people who discovered and developed this process into a highly successful strategy outlined by American Stewards of Liberty.[337] Margaret Byfield notes:

Unlike the 35-plus major environmental bills filed in the 90th and 91st Congress of the late 1960s, NEPA was not advocated by militant organized environmental activists. In fact, they paid little attention to the legislation until late in the process, when they recognized it could play a role in stopping unwanted projects. This is likely the reason the text emphasizes man's environment and the productive use of the environment. When read in its entirety, it is clear the intent of Congress was to ensure a healthy, productive environment for man's benefit.[338]

In other words, NEPA Environmental Impact Studies were never intended to be one dimensional, focusing solely on the natural environment. Section 4331(a) of NEPA also mandates that all this is to be done in order to "fulfill the social, economic and other requirements of present and future generations of Americans." Byfield notes that "every Environmental Impact Statement should include, but rarely does, detailed studies as to the impact that the action will have on the local economy, the community, and the safety of the citizens."[339]

Landowners and local governments are beginning to realize NEPA gives them a powerful tool to protect themselves from the federal assault on property rights and the economy of their local town or county. When a local government requires that the study be coordinated with them, the agency is required to follow the five criteria for coordination defined in the sister statute, the Federal Land Policy and Management Act (FLPMA). The Supreme Court has ruled that when Congress defines a word in one statute, uses the word in a sister statute and does not redefine this, then we are to presume Congress intended the same definition. So, the FLPMA criterion applies to the NEPA requirement for coordination as well.[340] In 43 United States Code Section 1712 Congress directs that the agency implement this requirement by doing the following:

1. Keep apprised of State, local and tribal land use plans;

2. Assure that consideration is given to local plans when developing a federal plan, policy or management action;

3. Provide early notification (prior to public notice) to local government of development of any plan, policy or action;

4. Provide opportunity for meaningful input by local government into development of the plan, policy or action; and

5. Make all practical effort to resolve conflicts between federal and local policy, and reach consistency.[341]

Local communities, usually counties, which have taken advantage of this provision, have found that when they develop their own county plans within the framework of NEPA, the federal agency must adjust the federal plan to be consistent with the local plan or explain why it cannot.

Although cities and townships have not yet done this with NEPA, the law and its opportunity applies equally for them. Towns and cities have used the process with state law, however, and the results have been nothing short of spectacular in some cases. Even if "coordination" language is not in state law, many, if not most state constitutions and laws also allow local control.

As important, if the state or local government accepts *any* federal money for planning or implementing abusive environmental regulations, they too come under the same NEPA requirements as federal agencies. If county government is abusive, such as a large city dominating decisions that affect rural residents within the county, citizens can organize their townships or school districts to protect their citizens. Citizens can also sue their local government for failure to coordinate properly with a federal agency.

Both the U.S. Code (U.S.C.) and the Code of Federal Regulations (C.F.R) provide powerful tools for local governments to intervene and protect its citizens through coordination in federal planning. For instance, Title 40 C.F.R. §1502.16(c) requires all federal agencies to identify and report "possible conflicts between the proposed action and the objectives of federal, regional, State and local (and… Indian tribe) land use plans, policies and controls for the area concerned."

Title 40 C.F.R §1506.2d goes on to say that environmental impact statements must discuss any "inconsistency of a proposed action with any approved State or local plan and laws (whether or not federally sanctioned). Where an inconsistency exists, the [Environmental Impact Statement] should describe the extent to *which the agency would reconcile its proposed action with the plan or law*." (Italics added)

Because of 40C.F.R. §1506.2, the local government no longer is merely an advisor or subordinate to the primacy of the federal agency in the planning process. The local government can be a *joint* partner with the federal agency in developing a plan to implement an environmental law. If the federal plan is *not* consistent with the county or community plan, the federal agency (*not* the local government) must identify that inconsistency and then mitigate the difference. *The burden is on the federal government,* not the local government! Once the joint plan is accepted by the federal agency, the agency is responsible for its administration—and its liability, not the local community.

One of the biggest obstacles to local citizens and elected officials applying these laws is their disbelief that they can legally do this. Local attorneys have a tendency to disbelieve anything unless there is case law to support it or it comes from another attorney. Even where this exists, attorneys often drag their feet because it requires a lot of work on their part learning how to proceed. Yet, where local government has forced the federal government to obey its own laws using the coordination process, it has worked to protect the local community! While the Rousseau model of an all-powerful federal government has not been totally reversed, the approach can severely constrain the arbitrary power of federal agencies. Similar abuse is also occurring at the state, county and city level.

Federal bureaucracies are disinclined to give up the Rousseau power they have enjoyed for decades. That is especially true in the Obama administration. Margret Byfield warns that federal and state agencies often resist local government's insistence that the study be coordinated with them, taking the position that they cannot discuss the details of the study with them until the draft study has been released. This is not only a violation of the coordination process, but a violation of the CEQ rules. At 40 CFR 1507.1(a) the regulations state that, "As part of the scoping process the lead agency shall: (1) *Invite the participation of affected Federal, State and local agencies...*" (italics added) This rule makes it clear that local governments are to be involved in a meaningful way *at the very beginning* of the study.[342]

However, unless the local government takes the agency to court, the stonewalling works. Most local governments cannot afford to go to court, so the use of NEPA and other environmental laws have only been partially successful. If the people in a county or community suffer from bureaucratic abuse of regulations, then it is imperative that the citizens elect representatives who are willing to stand up for their citizens and support a lawsuit. This is becoming easier as more local governments have established precedent.

Although change comes slow to bureaucracies, the various federal agencies administering NEPA are required to seek active involvement of local government in their planning process. Unfortunately, after decades of indoctrination by colleges and agency policy, most government resource regulatory employees believe that, rather than *serve* the people; their job is to protect the environment *from* American citizens regardless of the cost. That this imperative is part of the culture of federal agencies is evident in a Bureau of Land Management (BLM) 1994 internal working document. The working document required BLM employees to treat "human beings as a biological resource" when implementing ecosystem management.[343]

Although many federal employees believe they must protect the environment *from* people, they are generally not evil, contrary to the belief of many rural citizens. Likewise, most government employees certainly have no idea they are unwittingly helping to implement the global agenda. A shocking study done by Yale research psychologist Dr. Stanley Milgram clearly showed that "...*ordinary people, simply doing their jobs, and without any particular hostility on their part, can become agents in a terrible destructive process.*"[344] (Italics added) Milgram drew these conclusions from research designed to determine whether "normal" Americans would exceed personal moral limits of inflicting pain on others if they believed they were doing so under a higher authority, and for a good cause.

A graphic illustration of this is the April 2004 revelation of abuse by otherwise "normal" soldiers of Iraqi prisoners in Abu Ghraib prison. None of the soldiers would ever even think of doing what they did in any other circumstance. They believed they had to get good intelligence because Iraqi terrorists and Saddam loyalists were brutally killing civilian contractors and soldiers every day. And besides, the tactics they used were primarily mental, in no way morally comparable to the barbaric torture and beheadings used by the terrorists and Saddam loyalists. They certainly thought they had the blessings of their superiors. The soldiers had moral justification and perceived approval from a higher authority.

Both conditions also exist within the culture of federal agencies today. Already predisposed to Rousseau indoctrination, many, if not most federal resource use employees believe they are morally right in protecting the environment from "greedy" landowners. They also have the perceived authority from their superiors and the Rousseau-oriented laws themselves. Dr. Robert Lee, professor of sociology and natural resources at the University of Washington, warns that otherwise "normal" government employees can inflict "extreme human suffering" on people "for violating laws protecting nature by creating a minor disturbance in a wetland, cutting a tree, or building a road on an unstable slope."[345]

Government agents must learn they do not have the authority to treat landowners as "biological resources" subject to their decrees. Instead, federal employees need to learn that while they must enforce various environmental laws, they remain the *servants* of the very American citizens whom their decisions affect. As such, they must cooperate and coordinate with local citizens and governments to find ways to protect the environment *and* the local economy—as required by law.

Two Types of Agency/Community Interaction

Cooperation. Various federal agencies have already attempted to use Resource Advisory Committees and Stakeholder Councils to *cooperate* (not coordinate) with local citizens with varying levels of success. Attorney Fred Kelly Grant warns that "no version of the word 'cooperate' carries any connotation of equal parties striving for harmonious result as does coordinate and coordination. A superior party can cooperate with an inferior party. By the act of cooperation, the inferior party does not become equal to the superior. Unequal parties can "cooperate" by working together to accomplish their unequal goals."[346] Grant also warns that:

The federal agencies, particularly the Forest Service, seek to lure local government into a "cooperating agency" role. As such "cooperating agency," the local government sits at the planning table with the federal interdisciplinary planning team. The agency can provide input into the planning activity, and the federal team listens. But, then most often, the local input is ignored and never referred to in the planning document that emerges from the meetings.[347]

However, while the cooperation approach has value, unless the community controls the selection of the citizens appointed to the committees or councils so they are truly representative, agenda-driven special interest groups quickly dominate the process.

Additionally, because the agency invites local people to participate in the advisory committee or stakeholder council, the agency usually controls the process and forces decisions on the local people based on *the agency's custom culture and perceived mandates.*

At the same time, community representatives to the advisory committee or stakeholder council bring their own, often confusing, customs, culture and perceived economic realities to the process. To agency personnel, the community's confusing culture and perceived needs are bewildering compared to their own perceived clear-cut mandate. Since the agency controls the process they have no incentive to understand the community. Therefore, they minimize or ignore community input. It does not take long before the community representatives realize the agency is not taking them seriously and they have no real say in the final decisions. All too often they become frustrated, disenfranchised and angry, which in turn results in an ever-increasing cycle of conflict and adversarial relationships between citizens and government. Nonetheless, the process does have value, and some recommend the local government file for both Cooperative and Coordination status with the federal agency.

Coordination. Only when there is a level playing field can two groups having widely divergent customs, cultures and perceived needs successfully cooperate through collaboration. Almost all federal environmental laws include the clear provisions that require each federal agency to *coordinate* with local governments and fully resolve inconsistencies between proposed federal actions and local government policies.

Margaret Byfield warns that agencies attempt to argue that local governments can only have this level of participation in the study process if they are a "cooperative agency." This is a false position, as neither the rules nor statute state this level of participation is exclusive to those entities in a "cooperative" role. Certainly, a local government could ask the agency to participate as a "cooperator," but doing so does not preclude the local government from requiring that the study be coordinated.[348]

There is a reason that agencies discourage coordinating the study and encourage local governments into a cooperative role. The rules for cooperator agency status are spelled out at C.F.R. 1501.6. If a local government is accepted as a cooperative agency then it agrees to help develop analysis, make available staff support, and use its own funds in preparing reports for the study. Yet, there is no guarantee that the reports funded and produced by the local governments will be meaningfully considered, as they must be through coordination. In fact, many local governments that have participated in studies as cooperators have found the time and money wasteful. Some have withdrawn their cooperator status and instead required the agency to coordinate the study with them, where the full burden of the study preparation is on the federal or state agency. In a coordination role, the local government arguably has a better position to insist the local position is considered without being obligated to funding and staffing the study.[349]

Any *elected* local government typically charges an advisory committee with the task of developing a local resource plan. The plan incorporates local knowledge of environmental conditions and how best to protect the environmental attribute covered in the federal law, while also protecting the community's custom, culture and economic infrastructure.

Most federal environmental laws also require federal agencies to adopt or very strongly consider the local government's resource plan to protect the environment.[350] The law essentially levels the playing field between the local government and the federal government in the planning process. Because of the Rule of Law, the agency no longer directly controls the composition or the outcomes of the committee.

A word of caution is appropriate. Attorney Grant specifically warns that coordination is not Supremacy; "In the early days of local government's foray into the coordination concept established in the Federal Land Policy Management Act, local government urged that it had supremacy over the federal agency with regard to land lying within the boundaries of the unit of local government. The "county supremacy" doctrine was based not only on the language of FLPMA, but on the historical and traditional place of the county in the hierarchy of government. [That] notion was stricken down in *United States v. Nye County, 920 F. Supp. 1108.*"[351]

The law still provides federal agencies the authority to make final decisions and implementation of its plans. However, the law allows local government to have legal standing in the planning process. If a federal agency does not accept a local government's plan, it must legally explain why it cannot. The law usually allows the local government to request mitigation. Failing that, local government retains the option to pursue litigation against the federal agency. The process works because there is considerable pressure for both sides to find common understanding and work out win-win solutions.

How It Works

Coordination is performed by local units of government. These normally include counties, incorporated cities, water districts, school districts, or any legislatively, statutorily created government entity with local planning, taxing, enforcement, or regulatory authority. The first step is to identify which unit of government best serves your interests. Get to know them and their positions.

The majority of city councilmen, county commissioners/ selectmen or parish judges have been indoctrinated in Rousseau socialism and governance. The first step is to educate them, and if that does not work, vote them out of office and replace them with people who promise to uphold Constitutional principles. This is imperative. Elected officials who are fully indoctrinated with progressive liberal ideology will never support this approach. They will fight the process every step of the way because they want to *control* the people rather than *serve* them. Fortunately, it is much easier to elect people with a solid Constitutional understanding at the local level than it is to elect a state legislator or congressman. That is especially true today with the nation waking up to the damage being done to America by the progressive liberals.

The process is relatively simple, but foreign to most elected local officials. Since most work to date has been done at the county level, county government and commissioners will be used for discussion purposes. However, it can be any elected body of representatives of local government including school boards and water boards. Local citizens initially petition the county commission to create a local resource or land-use committee made up of a cross-section of interested local citizens. Its purpose is to develop and *recommend* a city, county, or even a school district resource or land-use plan to the city council, county commissioners or school board. In the case of a school district, parents of students as well as other interested people can be directly involved.

The plan, when developed, will consider how to meet federal and state environmental law in a way that protects the local culture and economy of the governing jurisdiction as well as the environmental issue the federal law encompasses. It must include representatives from all segments of the culture within local jurisdictions.

The committee is *not* comprised of the planning department, although a member of the planning department can be a member. Nor is the plan a comprehensive zoning plan unless required by law. It is important that the planning department not control the process. The education of most planners centers in Rousseau socialism which almost inevitably gravitates to government-controlled, forced compliance solutions that minimize private property rights.

The committee first explains to the county board or city council the purpose. If acceptable, the *elected* officials give the committee legal standing by resolution. There may be a need to modify the purpose somewhat to satisfy the elected board or council. However, if the elected officials refuse to sanction the committee, then it is time to elect new councilmen or county commissioners. Once accepted by the duly elected council or board of commissioners, the committee takes input from the citizens and builds its first plan. The initial plan does not have to be comprehensive if they must address an immediate crisis. It is possible to develop a working first plan in a relatively short period.

Once the first plan is completed, citizens and the elected government review and provide input to it. After making changes, the county commission or city council accepts the plan by resolution or ordinance. Once accepted, the federal government *must* accept the elected government's plan and coordinate it with their federal plan. However, to do this the local elected officials *must* send a certified or registered letter to the federal agency(ies) with which they desire coordinating status, requesting coordinating agency standing. Otherwise, the federal agency is under no legal requirement to extend coordinating agency standing to the local government. The agency will probably attempt to ignore or reject the request. Don't let them. They legally must accept the local government's request.

If the agency resists real government-to-government coordination, the local unit of government should send a second or third certified or registered letter to the next level up the chain of command until you reach the head of the federal or state agency. You may also eventually notify the Department of Justice as your final effort, so that they can clarify the coordination requirements to the agency.[352] Proper training and instructions of how to implement the process can be obtained from American Stewards of Liberty.[a]

Some counties have written two letters, one for coordinating standing, and the other for cooperating agency standing. In either case, the letter must include the legal citation of the law or regulation. The elected body can legally designate the resource committee as its representative to meetings of the federal agencies so elected officials do not have to be burdened with the task.

What is so powerful about this approach to local control is that most state laws also permit the same type of joint standing of the local government

---

a American Stewards of Liberty, P.O. Box 1190, Taylor, TX 76574. (512)-365- 2699. www.stewards.us.

with state agencies—especially if the state laws are linked to the National Environmental Policy Act through federal funding.[353] Experience has shown that the local government can be very effective in protecting its citizens from state mandates that affect their citizens.

11

Plan for Success

Show me that age and country where the rights and liberties of the people were placed on the sole chance of their rulers being good men, without a consequent loss of liberty! I say that the loss of the dearest privilege has ever followed, with absolute certainty, every such mad attempt.

— Patrick Henry

AMERICAN STEWARDS OF LIBERTY report in April of 2010 that they are directly involved in the coordination process of nearly 50 local governments throughout the Western United States. There undoubtedly are more. Since this is a new strategy, there have been the expected frustrations and ideas that do not work. These occur with any new approach to doing things. However, the strategy has already met with a high degree of success.

Owyhee County, Idaho. Under the guidance of attorney Fred Kelly Grant in American Stewards of Liberty, Citizens for Owyhee County in Southwestern Idaho developed one of the first and most successful plans. Local citizens organized a group of interested citizens who then went to the County Commissioners for a resolution to allow them to form a Resource

Advisory Committee that would develop a resource-use plan for the Owyhee County Board to approve later. [354]

The Owyhee County Resource Committee first wrote a quick plan to cover a regulation the federal Bureau of Land Management (BLM) was about to institute. The BLM plan would seriously, and unnecessarily impact ranchers in the county. Even though the first plan that was accepted by the Owyhee County Commissioners in 1991 was only about five-pages long, it was enough to force the BLM to the coordinating table and the affected regulations were stopped from being implemented.

The federal agencies are not the only group fighting private property rights. After years of trying to buck the process at every turn the BLM finally realized it could not roll over the county. When the BLM decided to work with Owyhee County, a radical environmental group began to file an unending list of biologically unfounded anti-grazing, anti BLM lawsuits against the BLM and the ranchers in Owyhee County. The judge hearing the cases was *extremely* supportive of the environmental group, and the judge not only found in their favor in almost every case, but awarded the environmental group a staggering amount of attorney fees abusively using the Equal Access to Justice Act (EAJA). The corruption of the court was obvious, but there was little either the BLM or the county could do.

To stop the assault, the BLM, county, other conservation and recreation groups actually joined forces, and after five years of collaboration, worked out a major piece of Congressional legislation introduced by Senator Mike Crapo (R-ID); the Owyhee Initiative Implementation Act of 2006. The legislation was beneficial to all the parties involved, except for the radical environmental group who wanted to eliminate all use of the land. The centerpiece of the legislation called for a major land swap between the BLM and certain ranchers who would trade their private land suitable for wilderness and recreation to the BLM, for BLM land that was great for grazing. Over 500 thousand acres of wilderness was created in the deal.[355]

The Owyhee legislation was combined into the Omnibus Public Land Management Act of 2009 and passed and signed into law in March of 2009.

The Omnibus Public Land Management Act of 2009 was another 1000 plus page bill combining 160 separate public land, water and natural resource bills that was steamrolled through the Senate and passed by the House without hearings on March 25. The Owyhee portion of the bill was about the only thing good about the legislation. Just like all the other bills passed in 2009, it was full of pork and special favors to bribe Senators and Congressmen from both parties to vote for it.

On the downside for resource users in the West, the Omnibus Public Land Management Act of 2009 also establishes a host of programs and restrictions that can severely affect landowners living in impacted areas. The thousands of families depending on these resources for their livelihoods will suddenly find themselves shut out.

The joint status provisions also work with federal laws like the Endangered Species Act. Grays Harbor County challenged the United States Fish and Wildlife Service (USFWS) in 2000. The USFWS proposed to list the coastal cutthroat trout as threatened under the Endangered Species Act. However, the proposed listing did not take the impact to the citizens of in the State of Washington into consideration, nor did it consider that research by the National Marine Fisheries Service (NMFS) found the trout was not even endangered in Grays Harbor County. That allowed the Grays Harbor County Commission to write a letter to USFWS on June 26, 2000, asking for joint lead- or coordinating agency status under NEPA.

The request by the county forced a delay in the listing until further studies could be done. By 2002 it was determined that the trout had sufficient numbers under the ESA that it didn't have to be listed in the county, saving hundreds of jobs and an important segment of the county's economy.

Walla Walla County, Washington. In another example, legal standing for the coordination process was established in the early 1990s in Walla Walla County, Washington. When the county began to notice significant federal intrusion into local affairs by the United States department of Interior, Bureau of Indian Affairs, Corps of Engineers and Forest Service (USFS) and others, the county commission followed the advice of attorney Karen Budd-Falen (now in Cheyenne, Wyoming) to utilize the NEPA process to protect their citizens. Bud-Falen is another of the small pool of attorneys who understood and developed the local government/ NEPA process.

A representative group of residents from Walla Walla County were charged with studying and using the Constitutional provisions of NEPA. The county established a resource committee made up of a cross-section of people from the county. Seven different sub-committees with 5-7 people each were formed for education, natural resources, culture, economy and so forth. In the case of Walla Walla, the subcommittees worked, but other counties found so many sub-committees proved to be unwieldy and counter productive.

The committee was charged with first defining Walla Walla County's environmental, social and economic issues and how to best manage them for the citizens of the county. The various committees then pooled their reports into one common report that would later evolve into what is known the Walla Walla River Basin Plan. After numerous public hearings the long and diligent work of this committee resulted in the passage of Walla Walla's Ordinance #219 by the County Commissioners. Columbia County, which borders Walla Walla County, used the Walla Walla ordinance as a template to create their own ordinance. Once the ordinances were passed, both counties petitioned the US Forest Service and Army Corps of Engineers to coordinate with them on the federal water management plan. Together, they came up with a common plan acceptable to the counties and federal agencies.

The process, now called the Walla Walla Way, worked so well for the two counties that Washington Wilderness Coalition, led by a green professor at Whitman College in Walla Walla sued the Army Corps of Engineers and the USFS in the Ninth District Court of the United States.[356] The lawsuit was designed to stop all uses of the Umatilla National Forest and the land along the Walla Walla River that were allowed by the joint county/federal management plan. The suit alleged the waters of the Walla Walla River Basin were being irreparably harmed.

Because the two Counties had a management plan which was coordinated with the federal management plan, the judge found that the two counties had standing in the court, while the environmental group did not. The court found in favor of the defendants and the lawsuit was dismissed in 1995.[357]

The Washington Wilderness Coalition appealed case to the 9th Circuit Court of Appeals in San Francisco and the decision by the lower court was upheld by the Circuit Court on January 10, 1996.[358] This was a major victory for the citizens of Walla Walla County. More importantly, however, it clearly shows that local governments have greater standing than do environmental groups in the NEPA process. The coordinating process offers a powerful tool for local communities.

Later Umatilla County in Oregon joined the process, so the process can even cross state lines. The success of the Walla Walla Way continues today, with the newly created Walla Walla Watershed Management Partnership established to join local governments, citizens and tribal leaders in a pilot effort to innovatively manage local water resources. The green group that originally sued the Corps of Engineers has seen the positive results and has joined the process.

With unanimous support of the Washington State Legislature in 2009, this unique, local governance structure was granted authority (RCW 90.92) to bank water and employ flexible water management practices outside of existing water law, to enhance stream conditions for fish, while also protecting irrigators from relinquishment of their water rights. In this challenging arena where personal property rights hit head-on with multiple layers of local, state and federal regulations, Walla Walla County endorses the Walla Walla Way as the ideal approach for collaborative, local problem-solving to maintain the ecological, cultural and economic health of their watershed. This type of coordinating plan will work in *any* county or group of counties in the United States.

The Trans Texas Highway. Perhaps the most powerful illustration of how the coordination approach can work to protect local communities didn't happen with the federal government, but with the State of Texas. It not only affected Texas, but the entire nation. It started with the expansion of NAFTA (North American Free Trade Agreement) to include Mexico in a 2005 agreement called the Security and Prosperity Partnership (SPP) during the Bush administration.[359] It is also popularly known as the North American Union. The machinations of the SPP would require another book, but suffice it to say that it is part of the larger effort to create economic and security regions patterned after the European Union discussed in previous chapters. That said, one of the first steps in this three-nation governing unit was to build what was called the NAFTA superhighway.

This extremely limited access highway was to be four football fields wide and extend from the southwestern Mexican port of Lazaro Cardenas and enter the United States at Laredo, Texas. It would follow the I-35 corridor northward and extend into Canada at the border north of either Duluth, Minnesota or Fargo, North Dakota (or both). The only customs stop would be in Kansas City at the new Smart Port complex, a facility being built for Mexico at a cost of $3 million to the U.S. taxpayers. The first segment of this super highway was to be built through Texas and was known as the Trans-Texas Highway. Construction was to have begun in 2007.[360]

The Trans Texas Highway was to be a 10-lane very limited-access road (five lanes in each direction) plus passenger and freight rail lines running alongside pipelines laid for oil and natural gas. It would have taken 80,300 privately owned acres out of production and split communities in half. The billions needed to build it were to be provided by a foreign company, Cintra Concessions de Infraestructuras de Transporte, S.A. of Spain. As a consequence, the TTC would have been privately operated by lease to the Cintra consortium to be operated as a toll-road.

The mammoth process was kept super quiet and almost no one outside certain Bush administration agencies, the Texas DOT (TXDOT) and Texas Governor Rick Perry even knew about it; including Congress and the Texas legislature. It wasn't until 2006 that citizens of Texas began to hear about it. *WorldNetDaily*'s Jerome Corsi broke the story and Lou Dobbs made it a national issue by producing a series of exposés on it. [361]

Led by attorney Fred Kelly Grant, the American Land Foundation and Stewards of the Range (now American Stewards of Liberty) used the NEPA process and a little used provision of Texas law—Chapter 391 of the Texas Local Government Code—to stop the process dead in its tracks. Five communities (some were school districts) joined together. They created what they called the Eastern Central Texas Sub-Regional Planning Commission (ECTSRPC) to demand coordination with the state and TXDOT.

The first item on ECTSRPC's agenda was to challenge the Environmental Impact Statement (EIS). As usual, the EIS's discussion of economic and cultural impacts was almost non-existent. Even though the highway would have ripped communities apart and caused tremendous economic dislocation, the draft study claimed this superhighway's effect on the "economic characteristics" of the areas "would be limited to land value changes."[362] That wording was the sum total of their discussion on the economic impacts of the largest transportation system ever conceived in America.

ECTSRPC found a quagmire of corruption, shortcuts, NEPA violations and outright illegal actions by TXDOT to ram this project through.[363] ECTSRPC also requested the EIS be rejected because TXDOT did not coordinate with the impacted cities as required by NEPA. Consequently, TXDOT violated the law when the conducted the EIS study. As an equal coordinator, ECTSRPC used the federal nexus to request that the Federal Highway Administration reject the EIS and force them to start over again. Millions of dollars were spent trying to defeat the ECTSRPC. President Bush pushed hard as did Governor Rick Perry, to no avail. Eventually TXDOT's project deadline expired and they no longer had any authority to implement the project.

On October 7, 2009, the project was declared dead. Attorney Fred Kelly Grant said that its defeat was "certainly the biggest victory ever won by the coordinating process."[364] The celebration was short-lived. Although TXDOT and the State of Texas have declared the project dead, TXDOT quietly requested the Federal Highway Administration not to rule on the EIS, but to issue a "no action" alternative. That ruling would allow TXDOT to reauthorize the project following the reelection of Governor Perry without having to do another EIS. The corrupted EIS would be in force, again bypassing the NEPA process.

Attorney Fred Kelly is neither surprised, nor very concerned. ECTSRPC will sue if that happens, and there is no way TXDOT and the Federal Highway Administration can win. TXDOT clearly violated the law.

Forcing state and federal government into the coordinating process works to protect local communities. However, to make it work, the community has to have local elected officials that understand Constitutional principles and the backbone to stand up to the Goliath's and protect their citizens. As important, citizens need to be willing to put in hundreds, sometimes thousands of hours over a fairly long period of time.[365]

Will Local Control Work?

Using the coordination process with local government will not cause the global agenda house of cards to come tumbling down. However, it will help keep the federal and sometimes state governments from further encroachment into the sovereignty of local communities. It can even help to reverse it where that federal encroachment has already caused harm to local citizens. It will also deflate the incredible power that environmental and social NGOs have been exerting over federal policy at the local level. Most importantly this approach will level the playing field with the global agenda while it is being exposed for what it is—a blatant attempt to use the Hegelian dialectic to trick the people of America and the world into accepting the Rousseau general will, and in so doing establishing and authoritarian, if not totalitarian, global governance.

The Elite Will React

Always remember that the opposition is very well organized and very well funded. Their most common strategy is the same as all tyrants throughout history—demonize and destroy the opposition when the facts don't back them up. Expect the elite to vilify and demonize both the efforts and the emerging leaders who oppose them. It is already happening.

When the Iron Curtain fell in the early 1990s and the Soviet records made public, it turns out that Joseph McCarthy was correct on many counts. Yet, the global cartel totally vilified and demonized him in the 1940s and 1950s. It worked with McCarthy because the mainstream media controlled the process—either through arrogant ignorance or deliberate action. The same has been true of the John Birch Society. True, neither was right on all accounts. That is impossible for any person or group. But records made available after the collapse of the Soviet Union proved them mostly correct. With the alternative media and an increasingly educated public, the evil consequence of this agenda can be avoided.

Be Alert and Educated

Every American can use the alternative media to stay informed of the story behind the story. Cancel your subscriptions and challenge the mainstream media with polite letters to the editor. The reader and viewership of the mainstream media is plunging. Some of it is due to free news on the internet, but most is because their progressive bias is so blatant that people treat it as propaganda rather than news. Challenge the expected outcomes when they are based on Rousseau socialism.

Never blindly trust the government. Patrick Henry warned us to "Guard with jealous attention the public liberty. Suspect every one who approaches that jewel. Unfortunately, nothing will preserve it but downright force. Whenever you give up that force, you are inevitably ruined."[366] As best you can, get the UN or government documents themselves on issues of interest. Then, as painful as it may be, read them to find their fatal flaws. Those flaws *will* be there. Then use their own documents and words against them.

The greatest danger is in the global cartel's ability to create a series of Hegelian crises to protect their agenda. We now know that the 9-11 tragedy was in part allowed to happen because intelligence agencies were more interested in protecting their turf and covering their tails than in protecting

American citizens. The Rousseau progressive liberals had emasculated the CIA, FBI and NSA intelligence agencies. But, is there more to it than that? Were our intelligence agencies deliberately allowed to misread the abundant clues leading up to 9-11? One of my employees wrote an article of the inevitable terrorist attack by Osama bin Laden on the United States in 1999, two years before it actually occurred.[367] Yet our intelligence agencies supposedly were caught totally off guard. Just who knew what and when? While it is very doubtful that the federal government was directly involved in this, were key agencies and a few people being manipulated by the cartel? These are troubling questions that will never be proven one way or the other, but given accumulating evidence, they cannot be ignored.

The very important warning given by Alexander Hamilton in *Federalist Papers*, No. 8 bears repeating:

Safety from external danger is the most powerful director of national conduct. Even the ardent love of liberty will after a time, give way to its dictates. The violent destruction of life and property incident to war—the continual effort and alarm attendant on a state of continual danger, will compel nations the most attached to liberty to resort for repose and security to institutions which have a tendency to destroy their civil and political rights. To be more safe, they at length become willing to run the risk of being less free."

History teaches that the global financial cartel knows this truth well, and has used it to their ends on numerous occasions. There is good evidence that the global financial cartel played both ends against the middle in World Wars I and II, Kosovo and many, many more.[368] It would be foolish not to be concerned that the global financial cartel, if threatened, would not attempt the same strategy once more. The Homeland Security Act passed on November 19, 2002 will allow the government to keep track of every financial transaction, every medical record, every event you attend, every complaint by nosy neighbors—everything![369] The overreach by the federal government following the 2008 financial crisis by both Bush and Obama follows the same pattern.

The federal government and others assure us that these dangerous powers will not be abused by going after American citizens, claiming they are potential terrorists or greedy bankers. Even if that had been true with the Bush administration—and it wasn't—what about future administrations? Almost everything Obama and the progressive leadership have done has been a misuse of power and a violation of the United States Constitution.

Patrick Henry was opposed to the Constitution of the United States because it provided too many doors open through which the federal government could become all-powerful. Once again, Patrick Henry warns; "Show me that age and country where the rights and liberties of the people were placed on the sole chance of their rulers being good men, without a consequent loss of liberty! I say that the loss of the dearest privilege has ever followed, with absolute certainty, every such mad attempt."[370]

Never forget the *global cartel essentially controls the money supply*, and therefore the economy, of the United States and the world. If the cartel collapsed the economy once, they can and may do it again. Would Americans give up even more of their freedom for security as Hamilton warned? The only way to prevent the elite from trying this tactic, or something like it, is to expose their agenda and put a spotlight on them so bright that they could not do it without global condemnation so severe that they would fear for their corporate survival.

While it might provide warm feelings to believe the people of the world could throw off the corporate banking noose from around their necks, it may be wishful thinking. The entire global financial system basically is in place. Together, the U.S. and England handle nearly half of all monetary exchanges in the world.[371] Link that type of control with the raw economic power of the U.S. and the Anglo-American banking axis is all-powerful. Some observers say that it is not unlike Daniel's vision of a future all-powerful global system that will crush all opposition.[372] To react suddenly to break this cartel's control over the people of the world without having a well thought out plan to replace it would be as bad as or worse than having them continue the status-quo.

Joseph Stieglitz, former Vice President and Chief Economist of the World Bank, provides evidence that this cartel of central bankers and financiers have already plundered and ravaged many third world nations through the IMF. After his stint as Vice President with the World Bank, Stieglitz warns;

> ...we have a system that might be called *global governance without world government*, one in which a few institutions—the World Bank, the IMF, the WTO—and a few players—the finance, commerce, and trade ministries, closely linked to certain financial and commercial interests—dominate the scene, but in which many of those affected by their decisions are left almost voiceless.[373]

The financial cartel that Carroll Quigley in his book *Tragedy and Hope* described in detail in 1967 is still alive and well. It is also very dangerous. Stieglitz says, "It's time to change some of the rules governing the international economic order, to think once again about how decisions get made at the international level—and in whose interests" they are made. Whatever the action taken, however, the world cannot permit these international bankers to take the final step to global control through a world government under the banner of UN global governance. To that end, the world was very fortunate that China and India were the spoilers preventing a consensus of the Copenhagen Agreement in December of 2009. It was the first agreement using the concept of a global government to enforce the treaty's mandates.

Although I am not an economist, and don't claim any special insight into this problem, the global banking system must be made truly and totally transparent. There are virtually no checks and balances on these supranational organizations. There was much verbiage during the International Conference on Financing for Development held in Monterrey, Mexico in March 2002 about making nations and corporations more transparent. However, the various institutions of the Bank of International Settlements (BIS) will monitor all of this. That is like putting the wolf in charge of guarding the hen house. Carroll Quigley revealed the BIS as the very apex of the global financial cartel that needs to be controlled!

Plan for Success

A series of checks and balances must be put into place that governs the global financial cartel as well as within individual nations to prevent the abuse of power that has been demonstrated the past one-hundred years. Eventually, fractional-reserve banking has to be eliminated. The problem in this, however, is that the bankers are the experts in this arena and they have demonstrated they cannot be trusted. President John Kennedy may have been attempting to do this in 1963 by issuing EO 11110 which allowed the U.S. Treasury to print silver certificates, backed by real silver, to compete with the debt-ridden Federal Reserve Notes.[374] That effort, however, abruptly ended with the assassination of President Kennedy five months later. [375]

Whatever is done will take many years to accomplish. In the meantime the United States needs a plan to stop the usurpation of our liberties while we slowly disassemble the system of chokeholds the global cartel has put into place over the past one hundred years. While Congress could act swiftly to do this, don't expect it to—at least not initially. It can only begin when we elect congressmen and women to office who have pledged to uphold the Constitution. Protection of the local community has to come from local government—using existing federal law.

In conclusion, I submit the same challenge issued by Winston Churchill upon entering into World War II:

If you will not fight for right when you can easily win without bloodshed; if you will not fight when your victory is sure and not too costly; you may come to the moment when you will have to fight with all the odds against you and only a precarious chance of survival. There may be a worse case. You may have to fight when there is no hope of victory, because it is better to perish than to live as slaves.

This process will not get America immediately back to the full Constitutional protections originally intended by the Founding Fathers. It will, however, slow down or even stop the attack on private property rights, regulatory abuse and the progressive liberal's insidious attack on the United States Constitution to replace it with Rousseau socialism and fascism.

Take Back America

If you are concerned about the attack on the Constitution of the United States and want to stop it, there are several things you *must* do.

- Share this book with others, especially those who consider themselves liberal, yet have open minds. Warn them they will initially be offended, but must continue to read. It provides an overview of the "what and how" this attack has been orchestrated.

- Understand that most progressives want to do the right thing. Their indoctrination merely leads them to make wrong decisions. Party affiliation is irrelevant.

- Only a small minority of progressives is so indoctrinated they are totally blind to reality. They will do all they can to force their ideas onto society, believing their previous failures are merely a consequence of not trying hard enough. Unfortunately, these people are in power and need to be voted out of office or removed from their positions of power.

- Challenge political candidates on their core beliefs about Constitutional limitations on government. Do not support any candidate, regardless of political affiliation, who does not pledge to uphold Constitutional principles. There can be no such thing as politics as usual. If the Republican Party is smart, it will realize this and field this slate of Constitutional candidates. However, Republicans seem to be so fixated on politics and seniority they cannot see out of the box. This will leave room for repentant Democrats to take the Constitutional lead.

- Don't dismiss the idea of running for office yourself. That includes the city council, county commission, and school board in addition to the more glamorous state legislature and congress.

- Attend city council, school board and county board meetings. Volunteer to be on your local planning board and other volunteer entities. If you don't progressives will.

- States are beginning to stand up for states rights embodied in the Tenth Amendment. Support that effort.

- Because of the Tenth Amendment, federal laws that impact state and local governments must have embedded in them language that allows the state and elected local governments (of any type) the right to coordinate and cooperate in deciding how federal laws are implemented within their jurisdictions. Many state laws have the same provision or are under the same rules because of federal grants. These Constitutional provisions offer incredible power to stop federal (even state) intrusion into local affairs.

- These methods are time tested and have actually been used to stop multibillion dollar plans forced on communities that do not want them.

We are in a battle for the very survival of the freedoms, liberties and wealth creation given to us by our Founding Fathers. We either start taking our nation back from those who want to control it this year, or we will lose our nation to a stagnant, all-controlling government. The choice is ours to make.

Appendix A

Although not exhaustive, a list of key successes and how they were implemented using the coordination process follows:

Owyhee County, Idaho

The Owyhee County Commission first adopted a five-page Interim Land Use Policy developed by the committee in late 1991. The policy cited the appropriate federal laws and regulations and defined their culture, economy and other key information needed to meet the federal requirements for several issues that were high priority at the time. The affected federal agencies immediately had to recognize the policy and work with the citizen's resource committee to ensure federal planning did not conflict with local planning.

By mid 1993, the County adopted the 29-page Interim Comprehensive Land Use and Management Plan written by the resource committee. Again, the federal agencies had to work with the county in this much more detailed management plan. In mid 1997, the county finally adopted Ordinance No. 97-01 as the Owyhee County Land Use and Management Plan for Federal and State Managed Lands.[376] That ordinance established the resource committee as a "standing advisory committee to continue advising the Board regarding the management of the federal and state managed lands lying within Owyhee County and the relationship of that management to continuation of the custom, culture and economic stability of the County."[377]

Owyhee County has shown that using federal law to stop federal abuse against local citizens clearly works. Yet, they caution that their plan is specific to Owyhee County and only provides an example for other counties or communities. For one, federal land makes up 83 percent of Owyhee County—mostly U.S. Bureau of Land Management (BLM). Over 61 percent of people employed in Owyhee County are dependent upon ranching, farming, mining and other job activities reliant upon the availability of natural resources for economic use. Therefore, their plan invokes a series of laws dealing with federal land management, the most important of which is the Federal Land Policy and Management Act (FLPMA).[378]

Since most counties in the U.S. do not have large blocks of federal land, each county or community will necessarily have a plan specific to their situation and conditions. Appendix—cites the necessary laws, regulations and Executive Orders, whether for the Endangered Species Act, Clean Water Act, or other federal environmental laws.

Using this approach does *not* make the county supreme over the management of federal land within the county. Even if the founding fathers intended for local governments to be supreme over the federal lands on local issues, and they did not, numerous federal court decisions have interpreted the division of powers very narrowly.[379] Federal law defines how federal land is to be managed, not the local government. In *Kleppe v. the United States* the Supreme Court ruled that although state and local governments retain important powers over federal lands, they are not absolute:

Absent consent or cession of a State undoubtedly retains jurisdiction over federal lands within its territory, but Congress equally surely retains the power to enact legislation respecting those lands pursuant to the Property Clause."[380]

While the process addresses local concerns about the application of federal laws, a county, city or township can also use it to affect how state or even county agencies interact with the local government as well. State or county environmental laws and actions fall under the NEPA process if there has been any federal funding in the process of enacting or enforcing the state law.[381] This is called a federal nexus. Failing the federal nexus test, many states will work with local government if the local government has demonstrated a history as a cooperating agency with the federal government.

One of the advantages of having an active committee is that all members of the committee are constantly watching news sources and official sources as well as unofficial sources for items of vital interest. One member of the Owyhee County Committee, for instance, saw a small notice in the Idaho Statesman (a Boise newspaper which has very limited distribution in Owyhee County) announcing a meeting before the Idaho Water Board to discuss and set minimum stream flows in the Owyhee River.

The issue of minimum stream flows was before the water board on a petition filed by Idaho Rivers United, a water environmentalist group. The notice gave very little time for preparation, so the advisory committee and the Board of Commissioners sent a representative to object to the hearing. They based their objection on the grounds the state's Idaho Water Board had not advised the county in advance and had not given the county adequate opportunity to prepare. In addition, the Commissioners also sent a letter to the water board complaining about the lack of notice and about the lack of coordination with the county. In response, the water board set a new hearing with substantial advance notice.

The advisory committee discussed the issue and three members of the committee prepared themselves to appear before the water board. They opposed the setting of minimum stream flows on the basis of failure to comply with the statutory burden of proof. At the conclusion of the public hearing, the Idaho Water Board denied the petition by the Idaho Rivers United and dismissed it. Had the planning process not been in place, there is little doubt the state would have established the minimum stream flows to the detriment of all farmers and ranchers who use water from the river, as well as other counties in the immediate area.

Grays Harbor County, Washington.

In 2000, the United States Fish and Wildlife Service (USFWS) proposed to list the coastal cutthroat trout as threatened under the Endangered Species Act. However, the proposed listing did not take the impact to the citizens of Grays Harbor County in the State of Washington into consideration. That allowed the Grays Harbor County Commission to write a letter to USFWS on June 26, 2000, asking for joint lead or cooperating agency status under NEPA.

The commission also wrote to the state supervisor for USFWS in Oregon asking why the agency was even considering listing the coastal cutthroat trout in Grays Harbor County. Information compiled by National Marine Fisheries Service (NMFS) indicated the only threatened populations of coastal cutthroat occurred in the lower Columbia Basin. The commission used the Freedom of Information Act to request specific information about the potential listing. The request included data specific to Grays Harbor about cutthroat populations, habitat and genetic information to indicate differences between one ESU and any other within Washington State. The letter further requested a public hearing in Grays Harbor County to consider the possible listing.

Through the diligent work of the Grays Harbor commissioners and a one-year moratorium on new listings, the coastal cutthroat trout listing was delayed until 2002. Review of research data in 2002 indicated sufficient numbers of cutthroat trout in Grays Harbor to deny the threatened status for this fish under the guidelines of the Endangered Species Act.

Modoc County

The county planning process can also pit one federal agency against another. In the mid-1990s the USFWS worked out an agreement with the Modoc National Forest in northern California on grazing management allotments. The agreement identified grazing a management strategy to protect the endangered Lost River, Short-Nose and Modoc suckerfish within allotments that had streams containing the endangered fish. The joint task force devised a grazing strategy and for the next three years, both the Modoc National Forest and the USFWS carefully monitored the results. The data clearly showed an upward trend toward desired condition and increased recruitment of juvenile fish.

In spite of the improving fish numbers, the USFWS arbitrarily persisted in their mandate to increase the restrictions by reducing stream bank alteration from twenty percent to ten percent. Ten percent would render the allotments economically unviable for grazing 2000 cattle and 6000 sheep. Using the section in the Endangered Species Act that allows for adoption of a local recovery plan, Modoc County adopted the Modoc National Forest Biological Assessment. Since that assessment allowed 20 percent alterations in its local recovery plan, the county filed a notice of intent to sue the USFWS.

The ESA states that the USFWS cannot develop or change a recovery plan without showing that a local plan is not working. The Modoc National Forest monitoring had already showed that the current plan was successful. Three days after the filing, the Department of Justice called the county and suggested they could work this out on the ground. A subsequent meeting that included the Regional Forester and Regional Director of USFWS determined that the current standards were adequate for protecting the fish. By developing their own resource plan, Modoc County was able to stop an arbitrary imposition of a rule that would have seriously harmed its citizens.

In another example concerning the Clean Water Act, the Idaho Department of Environmental Quality (DEQ), working as the lead agency for watershed management planning in Idaho, established local and regional groups for providing local input into development of a TMDL plan. A TMDL (Total Maximum Daily Load) is the maximum amount of pollution that a water body can assimilate without violating state water quality standards as mandated by Section 303(d) of the Clean Water Act.[382]

The Idaho Watershed Advisory Group (WAG) included the nominations submitted to DEQ by the Natural Resources Committee of Owyhee County.

The format for development of the plan used by DEQ did not provide any real local input from the WAG, but merely had WAG members comment on the draft plan when completed by the department. Thus, agency personnel would control the preparation of the draft plan, not the affected citizens or their local representative government.

The WAG members from Owyhee County, well trained in the planning process in the county, objected to this process and requested that the Owyhee Board of Commissioners insist upon *direct* involvement in the actual writing of the plan. The state director of DEQ and the regional director in charge of TMDL planning appeared before the Board of Commissioners. Before the meeting ended, the state director agreed that because of the long planning experience in Owyhee County, members of the WAG had sufficient expertise and involvement to participate in development of the plan. Because of this, the draft of the plan was withdrawn, the WAG comments were considered, members of the WAG met with DEQ staff, and the joint WAG-DEQ task force revised the draft plan to include the comments and input provided by the county. None of this would have been possible but for the planning process in place in the county.

The joint lead and/or cooperating agency standing protected the local residents of Grays Harbor, Modoc and Owyhee Counties from decisions made in a vacuum by federal and state bureaucrats not concerned about local concerns and issues. Had Monterey County, California followed this same process and used a resource plan developed by the people rather than misguided professionals, they too could have had equal standing with the state and federal agencies. They still can. So can every elected government for their community.

Wallowa County, Oregon

In 1992 the first listing of the Snake River Chinook Salmon as threatened under the Endangered Species Act was about to occur. The Wallowa County Court (name changed to Commission in 1995) and the Nez Perce Tribe had the foresight to recognize the economic devastation the community would suffer as a result of the listing. Their solution was to take a pro-active approach in creating a plan that would result in resource management and use that would again stimulate their economy. A committee of 17 local individuals wrote *The Wallowa County-Nez Perce Salmon Habitat Recovery Plan (Salmon Plan)* in August of 1993, which covered all lands in Wallowa County, Oregon, including federal, state and private lands.

The mission statement of the Salmon Plan states: "*To develop a management plan to assure that watershed conditions in Wallowa County provide the spawning, rearing, and migration habitat required to assist in the recovery of Snake River salmonids by protecting and enhancing conditions as needed. The plan will provide the best watershed conditions available consistent with the needs of the people of Wallowa County, the Nez Perce Tribe, and the rest of the United States, and will be submitted to the National Marine Fisheries Service for inclusion in the Snake River Salmon Recovery Plan*".

The Salmon Plan strategy is designed to create guidelines for habitat improvement through adaptive management. These guidelines are intended to include all ownerships, reduce bureaucracy, and expedite approvals. This process starts with a watershed analysis of current conditions, identifies watershed issues and site-specific problems and then offers possible solutions. It is designed to be ridgetop-to-ridgetop and to consider the cumulative effects including short-term requirements and long-term goals for habitat improvement.

All federal laws governing forest management require that local governments must be included in the decision-making process. The Endangered Species Act (ESA) gives local governments the latitude to develop recovery plans that **must be** considered. The Wallowa County Board of Commissioners, not sure what ordinances were required, adopted ordinances that include: The right to farm; designation of Wallowa County Court as a land resource management agency; and preservation of custom, culture and community stability in Wallowa County.[a]

---

a   While Wallowa County used the ordinance approach, it should be noted that it is not necessarily needed to coordinate with federal agencies.

Wallowa County's Land Use Plan states that Wallowa County "shall develop and implement habitat conservation plans or similar plans for the protection of threatened and endangered species within the County and that state and federal agencies shall coordinate their management activities and plans with the County." Implementation measures for the Salmon Habitat Recovery Plan are included in the zoning articles of Wallowa County. As a result of the ordinances, Wallowa County has been able to proceed in an orderly, common-sense manner to implement land-use planning on an equal footing with federal agencies.

In 1995 the Wallowa County Commission, the Nez Perce Tribe, and Wallowa-Whitman National Forest signed a resolution to implement the *Wallowa County-Nez Perce Salmon Habitat Recovery Plan* within all lands in Wallowa County, and a Memorandum of Understanding (MOU) has been signed granting Wallowa County Commission government-to-government consultation status with the US Forest Service.

In 1995, the Wallowa County Court appointed a Natural Resource Advisory Committee (NRAC) to primarily coordinate the implementation of the Salmon Plan, assist landowners in the development of comprehensive resource management plans and to review and monitor on-the-ground projects. This committee of 20 diverse individuals meets two to three times a year when significant issues arise or large projects are ready to move ahead. Two subcommittees were developed – The Standing Committee, who reviews and makes recommendations to the commissioners on political issues and the Technical Committee, who ensures various project proposals concerning natural resources, meet the guidelines of the Salmon Plan. Both committees have met once a month since their development.

Today the Wallowa County NRAC is still moving ahead with its charge of advising the Board of Commissioners, developing projects that will help the voice of the local community be heard in federal and state agency actions. It continues to educate folks, both in-county as well as out of county about the need for good watershed management and how to be effective in a local effort.

Appendix A

Wallowa County has seen major changes in the community since the writing of Wallowa County Nez Perce Tribe Salmon Habitat Recovery Plan and the inception of the NRAC. Over $16 million dollars has been spent on watershed improvement projects through the various agencies and entities including over $5 million of private dollars.

Paramount from this process is not only the need for watershed improvements but for economic activity generated from those projects that would support the local community. As stated to the Chief of the U.S. Forest Service during his visit in May of 2003, there is a sense of urgency from the community that it needs a volume of timber harvesting and other work from the federal lands that not only is of sufficient volume to have a significant impact on our economy but that it needs to be done soon before we lose our capacity of workers and infrastructure. The volume of work must be sustained long enough for our community to continue to invest in the infrastructure such as logging equipment, mills and roads.

Another major USFS project being imposed on the local communities is the US Forest Service Travel Management Plan (TMP). This process will develop a Travel Management Plan for all national forest lands in the county designating which roads stay open and which will close. In the TMP process, the county took the following steps to make sure the local input had the most influence possible:

- Since the USFS planned to accomplish this without doing an on-the-ground assessment of the roads, Wallowa County felt the need to submit their own alternative based on factual information. The NRAC, with the help of citizen volunteers, completed the on-the-ground assessments of all roads on national forest land (over 1200 roads). The County Board of Commissioners finalized the evaluation of the input and amended the local land use plan adding the counties travel plan for federal lands in Wallowa County.

- The county, worked with five other counties in the area to file for cooperating agency status

- Together, they worked with USFS to assure that coordination continued between the county and the Forest Service

After nearly 15 years of implementation of the Wallowa County Nez Perce Tribe Salmon Habitat Recovery Plan the Wallowa County Process has an impressive record of watershed improvements and countless times they have intervened or given input on the processes dealing with natural resource management.

However, in spite of the improving watersheds and continuous participation, Wallowa County is not ready to "write a success story." For that to happen they will need to see significant activities occurring on the federal lands, enough to see a real economic return to the community for a sustained time. One county commissioner stated "to engage in the natural resource issues as we have requires patience and hope." Hope seems to run eternal in Wallowa County, patience…sometimes those involved have to search for that.

Local Governments Still Retain Police Power

While local governments are not supreme over federal laws, federal laws are often superseded by treaties and original laws that provide a bundle of property rights for citizens. Local governments retain most police powers even on federal land; "A state may enforce its criminal and civil laws on federal lands as long as it exercises its powers in a manner that does not conflict with federal law."[383]

The Federal Land Policy and Management Act of 1976 (FLPMA) specifically states in 43 U.S.C. §1701 that: "Nothing in this Act shall be construed as …a limitation upon the police power of the respective States, or as derogating the authority of a local police officer in the performance of his duties, or as depriving any State or political subdivision thereof of any right it may have to exercise civil and criminal jurisdiction on the national resource lands."[384] Owyhee County, for instance, claims in its Land Use Management Plan:

Appendix A

Increasingly, the Bureau of Land Management and other Federal agencies have become involved in law enforcement activities in Owyhee County, acting as peace officers and enforcing Federal laws and regulations in addition to state and local laws. These activities have become of increasing concern to the citizens of Owyhee County, who feel that federal agencies have become increasingly difficult and dangerous to work with...

The Federal Land Policy and Management Act of 1976 requires the Bureau of Land Management and other agencies under the authority of the Secretary of Interior to coordinate ALL land management activities with county and state governments involved with land use planning USC 1712(c)(9). The Owyhee County Sheriff is authorized as the primary law enforcement agent in the county under Idaho Code 31-2227, and the Owyhee County Land use Planning Committee will assist the County Sheriff in his attempts to secure coordination by federal agencies... Federal laws that simply duplicate existing state and local laws are still within the primary law enforcement jurisdiction of the state, a field Congress did not intend to usurp...

This police power has some real teeth. As discussed in chapters 8 and 10, federal land management agencies like the U.S. Forest Service and Bureau of Land Management are loaded with people having nature-knows-best conservation degrees. Many of these are extremely hostile to *any* human activity on federal land because of incorrect teaching that man is destroying the earth. As detailed in chapter 8, western ranchers like Wayne Hage have found that these federal bureaucrats will do almost anything to force them off the land. However, as Hage, now deceased, relates in a personal story, they have no authority over the local sheriff:

My wife Helen and I were in the town of Eureka, Nevada, about eighty miles from our ranch headquarters. We received a call from my son at the ranch saying there were two BLM people there who were claiming to be law enforcement officers. They wanted, he said to see Helen and me. I told my son to call the sheriff. My son said, "I already have. The deputy is on his way." He added, "I have told them to get off the ranch property and wait out on the public road."

Helen and I proceeded to the ranch arriving about an hour and a half later. On the way I called the Nye County sheriff, Tony DeMeo, and told him I thought the BLM was trying to create a confrontation and requested he send back up. When we arrived there were two BLM vehicles out on the road marked with large letters spelling out the words law enforcement, light bars and all. Two BLM employees were there, a man and a woman, wearing guns, badges, mace and clubs. Also three Nye County deputies including the sheriff's lieutenant were on the scene.

The sheriff's lieutenant walked over to our car and said, "We've got it taken care of. Their people will be out of here in about five minutes. With that, the woman BLM employee announced she was going to call the U.S. Attorney on her radio phone. When she got the U.S. Attorney on the line she called the sheriff lieutenant over and said, "the attorney wants to talk to you." The U.S. Attorney started out by asking the sheriff lieutenant if he knew he was interfering with a federal law enforcement action. The sheriff lieutenant acknowledged that he understood. The U.S. attorney then threatened to have the U.S. marshals come out and arrest the Hages and the sheriff too.

The sheriff lieutenant replied; "you know where we are. Do what you have to do." Then he explained to the U.S. attorney a very simple premise of law. The U.S. including the BLM does not have a general grant of law enforcement authority; and if they had any citations to issue or arrest warrants, they could go through him. "BLM people," he went on, "are not allowed to impersonate police officers in Nye County." With that, the U.S. Attorney cooled down and explained to the sheriff lieutenant that he was just doing his job and he realized the sheriff was doing his. The BLM employees left the scene.

Helen and I and the family certainly appreciate the fact that Nye County has a sheriff that knows what his jurisdiction is and what the federal government's jurisdiction is not.[385]

Ironically, the fracas between Hage and the BLM was over something that did not affect the BLM at all, even if they had enforcement jurisdiction. As with most ranches dozens of miles from the nearest town, the Hage ranch had its own trash dump on its own fee lands. The dump had been in use since 1865. However, the BLM had apparently just issued a new rule about dumping trash on "public" land. In their haste to harass the Hages again, they somehow included Hage's private land into the new rule. Said Hage, "They [the BLM] could not make the distinction between public and private lands."

Federal employees also collaborate with anti-ranching environmental groups. These anti-ranching organizations sue the federal agency to impose unneeded, but stricter grazing regulations so that it becomes economically impossible for the rancher to stay in business.

In another example of the power of sheriffs, ranchers in Owyhee County have been under heavy and repeated attack by members of anti-grazing organizations. During his investigation of this harassment, Owyhee County Sheriff Gary Aman found that BLM employees were transporting radical, anti-ranching environmentalists across private property to review grazing allotments. In one case, a "supervising range 'expert' of the BLM spent long hours briefing a representative of one of the organizations which had sued the BLM in a lawsuit charging ineptness in management of the lands."[386] While BLM has a general provision to permit "reasonable administrative access across private and leased lands," BLM employees do not have the right to transport non-BLM employees across private land—especially those people who intend to arbitrarily put the private landowner out of business!

Sheriff Aman served notice that in order to protect private property BLM employees can no longer transport non-BLM employees across private *or* leased property without prior permission. They must first secure oral or written permission of the owner or lease holder of private property with evidence of the permission provided to the Sheriff—*five days* before the proposed crossing! The permission must include the purpose of the crossing and the names and status of the non-BLM employees. If the crossing is on foot, BLM employees "must be present and in direct supervision and control" of the non-employees.[387] In issuing the notice, Sheriff Aman said:

> The nature of our western county and the livelihood and traditions of our citizens make it necessary that private property rights be respected. [He stated his determination] to not stand idly by while property rights were violated. The BLM employees are not above the law. They expect ranchers to obey the law. I expect the same of them.[388]

This may seem petty, but when there is a blatant alliance between a regulating agency and radical environmentalists who openly say they want, in essence, to destroy your business, the evoking of such police powers can be an effective tool. It worked. BLM management at first balked at complying with the Sheriff's policy. When it became clear, however, that the Sheriff,

> was going to stand by it, had every intention of enforcing it, and was backed fully by the Commissioners in his pledge to defend the policy to the highest courts, the BLM put together an internal policy relating to escorting persons on tours and announced that it had no intention of challenging the Sheriff's policy.[389]

The confiscation of cattle by federal bureaucrats for some alleged infraction unfortunately is common throughout the west. Sheriff Aman advised the BLM that the county would not allow them to seize and confine trespassing livestock, the most common infraction, without going through his office and upon proper due process. The BLM balked and claimed it had the authority to gather and confine such livestock. Nevertheless, faced with his legal analysis of Idaho law, the BLM capitulated, and now the BLM gives Sheriff Aman advance notice of even a potential trespass situation.

The sheriff has also advised the BLM that their "law enforcement officers" only had the authority in the County which *he* allowed them. Any of their investigative or enforcement activities had to be cleared with him. Again, the BLM balked and threatened legal resistance, but the Sheriff held firm, and BLM capitulated.[390]

Sheriff Aman is on solid ground. Technically, federal agents conducting legitimate police work in local jurisdictions are required to check in with the county sheriff or city police when they enter the jurisdiction. Because of the inconvenience, there is a loose understanding between federal and local law enforcement agencies whereby the requirement is not generally followed. However, the sheriff does have a right to enforce the provision if the federal agents become abusive.

Robert Herd, former sheriff for Tehama County, CA, demonstrated this right. He arrested, disarmed and threw out of the county federal agents of the ATF, IRS, and EPA who had come in to his county to shake down and otherwise harass his constituency. None of the agencies mentioned had bothered to sign a memorandum of understanding with him that requires federal agents to state their purpose with the sheriff before conducting business in the sheriff's county.[391]

Abuse by federal police agents had gotten so bad in Wyoming during the Clinton administration that most county sheriff's insisted that all federal law enforcement officers and personnel from federal regulatory agencies clear *all* their activities with the sheriff. In a U.S. District Court ruling in Wyoming, the court stated, "Wyoming is a sovereign state and the duly elected sheriff of a county is the highest law enforcement official within a county and has law enforcement powers exceeding that of any other state or federal official."[392]

The Wyoming sheriffs demanded access to all BATF files to verify that the agency is not violating provisions of Wyoming law that prohibit the registration of firearms or the keeping of a registry of firearm owners. They also demanded that federal agencies immediately cease the seizure of private property and the impoundment of private bank accounts without regard to due process in state courts. During a press conference following the court decision, Bighorn County Sheriff Dave Mattis said,

> I am reacting to the actions of federal employees who have attempted to deprive citizens of my county of their privacy, their liberty, and their property without regard to constitutional safeguards. I hope that more sheriffs all across America will join us in protecting their citizens from the illegal activities of the IRS, EPA, BATF, FBI", or any other federal agency that is operating outside the confines of constitutional law. Employees of the IRS and the EPA are no longer welcome in Bighorn County unless they intend to operate in conformance to constitutional law.[393]

This case is not some melodrama from a rural state. This is a core issue even for urbanites. It is further evidence that the Tenth Amendment is still alive: "The powers not delegated to the United States by the Constitution, nor prohibited by it to the States, are reserved to the States respectively, or to the people." Though atrophied, states and local governments still have the power to enforce their own laws. The Constitution never gave that power to the federal government. It is extremely significant that the powers exercised by a sheriff are an extension of the unalienable rights which the Tenth Amendment explicitly reserves to the People.

Protect Yourself Using Lawsuits

Even if the local county commission and sheriff will not protect their citizen's constitutional rights, the federal, state or local bureaucrats who conspire to deny specific citizens their constitutional rights can find themselves faced with prison. On January 20, 2004, Wyoming Federal District Judge, Clarence Brimmer ruled that the Bureau of Land Management (BLM) employees could be sued individually by Frank Robbins for violating his constitutional rights. According to Robbins, the named employees used the power of their federal employment to attempt to acquire an easement across Robbins' private property. Because he refused their demand, the employees set out to destroy him to accomplish their goals. The charges included unlawful retaliation and attempted extortion by the wrongful use of fear or under color of official right. The judge ruled these federal employees were *not* protected by the qualified immunity of their BLM employment and that the BLM employees would have to stand trial, by jury. Robbins' suit named several current and past BLM employees under the Racketeering, Influenced and Corrupt Organizations Act ("RICO") and *"Bivens v. Six Unknown Nacotics Agents."*[394]

The Defendants claimed that because they acted while they were employed by the BLM, they were protected from individual liability. However, the Court agreed with Frank Robbins and rejected that blanket immunity argument. According to the Court, "qualified immunity protects federal officials from individual liability unless the officials violated a clearly established constitutional or statutory right of which a reasonable person would have known."[395] Although the Court noted that Mr. Robbins had a "heavy burden" in proving his claims, the Court agreed that Mr. Robbins presented factual evidence that reasonable BLM employees would have known that they were violating Mr. Robbins' rights with their actions. The Court cited to the 248 exhibits attached to Mr. Robbins brief and stated that "Plaintiff [Mr. Robbins] provides a significant amount of evidence which would lead a jury to conclude that Defendants did intend and agreed to extort and punish Plaintiff."[396]

In its footnote, the Court went on that "Plaintiff has submitted evidence of Defendants' alleged motive and intent, threats, lies, trespass, disparate treatment and harassment in the form of various depositions, including a deposition of a former BLM employee Ed Parodi, various letters, criminal trial transcripts and trespass notices." Although each BLM employee affirmatively denied that he or she "'did not conspire or agree with anyone at any time for any purpose with regards to Plaintiff, particularly to commit any alleged predicate acts of extortion or retaliation,'" the Court "will not solely rely upon the statements of the individual employees."[397] This case will go to a jury.

After decades of abuse without consequence, arrogant federal bureaucrats will be held criminally responsible for their deliberate and autocratic acts to deny a citizen of the United States their Constitutional rights. This case should have sent a very strong message to government bureaucrats that arrogance and abuse of power can send them to prison. However, the decisions by the Court have been uneven since the Bivens decision, so its protections are still not automatic. Although Congress has not done so, there is a general recognition that legislation that offers a clearer line upon which federal employees might be held personally responsible would be of help.[398]

About The Author

 Dr. Michael Coffman has taught and conducted research at the University level as well as leading a multimillion dollar research effort to determine the effects of global warming on our nation's ecosystems. As president of Environmental Perspectives, Inc. and CEO of Sovereignty International he is now attempting to warn America of the dangers behind a warped worldview and a blind agenda to transfer power to first the federal government and ultimately a world government. He played the instrumental role in stopping the ratification of the United Nations Convention on Biological Diversity one hour before the vote was scheduled in the U.S. Senate. He has also written several books and produced DVDs on the subject.

Endnotes

Chapter 1

1. William Ayres. Discover the Networks. No date. http://www.discoverthenetworks. org/individualProfile.asp?indid=2169

2. Brad Wilmouth. Matthews: Obama Speech Caused 'Thrill Going Up My Leg." NewsBusters, Media Research Center. February 13, 2008. http://newsbusters.org/ blogs/brad-wilmouth/2008/02/13/matthews-obama-speech-caused-thrill-going-my-leg

3. YouTube video of Obama Joe the Plumber exchange. http://www.youtube.com/ watch?v=BRPbCSSXyp0

4. Candidate Barak Obama's transforming the United States of America campaign promise. http://www.youtube.com/watch?v=xvJJP9AYgqU

5. Senate Panel Approves Climate Change Bill Despite GOP Boycott, FoxNews. com. November 05, 2009. http://www.foxnews.com/politics/2009/11/05/senate-panel-approves-climate-change-despite-gop-boycott/

6. Michael Coffman. Cap and Trade Looms Large. Range Magazine. Fall 2009, pp 52-55. http://www.rangemagazine.com/features/fall-09/fa09-cap_trade.pdf

7. Susan Davis. WSJ/NBC News Poll: Tea Party Tops Democrats and Republicans. Wall Street Journal Blogs, Washington Wire. http://blogs.wsj. com/washwire/2009/12/16/wsjnbc-news-poll-tea-party-tops-democrats-and-republicans/

8. Obama's Approval Most Polarized for First-Year President. Gallup, January 25, 2010. http://www.gallup.com/poll/125345/obama-approval-polarized-first-year-president.aspx

9. Distrust, Discontent, Anger and Partisan Rancor, Pew Research Center, April 18, 2010. http://people-press.org/report/606/trust-in-government

10. Weinstein, Kenneth. Individual Rights v. The General Will CFACT, 2002, Briefing Paper 111. Wells, H. G. Experiment in Autobiography, (New York: The Macmillian Company, 1934).

11. Locke, John. Second Treatise Government. Chapter Nine, 1690. http://www. constitution.org/jl/2ndtr09.htm

12. For a full discussion of God's Law and Nature's Law, see Cleon Skousen, The Majesty of God's Law (Salt Lake City: Ensign Publishing, 1996).

13. Thomas Sowell. The Quest for Cosmic Justice (New York: Free Press, 1999). Also see quote at http://www.conservativeforum.org/authquot.asp?ID=158

14. James Gwartney, el. al. Economic Freedom of the World, 2009 Annual Report.

    http://www.freetheworld.com/2009/reports/world/EFW2009_BOOK.pdf

15. List of Countries by GDP (PPP) per capita. Wikipedia http://en.wikipedia.org/ wiki/List_of_countries_by_GDP_%28PPP%29_per_capita.

16. Amelia Karabegović et. al. Economic Freedom of North America, 2008 Annual Report (US Edition). 2008. p. ix.

17. Rousseau, Jean-Jacques. The Social Contract, Or Principles Of Political Right, Book I, 6—The Social Compact Paragraph 10 and 11. 1762. http://www. constitution.org/jjr/socon_01.htm

18. Ibid.

19. Ibid.

20. Ibid.

21. Ibid. The Sovereign, Paragraphs 8 and 9

22. Ibid.

23. Jean-Jacques Rousseau. Discourse on the Origin of Inequality, Part II, paragraph 1. 1754. http://www.constitution.org/jjr/ineq_04.htm

24. Ibid, paragraph 38.

25. Coffman, Saviors of the Earth?, pp. 273-274.

26. James Madison. Speech before the Virginia State Constitution Convention, December 1 1829. Inscribed on the walls of Madison Building, Library of Congress. http://www.loc.gov/loc/walls/madison.html

27. Becky Akers. Green Government. The New American, February 1, 2010, Vol 26(3):17-22.

28. John Rapanos, et ux., Et al. Vs. United States. Amicus Curiae Brief of the Cato Institute in Support of Petitioners. http://www.cato.org/pubs/legalbriefs/ Rapanos3.pdf

29. John Rapanos Agrees to Pay for Clean Water Act Violations. EPA News Release, December 29, 2008. http://yosemite.epa.gov/opa/admpress.nsf/0/ B029AB82BF92CD5F8525752E0072FC60

Chapter 2

31. Thomas Jefferson. from: Bergh, Albert Ellery, ed. The writings of Thomas Jefferson, 20 Vols. (Washington: Thomas Jefferson Memorial Association, 1907), 15:278

32. Star Parker. Back on Uncle Sam's Plantation. Scripps Howard News Service, February 6, 2009. http://www.scrippsnews.com/node/40710

33. Dana Blanton. Fox News Poll: Obama Approval Up; Most Say Stop Blaming Bush. Fox News, April 22, 2010. http://www.foxnews.com/politics/2010/04/22/fox-news-poll-obama-approval-say-stop-blaming-bush/-say-stop-blaming-bush/?test=latestnews

34. Rossiter, Lyle Jr. M.D. The Liberal Mind; The Psychological Causes of political Madness. Free World Books, LLC. 2006, p 329.

     Benjamin Franklin, Quotation Reference. No date. http://www.quotationreference.com/quotefinder.php?byax=1&strt=1&subj=Benjamin+Franklin

35. Video. Arizona Chastised for Immigration Law. Fox News, May 19, 2010. http://video.foxnews.com/v/4203916/arizona-chastised-for-immigration-law

36. Ibid.

37. Dana Blanton. Fox News Poll: States Should Have the Right To Make Immigration Laws. Fox News. May 20, 2010. http://www.foxnews.com/politics/2010/05/20/fox-news-poll-states-right-make-immigration-laws/

38. Video. Congress Gives Calderone Standing Ovation for Bashing AZ. StandWithArizona.org, You Tube. May 20, 2010. http://www.youtube.com/watch?v=gLt3GgDQgVY

39. Associated Press. Obama's Border Plan Looks Similar to Bush's. Fox News, May 26, 2010. http://www.foxnews.com/politics/2010/05/26/ap-obamas-border-plan-looks-similar-bushs/

40. Rossiter, Lyle Jr. M.D. The Liberal Mind; The Psychological Causes of political Madness. Free World Books, LLC. 2006, p 330.

41 .Scott Hodge and Andre Dammert. U.S. Lags While Competitors Accelerate Corporate Income Tax Reform. Tax Foundation, Fiscal Fact No. 184. August, 2009. http://www.taxfoundation.org/files/ff184.pdf

42. Gerald Prante. Summary of Latest federal Individual Income Tax Data. Tax Foundation, Fiscal Fact No. 183. July 30, 2009. http://www.taxfoundation.org/news/show/250.html

43. Tom Palmer. Realizing Freedom: Libertarian Theory, History, and Practice. (Washing DC: Cato Institute, 2009), p 303. http://store.cato.org/pdfs/Pages%20from%20Realizing%20Freedom.pdf

44. Letter by Adams published in the Boston Gazette, September 5, 1763. http://www.conservativeforum.org/authquot.asp?ID=846

45. Alex Ritz. Government Jobs outnumber Private Sector. The Ritz Report. January 12, 2010. http://www.ritzreport.com/2010/01/government-jobs-out-number-private-sector/

46. Ibid, p 333.

47. Barack Obama Public Radio interview on January 18, 2001 on positive and negative rights and redistribution of wealth. You can listen to it on YouTube: http://www.youtube.com/watch?v=iivL4c_3pck&feature=player_embedded#

48. Jeffrey Crowley. All the President's Czars. Whistleblower Magazine, November 2009, (18)2:8-35

49. Mark Whittington. Barack Obama and "The Second Bill of Rights." Associated Content News. October 28, 2010. http://www.associatedcontent.com/article/1158059/barack_obama_and_the_second_bill_of.html?cat=9

50. Rossiter, Lyle Jr. M.D. The Liberal Mind; The Psychological Causes of political Madness. Free World Books, LLC. 2006, p 322.

51. Historical Poverty Tables. Bureau of Census, 2009. http://www.census.gov/hhes/www/poverty/histpov/hstpov2.html

52. Benjamin Franklin. On the Price of Corn, and Management of the Poor. The London Chronicle, November 29, 1766.

53. Health Care Law. Rasmussen Reports. April 5, 2010. http://www.rasmussenreports.com/public_content/politics/current_events/healthcare/march_2010/health_care_law

54. Pelosi Says She'll 'Pole Vault' Obamacare Through Congress. Fox Nation, January 28, 2010. http://www.thefoxnation.com/health-care/2010/01/29/pelosi-says-she-ll-poll-vault-obamacare-through-congress

55. Dan Pfeiffer. Obama Executive Order on Abortion Funding. White House. March 21, 2010. http://whitehouse.blogs.foxnews.com/2010/03/21/obama-executive-order-on-abortion-funding/

56. Chad Pergram, Dominique Pastre and the Associated Press. Rep. Bart Stupak Announces His Retirement After Health Care Controversy. Fox News, April 9, 2010. http://www.foxnews.com/politics/2010/04/09/rep-bart-stupak-retire/

57. Aaron Task. Health Care Fight All Over But the Shouting…and the Double-Counting. Yahoo! Finance, March 22, 2010. http://finance.yahoo.com/tech-ticker/article/446244/Health-Care-Fight-All-Over-But-the-Shouting-…-and-the-Double-Counting

58. Ibid.

59. Obama's Approval Most Polarized for First-Year President. Gallup, January 25, 2010. http://www.gallup.com/poll/125345/obama-approval-polarized-first-year-president.aspx

Chapter 3

60. Bergh, Albert Ellery, ed. The writings of Thomas Jefferson, 20 Vols. (Washington: Thomas Jefferson Memorial Association, 1907), 15:278

61. Forrest McDonald. Novus Ordo Seclorum: The Intellectual Origins of the Constitution. University Press of Kansas (1986). p 276

62. B.L. Rayner. Life of Thomas Jefferson; 20. Turmoil and Change in America. (Boston: Lilly, Wait, Colman, & Holden, 1834), 6:274. Written by Jefferson on September 16, 1787. http://etext.virginia.edu/jefferson/biog/lj20.htm

63. Bergh, Albert Ellery, ed. The writings of Thomas Jefferson, 20 Vols. (Washington: Thomas Jefferson Memorial Association, 1907), 15:278

64. Frederic Bastiat. The Law. (Irvin-on-the-Hudson, NY: Foundation for Economic Education, 1998), p. 52. Ibid, L.174-175 http://www.econlib.org/library/Bastiat/basLaw1.html#The%20Law, L 9-11.

65. Ibid, p 2

66. Ibid, p. 5. Ibid, L.13

67. 4 Letters and Other Writings of James Madison, 174. Taken from the essay "Property" written in 1792 and published in the National Gazette, March 27, 1792. See also The Papers of James Madison 266 (Riland, ed, 1977) http://press-pubs.uchicago.edu/founders/documents/v1ch16s23.html

68. Joel GehRkie, Jr. Pelosi Blames Bush Administration for BP Oil Spill. Washington Examiner, May, 29, 2010. http://www.washingtonexaminer.com/opinion/blogs/beltway-confidential/pelosi-blames-bush-administration-for-bp-oil-spill-95175304.html

69. Obama Extends Moratorium on Offshore Drilling. CBS News/AP, May 27, 2010. http://www.cbsnews.com/stories/2010/05/27/politics/main6523412.shtml

70. Darrell Issa. Committee on Oversight and Government Reform Report. U.S. House of Representatives, February 18, 2010. http://republicans.oversight.house.gov/images/stories/Reports/20100218followthemoneyacornseiuandtheirpolitical allies.pdf

71. Ibid.

72. Ralph Brauer. Bill Clinton, Glass-Steagall and the Current Foreclosure and Financial Crisis, Part 1. The Strange Death of Liberal America. May 8, 2008. http://thestrangedeathofliberalamerica.com/bill-clinton-glass-steagall-and-the-current-foreclosure-and-financial-crisis-part-one.html

73. Ibid.

74. Porter Stansberry. How AIG's Collapse Began a Global Run on the Banks. Daily Wealth. http://www.dailywealth.com/archive/2008/oct/2008_oct_04.asp

75.   Rick Newman. A User's Guide to Financial Reform. U.S. News and World Report, April 23, 2010. http://www.usnews.com/money/blogs/flowchart/2010/04/23/a-users-guide-to-financial-reform.html

76.   Frank McGuire and Dan Weil. Sen. Gregg: Finance Reform Bill a 'Disaster.' MoneyNews.com, May 25, 2010. http://www.moneynews.com/StreetTalk/Gregg-Finance-Reform-bill/2010/05/25/id/360037?s=al&promo_code=9F21-1

77.   Rick Newman. A User's Guide to Financial Reform. U.S. News and World Report, April 23, 2010. http://www.usnews.com/money/blogs/flowchart/2010/04/23/a-users-guide-to-financial-reform.html

78.   Frank McGuire and Dan Weil. Sen. Gregg: Finance Reform Bill a 'Disaster.' MoneyNews.com, May 25, 2010. http://www.moneynews.com/StreetTalk/Gregg-Finance-Reform-bill/2010/05/25/id/360037?s=al&promo_code=9F21-1

79.   Rick Newman. A User's Guide to Financial Reform. U.S. News and World Report, April 23, 2010. http://www.usnews.com/money/blogs/flowchart/2010/04/23/a-users-guide-to-financial-reform.html

80.   Mary Papenfuss. Critics Rip White House Links to Goldman Sachs. Newser, April 22, 2010. http://www.newser.com/story/86727/critics-rip-white-house-links-to-goldman-sachs.html

81.   Frederic Bastiat. The Law. (Irvin-on-the-Hudson, NY: Foundation for Economic Education, 1998), p. 4-5. Ibid, L.16

82.   Ibid, p. 7. Ibid, L.27

83.   Ibid, p. 7-8. Ibid, L.29

84.   Ibid, p. 14. Ibid, L.54-55

85.   Obama's Approval Most Polarized for First-Year President. Gallup, January 25, 2010. http://www.gallup.com/poll/125345/obama-approval-polarized-first-year-president.aspx

Chapter 4

86.   Dana Blanton. Fox News Poll: Obama Approval Up; Most Say Stop Blaming Bush. Fox News, April 22, 2010. http://www.foxnews.com/politics/2010/04/22/fox-news-poll-obama-approval-say-stop-blaming-bush/-say-stop-blaming-bush/?test=latestnews

87.   Distrust, Discontent, Anger and Partisan Rancor, Pew Research Center, April 18, 2010. http://people-press.org/report/606/trust-in-government

88.   Laurence J. Kotlikoff. Is The United States Bankrupt? Federal Reserve Bank of St. Louis Review, July/August 2006, 88(4), pp. 235-49.

89.   Curtis Dubay. America Celebrates Tax Freedom Day," Special Report No. 152, Tax Foundation, April 2007. http://www.taxfoundation.org/files/sr152.pdf

Endnotes

90.   Ibid. Also: Effective Marginal Tax Rates on Labor Income. Congressional Budget Office, 2005. http://www.cbo.gov/ftpdocs/68xx/doc6854/11-10-LaborTaxation. pdf

91.   Letter from the Congressional Budget Office to the Honorable Jeb Hensarling, March 8, 2007. http://www.cbo.gov/ftpdocs/78xx/doc7851/03-08-Long-Term%20Spending.pdf

92.   Clyde W. Crews, Jr. Ten Thousand Commandments, An Annual Policymaker's Snapshot of the Federal Regulatory State. 2004 Edition (Washington D.C.: The CATO Institute, 2002), pp. 1-2. http://www.cato.org/tech/pubs/10kc_2004.pdf

93.   Ronald Utt and Wyndell Cox. City Limits: Putting the Brakes on Sprawl: A Contrary View, WebMemo#20, Heritage Foundation. June 29, 2001. http://www. heritage.org/Research/SmartGrowth/WM20.cfm

94.   Hernando de Soto. The Mystery of Capital (New York: Basic Books, 2000), pp. 6-7, 20-21, 35.

95.   Paul Driessen. Eco-Imperialism, Green Power Black Death (The Free Enterprise Press, 2003)

96.   Kimberley Strassel, "Rural Cleansing," The Wall StreetJournal, July 26, 2001.

97.   Ann Forest Burns, Equal Access to Justice Act Abuse. American Forest Resource Council. November 25, 2009 http://www.amforest.org/resource/newsletters/ AFRC%20Newsletter%2011-25-09.pdf

98.   John Mauldin. "Those Magic Unemployment Numbers," InvestorsInsight. March 5, 2004. http://www.investorsinsight.com

99.   Ibid.

100.   Ibid.

101.   United States Public Debt. Wikipedia, 2008. http://en.wikipedia.org/wiki/United_ States_public_debt

102.   AP. Senate Lifts Federal Debt Ceiling by $1.9 Trillion. Fox News. January 28, 2010. http://www.foxnews.com/politics/2010/01/28/senate-lifts-federal-debt-ceiling-trillion/

103.   Table 1.1.5 Gross Domestic Product. Bureau of Economic Analysis, U.S. Department of Commerce. National Economic Accounts. http://www.bea.gov/ national/index.htm#gdp

104.   US Debt Clock. http://www.usdebtclock.org/

105.   Laurence J. Kotlikoff. Is The United States Bankrupt? Federal Reserve Bank of St. Louis Review, July/August 2006, 88(4), pp. 235-49.

106.   Doug Mataconis. Obama's Fist Year Increase in Nation Debt Already Record Setting. Below the Beltway. http://belowthebeltway.com/2010/01/21/obamas-first-year-increase-in-national-debt-already-record-setting/

107.   United States Public Debt. Wikipedia, 2008. http://en.wikipedia.org/wiki/United_ States_public_debt

108.   William Jasper. No Pennies Saved; Obama's Debt Commission. New American, April 26, 2010. pp 21-24.

109.   Ibid.

110.   Chris Edwards. Federal Pay Continues Rapid Ascent. CATO at Liberty. http://www.cato-at-liberty.org/2009/08/24/federal-pay-continues-rapid-ascent/

111.   The United States Dollar. Wikipedia. 2008. http://en.wikipedia.org/wiki/United_States_dollar

112.   Dana Blanton. Fox News Poll: 79% Say U.S. Economy Could Collapse. Fox News, March 23, 2010. http://www.foxnews.com/politics/2010/03/23/fox-news-poll-say-economy-collapse/

113.   Ibid.

114.   Saul Alinsky: Prophet of Power to the People. Time Magazine, March 2, 1970. http://www.time.com/time/magazine/article/0,9171,904228,00.html

115.   Scott Herron. Saul Alinsky [s Rules for Radicals. Heirs of Liberty Press. May 9, 2009 http://www.heirsoflibertypress.org/article.php?id=52

116.   Ibid.

117.   Saul Alinsky: Prophet of Power to the People. Time Magazine, March 2, 1970. http://www.time.com/time/magazine/article/0,9171,904228,00.html

118.   Glenn Beck. Manufacturing Czar Says "the Free Market is Nonsense." The Glenn Beck Program. October 20, 2009. Beck played an actual recording of Bloom's speech. http://www.glennbeck.com/content/articles/article/198/32133/

119.   Saul Alinsky: Prophet of Power to the People. Time Magazine, March 2, 1970. http://www.time.com/time/magazine/article/0,9171,904228,00.html Rules for Radicals. Heirs of Liberty Press. May 9, 2009 http://www.heirsoflibertypress.org/article.php?id=52

102.   Nina Easton. What's really behind SEIU's Bank of America Protests? Fortune. May 19, 2010. http://money.cnn.com/2010/05/19/news/companies/SEIU_Bank_of_America_protest.fortune/index.htm

121.   Glenn Beck. Obama Is Transforming Us. The Glenn Beck Program. July 29, 2009. Beck played actual video of Obama's speech. http://www.glennbeck.com/content/articles/article/198/28610/

122.   Capital Confidential. Police Report on "Gladney Beatings by SEIU Thugs. Big Government.com. November 9, 2009. http://biggovernment.com/capitolconfidential/2009/11/09/exclusive-police-report-on-gladney-beating-by-seiu-thugs/

123.   Sammy Benoit. Obama, ACOPRN, and the SEIU? They Go Way Back. Pajamas Media., August 18, 2009. http://pajamasmedia.com/blog/obama-acorn-and-the-seiu-they-go-way-back/

124.   Capital Confidential. Police Report on "Gladney Beatings by SEIU Thugs. Big Government.com. November 9, 2009. http://biggovernment.com/

capitolconfidential/2009/11/09/exclusive-police-report-on-gladney-beating-by-seiu-thugs/

125. Saul Alinsky: Prophet of Power to the People. Time Magazine, March 2, 1970. http://www.time.com/time/magazine/article/0,9171,904228,00.html

126. Ibid.

127. Richard Cloward and Frances Piven. The Weight of the Poor, A Strategy to End Poverty. Discover the Networks, May 2, 1966. http://www.discoverthenetworks. org/Articles/A%20Strategy%20to%20End%20Poverty2.html

128. The Cloward-Piven Strategy. Discover The Networks, no date. http://www. discoverthenetworks.org/groupProfile.asp?grpid=6967

129. Richard Cloward and Frances Piven. The Weight of the Poor, A Strategy to End Poverty. Discover the Networks, May 2, 1966 http://www.discoverthenetworks. org/Articles/A%20Strategy%20to%20End%20Poverty2.html

130. The Cloward-Piven Strategy. Discover The Networks, no date. http://www. discoverthenetworks.org/groupProfile.asp?grpid=6967

131. Ibid.

132. Ibid.

133. Ibid.

134. Association of Community Organizations for Reform Now (ACORN). Discover The Networks, no date. http://www.discoverthenetworks.org/groupProfile. asp?grpid=6968

Chapter 5

135. Carroll Quigley. Tragedy & Hope, A History of the World in Our Time. (New York: The Macmillan Company, 1966),p. 324.

136. Ibid, p. 950.

137. Ibid, p. 324.

138. Gurudas. Treason, The New World Order. (San Rafael, California: Cassandra Press, 1996), p. 17.

139. Ibid,

140. Kofi Annan, Sec. Gen of UN. "Towards a stable international financial system, responsive to the challenges of development, especially in the developing countries." Report of the Secretary General, A/55/187. July 27, 2001, paragraph 24, 32, 40, 71 p. 8-10, 16.

Also: See General Assembly Resolution: Towards a strengthened and stable international financial architecture responsive to the priorities of growth and development, especially in developing countries, and to the promotion of economic and social equity. A/RES/55/186. January 25, 2001.

And: General Assembly Resolution: "Role of the United Nations in promoting development in the context of globalization and interdependence." A/RES/55/212. February 22, 2001.

And: International Conference on Financing for Development. March 18-22, 2002.

And: Monterrey Consensus, (The); Report of the International Conference on Financing for Development. UN General Assembly A/CONF.198/11. January 27, 2002. http://ods-dds-ny.un.org/doc/UNDOC/GEN/N02/392/67/PDF/N0239267. pdf?OpenElement

141. Monterrey Consensus of the International Conference on Financing for Development, numerous pages. http://www.un.org/esa/ffd/monterrey/ MonterreyConsensus.pdf

142. Carroll Quigley. The Anglo-American Establishment (NY: Books in Focus, 1981), preface, p. xi. In: Stanley Monteith, Brotherhood of Darkness, (Oklahoma City: Hearthstone Publishing, 2000), p. 107.

143. Gurudas. Treason, The New World Order. (San Rafael, California: Cassandra Press, 1996), p. 17.

144. Carroll Quigley. The Anglo-American Establishment, p. 32. In Monteith, p. 106.

145. Ibid, Preface x, Ibid, p. 107.

146. Antony Sutton. America's Secret Establishment, (Waterville, Oregon: Trine Day:, 1983, 1986, 2002), pp.1-58.

147. Carroll Quigley, Tragedy and Hope, A History of the World in Our Time. (New York: The Macmillan Company, 1966) p. 539.

148. Ibid, p. 950.

149. Ibid, p. 60-61.

150. Ibid, p. 51.

151. Ibid, p. 956.

152. Ibid, p. 72.

153. Ibid, p. 539-540.

154. Paul Dobson. UK. Currency Trading Climbed to $1.43 Trillion a Day. Bloomberg.com. January 25, 2010. http://www.bloomberg.com/apps/ news?pid=20602097&sid=asINz4eE_CGs

155. Christopher Swan. "London Still Dominant as Finance Center." Bank of International Settlements, October 10, 2001.

156. Carroll Quigley, Tragedy and Hope, p. 956.

157. Gurudas, p. 15.

158. Ted Flynn, p. 82.

159. Ibid.

160. Ibid, p. 83. In: G. Edward Griffin. The Creature from Jekyll Island. (Westlake Village, California: American Media, 1994), p. 269.

161. Ibid, p 76.

162. Carroll Quigley, Tragedy and Hope, p 216.

163. Ibid, pp 342-350.

164. Ibid, p. 952.

165. Ibid, p. 950-951.

166. G. Edward Griffin. The Creature From Jekyll Island (Appleton, Wisconsin: American Opinion Publishing, Inc., 1994-1995), p. 240.

167. James Perloff. Council on Foreign Relations. New American, July 23, 2009. http://www.thenewamerican.com/index.php/usnews/foreign-policy/1462

168. Obama's Cabinet Full of CFR, Trilateral Commission and Bilderberg Members. The Future, December 16, 2008. http://futurestorm.blogspot.com/2008/12/obamas-cabinet-full-of-cfr-trilateral.html

169. David Rockefeller. Wikipedia. http://en.wikipedia.org/wiki/David_Rockefeller#Bilderberg.2C_Council_on_Foreign_Relations_and_Trilateral_Commission

    The Green Agenda. GreenAgenda.com, http://green-agenda.com/globalrevolution.html

170. The Green Agenda. GreenAgenda.com, http://green-agenda.com/globalrevolution.html

171. Ibid.

172. Bob Unrah. These People Want Empire. WorldNetDaily. June 1, 2010. http://www.wnd.com/index.php?fa=PAGE.view&pageId=161377

173. "David Rockefeller." Wikipedia, http://en.wikipedia.org/wiki/David_Rockefeller

174. Patrick Wood, Editor. Obama: Trilateral Commission Endgame. The August Review. January 30, 2009. http://www.augustreview.com/news_commentary/trilateral_commission/obama:_trilateral_commission_endgame_20090127110/

175. Patrick Wood, Editor. Obama and McCain: Pawns of the Global Elite? The August Review. August 5, 2008. http://www.augustreview.com/news_commentary/u.s._elections/obama_and_mccain%3a_pawns_of_the_global_elite?_2008080597/

176. Ibid.

177. Carroll Quigley, Tragedy and Hope, pp 1247-1248.

178. Ibid, p 866.

179. Hon. Carroll Reece, Chr. The Reece Report, p. 27. In: Rene Wormser. Foundations, Their Power and Influence (Sevierville, TN, Covenant House Books, 1958, 1977, 1993). p 48.

180. Ibid. Ibid, p. 303.

Chapter 6

181. Gurudas. Treason, The New World Order. (San Rafael, California: Cassandra Press, 1996), p. 17.

182. Charlotte Thomson Iserbyt, The Deliberate Dumbing Down of America, (Ravenna, Ohio: Conscience Press, 1999), p. 27, 28

183. William K. Medlin, et. al. Soviet Education Programs: Foundations, Curriculum, Teacher Preparation, Office of Education, OE-14037, Bulletin, 1950, No. 17. In: Charlotte Iserbyt, p. 57, 72.

      Charlotte Iserbyt, p 72.

184. Robert Muller. World Core Curriculum Manual (Arlington, TX: Robert Muller School, 1986), preface

      Also see Kristie Snyder, "Creating the Global Student," Discerning the Times Digest, October, 1999, Vol 1(9):3. http://www.discerningtoday.org/members/ Digest/1999Digest/October/Creating%20the%20Gobal%20Student.htm

      Also see "The Occult--Goals 2000 and Educating the Global Child," Discerning the Times Digest, Editor's Commentary December, 1999, Vol 1 (11):3. http:// www.discerningtoday.org/members/Digest/1999Digest/December/The   Occult. htm

185. Charlotte Thomson Iserbyt, The Deliberate Dumbing Down of America, (Ravenna, Ohio: Conscience Press, 1999) see "Futurism as a Social Tool and Decision-Making by an Elite," p. 248-255. and p. A-25.

186. Ibid, p. 259. Ibid.

187. Ibid, p. 261. Ibid.

188. Carroll Quigley, Tragedy and Hope, pp. 551, 553.

189. Berit Kjos, Brave New Schools, (Eugene, OR: Harvest House, 1995), p. 60.

190. Orlean Koehle, President of Eagle Forum of California. Quote used in Eagle forum of Santa Rosa annual meeting, March 9, 2002.

191. Ted Flynn. "Hope for the Wicked, The Master Plan to Rule the World." (Sterling, Virginia: MaxKol Communications, Inc., 2000), p. 4.

192. Charlotte Thomson Iserbyt, The Deliberate Dumbing Down of America, (Ravenna, Ohio: Conscience Press, 1999) p. 29.

193. Ibid, p. xiv.

194. Ibid, p. 7.

195. H.R. 1804. Goals 2000: Educate America Act. http://www2.ed.gov/legislation/ GOALS2000/TheAct/index.html

196. H.R. 2884. Bill Summary and Status for the 103rd Congress. School-to-Work Act. http://thomas.loc.gov/cgi-bin/query/z?c103:H.R.2884: |

Endnotes

197. H.R. 6. Bill Summary and Status for the 103rd Congress. Elementary and Secondary Education Act. http://frwebgate.access.gpo.gov/cgi-bin/getdoc.cgi?dbname=103_cong_bills&docid=f:h6eh.txt.pdf

198. H.R. 1617. To consolidate and reform workforce development and literacy programs, and for other purposes. http://frwebgate.access.gpo.gov/cgi-bin/getdoc.cgi?dbname=104_cong_bills&docid=f:h1617rfs.txt.pdf

199. Title X, Section 10601 a. In: Allen Quist. Fed Ed, The New Federal Curriculum and How It=s Enforced (Glencoe, MN: NuCompass Publishing, 2002), p. 16. Bold added for emphasis in original.

200. Ibid. Ibid, p. 17. Bold added for emphasis in original.

201. Allen Quist, Fed Ed, p. 17.

202. Ibid, p. 26.

203. Ibid, p. 29.

204. Phyllis Schlafly. Eagle Forum. http://www.eagleforum.org/educate/marc_tucker/marc_tucker_letter.html

205. Charlie Butts. America's Christian Roots – A Myth? One News Now, January 15, 2010. http://www.onenewsnow.com/Education/Default.aspx?id=854370

206. Charlie Butts. Religious References Restored to textbooks. One News Now, January 15, 2010. http://www.onenewsnow.com/Education/Default.aspx?id=855932

207. Jim Brown. Texas Doesn't Take the Bait. One News Now, January 18, 2010. http://www.onenewsnow.com/Education/Default.aspx?id=856346

208. Molly Henneberg. North Carolina Schools May Cut Chunk Out of U.S. History Lessons. Fox News, February 3, 2010. http://www.foxnews.com/story/0,2933,584758,00.html?loomia_ow=t0:s0:a4:g4:r1:c0.000000:b0:z5

209. Congressional Record. Second Session, Sixty-Fourth Congress, Volume 54, February 9, 1917, p.. 2947-48

210. Carroll Quigley, Tragedy and Hope, p. 953.

211. Bernard Goldberg. Bias, A CBS Insider Exposes How the Media Distort the News. (Washington, DC: Regnery Publishing, Inc., 2002), p. 16.

212. Ibid, p. 24.

213. Ibid, p. 222.

214. NBC News/Wall Street Journal Poll, October 16, 2009. http://www.pollingreport.com/media.htm

215. David Limbaugh, December 14, 1999. http://www.wnd.com/news/article.asp?ARTICLE_ID=18944

216. Ibid.

217. Bob Kohn. "The New York Times: Democrat Apologists," WorldNetDaily, July 29, 2003. http://www.wnd.com/news/article.asp?ARTICLE_ID=33787

218. Danny Shea. Fox News Dominates 3Q 2009 Cable News Ratings. Huffington Post, September 30, 2009. http://www.huffingtonpost.com/2009/09/30/fox-news-dominates-3q-200_n_304260.html

219. Robert Ringer. Glenn Beck's Departure from Fox News, Part 1. World Net Daily, May 26, 2010. http://www.wnd.com/index.php?fa=PAGE.view&pageId=158721

220. Joseph Farah. "Old Media vs New Media," Whistleblower magazine, May 2002, p. 6.

221. Joseph Farah. "The Free Press in a Free Society," Whistleblower magazine, May 2002, p. 45.

222. Joseph Farah. "Old Media vs New Media," p. 9.

223. Ibid.

224. Internet News Audience Highly Critical of News Organizations. The Pew Research Center for the People & the Press, August 9, 2007. http://people-press.org/report/348/internet-news-audience-highly-critical-of-news-organizations

225. Ibid.

226. Josh Benson. "Gore's TV War: He Lobs Salvo At Fox News." New York Observer, December 2, 2002, page 1. http://www.observer.com/pages/story.asp?ID=6665 Also see, Carl Cameron, "Gore Criticizes Media for Turning Its Collective Back on Him, Democrats. Fox News, November 28, 2002. http://www.foxnews.com/story/0,2933,71633,00.html

227. Fox News. White House Escalates War of Words With Fox News. Fox News, October 12, 2009. http://www.foxnews.com/politics/2009/10/12/white-house-escalates-war-words-fox-news/

228. Associated Press. White House Steps Up Attacks on Fox News. MSNBC. October 19, 2009. http://www.msnbc.msn.com/id/33376836/ns/politics-white_house/

229. Joseph Lawler. Anita Dunn: Mao Tse Tung Fan? The American Spectator. OCTOBER 15, 2009. http://spectator.org/blog/2009/10/16/anita-dunn-mao-tse-tung-fan

230. Glenn Beck. We're Raising a Generation of Would-be Killers. Segment recorded on October 26, 2009. Video clips of Dunn and Bloom were played saying Mao was their favorite historical person. http://www.foxnews.com/story/0,2933,569689,00.html

231. Andrea Tantaros. Anita Dunn and the Obama White House: Outfoxed. Fox News, November 10, 2009.

232. All the President's Czars. Whistleblower Magazine, November 2009, Vol 18(11):8-35.

233. Robert Ringer. Glenn Beck's Departure from Fox News, Part 1. World Net Daily, May 26, 2010. http://www.wnd.com/index.php?fa=PAGE.view&pageId=158721

Chapter 7

234. Brooks Alexander, "The View from Iron Mountain, Planning Global Ecowar," Spiritual Counterfeits Project Journal, 1992, 17(3):43.

253. Leonard Lewin, p. 35. http://projectcamelot.org/Report_from_Iron_Mountain. pdf, p. 34

236. Ibid, pp. 40 - 41. http://projectcamelot.org/Report_from_Iron_Mountain.pdf, p. 37

237. Lyle Rossiter, JR., M.D. The Liberal Mind; The Psychological Causes of Political Madness. (St Charles, IL: Free World Books, 2006. 418 pages.

238. Leonard Lewin, Report From Iron Mountain, p. 67. Ibid. http://projectcamelot. org/Report_from_Iron_Mountain.pdf, p. 51

239. Ibid, p. 66-67. http://projectcamelot.org/Report_from_Iron_Mountain.pdf, http:// projectcamelot.org/Report_from_Iron_Mountain.pdf, p. 51

240. Joan Veon, Blueprint for Global Governance: Y2K & the Report from Iron Mountain. Video taped at the Granada Forum, October 21, 1999. The final answer was from the actual tape recording of Cleveland.

241. Carroll Quigley, Tragedy and Hope, pp. 551, 553.

242. "Environmental Donors Set Tone—Activists Affected by Quest for Funds," by Scott Allen, Boston Globe, Monday, October 20, 1997, p. A1.

243. The Story of the Club of Rome. The Club of Rome. No date. http://www. clubofrome.org/eng/about/4/

   Also: Club of Rome Organization. http://www.nndb.com/org/142/000056971/

244. William K. Reilly. Use of Land: A Citizen's Policy Guide to Urban Growth (New York: Tomas Y Crowell Co., 1973), pp 15-16.

245. Ibid, p 25.

246. Anthony D'Elia, The Adirondack Rebellion (New York: Onchiota Books, 1979). pp 197-199

247. Plattsburg Press, August 19, 1991; and Adirondack Daily Enterprise, October 8, 1993.

248. Randal O'Toole. "Is Urban Planning "Creeping Socialism"? The Independent Review, Vol. IV, n. 4, Spring 2000, p. 504. http://www.independent.org/pdf/tir/ tir_04_4_otoole.pdf

249. Edward Glaeser and Joseph Gyourko. The Impact of Zoning on Housing Affordability. Harvard Institute of Economic Research. Discussion Paper Number 1948. March 2002. http://www.economics.harvard.edu/pub/hier/2002/HIER1948. pdf

250. Ibid.

251. Randal O'Tool. The Planning Penalty. The American Dream Coalition. March, 2006. http://americandreamcoalition.org/Penalty.pdf

252. Tape recording of the official Town of Falmouth Maine's Study Area Committee Meeting in September, 2002. Tape recording provided by Mary Alice Davis, an attendee of the meeting.

253. Agenda 21. Un Department of Economic and Social Affairs, Division for Sustainable Development. 1992. http://www.un.org/esa/dsd/agenda21/res_agenda21_00.shtml

254. Report of Habitat: United Nations Conference on Human Settlements, Chapter IID, Preamble. Vancouver May 31 to June 11, 1976. http://freedom.org/reports/human-settlements/land.html

255. Elaine Dewar. Cloak of Green. (Toronto: James Lorimer & Company, 1995), pp 252-273.

256. Steven C. Rockefeller and John C. Elder, Spirit and Nature: Why the Environment Is a Religious Issue, (Boston: Beacon, 1992), p. 134.

Chapter 8

257. Michael Soule. "History and purpose of the society of conservation biology." Conservation Biology, 1(1987):4-5.

258. Henry Lamb and Michael Coffman. How the Convention on Biodiversity Was Defeated. Sovereignty International, Inc. 1994. http://www.sovereignty.net/p/land/biotreatystop.htm

259. V.H. Heywood and R.T. Watson, ed. C Global Biodiversity Assessment, World Resources Institute and UN Environmental Program (London, New York: Cambridge University Press, 1995). Section 13.4.2.2.3, p. 993

260. Ibid.

261. Henry Lamb. The Convention on Biological Diversity: Cornerstone of the New World Order. Eco●Logic Special Report, November 4, 1994 http://freedom.org/reports/srbio.htm

262. Stephen McIntyre and Dr. Ross McKitrick. The IPCC, the "HOCKEY Stick" Curve, and the Illusion of Experience. George Marshall Institute. November 18 2003. http://www.marshall.org/article.php?id=188

263. Ross McKitrick: Defects in Key Climate Data Are Uncovered. Financial Times. October 1, 2009. http://network.nationalpost.com/np/blogs/fpcomment/archive/tags/hockey+stick/default.aspx

264. Anthony Watts. Ding Dong, the Stick is Dead. Watts Up with That? September 29, 2009. http://wattsupwiththat.com/2009/09/27/quote-of-the-week-20-ding-dong-the-stick-is-dead/

Endnotes

265. Noel Sheppard. ClimateGate's Michael Mann Received Stimulus Funds. The Wall Street Journal. January 15, 2010. http://online.wsj.com/article/SB1000142405274 8703657604575005412584751830.html

266. Michael S. Coffman. Lies and Damned Lies. Range Magazine. Spring, 2010. p 44. http://www.rangemagazine.com/features/spring-10/sp10-range-damned_lies.pdf

For original emails go to http://www.eastangliaemails.com/emails.php?eid=1044 &filename=1255095172.txt

267. Ibid, pp 45-46.

268. Michael Coffman. The Urban Heat-Island Effect. Range Magazine, Spring, 2010. p 46. http://www.rangemagazine.com/features/spring-10/sp10-range-damned_lies.pdf

269. Ibid, pp 46-47. and also see http://climateaudit.org/2007/08/04/1859/

270. Joseph D'Aleo. Climategate: Leaked Emails Inspired Data Analyses Show Claimed Warming Greatly Exaggerated and NOAA, not CRU is Ground Zero. Icecap. No date; circa January 15, 2010. http://icecap.us/images/uploads/NOAAroleinclimategate.pdf

271. Nitin Sethi. Ramesh Turns Heat on Pachauri Over Glacier Melt Scare. Times of India, January 19, 2010. http://timesofindia.indiatimes.com/india/Ramesh-turns-heat-on-Pachauri-over-glacier-melt-scare/articleshow/5474586.cms

272. David Rose. Glacier Scientist: I Knew Data Hadn't Been Verified. Mail Online. January 24, 2010. http://www.dailymail.co.uk/news/article-1245636/Glacier-scientists-says-knew-data-verified.html

273. Jonathan Leake. UN Wrongly Linked Global Warming to Natural Disasters. London Times Online. January 24, 2010. http://www.timesonline.co.uk/tol/news/environment/article7000063.ece

274. Gene Koprowski. UN's Global Warming Report Under Fresh Attack for Rainforest Claims. Fox News. January 28, 2010. http://www.foxnews.com/scitech/2010/01/28/save-rainforest-climate-change-scandal-chopped-facts/?utm_source=feedburner&utm_medium=feed&utm_campaign=Feed%253A+foxnews %252Fscitech+%2528Text+-+SciTech%2529

275. IPCC Used My Thesis for Glacier Report. Times Now. February 2, 2010. http://www.timesnow.tv/IPCC-used-my-thesis-for-glacier-report/articleshow/4337601.cms

276. Margaret Wente. The Great Global Warming Collapse. The Globe and Mail. February 5, 2010. http://www.theglobeandmail.com/news/opinions/the-great-global-warming-collapse/article1458206/

277. Craig Idso and Fred Singer, Lead Authors. Climate Change Reconsidered: 2009 Report of the Nongovernmental International Panel on Climate Change. (Chicago, IL: The Heartland Institute, 2009). Pp 106-107.

Also, Fred Singer, Ed. Nature, Not Human Activity Rules the Climate. Science and Environmental Policy Project and The Heartland Institute. 2007, pp 5-6. http://www.epi-us.com/NIPCC.pdf

278.   Arthor Robinson. Global Warming Petition Project. http://www.petitionproject. org/

279.   Michael Madden. Follow Global Warming Money. Casper Tribune. February 8, 2010. http://www.trib.com/news/opinion/mailbag/article_f137b016-446e-578d-aff6-d2d3533aab0e.html

280.   Senator James Inhofe. Over 400 Prominent Scientists Disputed Man-Made Global Warming Claims in 2007. U.S. Senate Committee on Environment & Public Works. December 20, 2007, Updated March 6, 2008. http://epw.senate.gov/ public/index.cfm?FuseAction=Minority.SenateReport#report

281.   Arthur Robinson. How Government Corrupts Science. Whistleblower. February 1020, vol. 19(2):14-21.

282.   Michael Coffman. Obama's EPA Threat. Range, Spring, 2010. p 47. http://www. rangemagazine.com/features/spring-10/sp10-range-damned_lies.pdf

283.   Gabriel Calzada Álvarez, et. Al. Study of the Effects On Employment of Public Aid to Renewable Energy Sources. University of Rey Jan Carlos, Madrid Spain. March 2009. http://www.nocapandtrade.us/Spain-employment.pdf

284.   James Taylor. The Cap & Trade Handbook. The Heartland Institute. February, 2010, p 4.

285.   Michael Coffman. Cap and Trade Looms Large. Range Magazine. Fall 2009, pp 52-53. http://www.rangemagazine.com/features/fall-09/fa09-cap_trade.pdf

286.   Jon Myers. Clean Energy is Pure Fantasy. Personal Liberty Digest. November 18, 2009. http://www.nocapandtrade.us/clean_energy_is_pure_fantasy.htm (link to Personal Liberty Digest does not work)

287.   Michael Coffman. Cap and Trade Looms Large. Range Magazine. Fall 2009, pp 52-53. http://www.rangemagazine.com/features/fall-09/fa09-cap_trade.pdf

288.   Joshua Miller. Fraud in Europe's Cap and Trade System a 'Red Flag,' Critics Say. Fox News. December 19, 2010. http://www.foxnews.com/politics/2009/12/14/ fraud-europes-cap-trade-red-flag-critics-say/?loomia_ow=t0:s0:a16:g2:r1:c0.100 073:b29429832:z10

298.   Patrick Wood. Carbon Currency: A New Beginning for Technocracy? The August Review. January 26, 2010. http://www.augustreview.com/issues/technocracy/ carbon_currency:_a_new_beginning_for_technocracy?_20100125155/

290.   Mario de Queniroz. Portugal Looking More Like Greece. IPS News. May 7, 2010. http://ipsnews.net/news.asp?idnews=51355

291.   Mark Memmott. Spain's Credit Rating Downgraded. National Public Radio (NPR) April 28, 2010. http://www.npr.org/blogs/thetwo-way/2010/04/spain_ debt_downgraded_stocks_f.html

Endnotes

292.   Richard Watchman and Nick Fletcher. Standard & Poor's Downgrade Greed Credit Ratings to Junk Status, Guardian, April 27, 2010. http://www.guardian.co.uk/business/2010/apr/27/greece-credit-rating-downgraded

293.   Simon Johnson and Peter Boone. The Greek Tragedy That Changed Europe. Wall Street Journal, Feb 13, 2010. http://online.wsj.com/article/SB10001424052748703525704575061172926967984.html?mod=WSJ_hp_mostpop_read

294.   Nina Mehta and Christ Nagi. Market fragmentation May get Review After Stock Drop. Bloomberg. May 7, 2010. http://www.bloomberg.com/apps/news?pid=20601103&sid=an66X1CjybPU

295.   United Nations. Toward A New International Financial Architecture. Report of the Task Force of the Executive Committee on Economic and Social Affairs of the United Nations. United Nations, Office of the Under-Secretary General. January 21, 1999. http://www.un.org/esa/desa/ousg/articles/pdf/intlfinar.htm

296.   United Nations. Monterrey Consensus of the International Conference on Financing for Development. United Nations Dept. of Economic and Social Affairs, March 18-22, 2002. http://www.un.org/esa/ffd/monterrey/MonterreyConsensus.pdf

297.   Joan Veon. World Globalization of the Banking & Regulatory Structure, Part II, News With Views, June 30, 2009. http://www.newswithviews.com/Veon/joan166.htm

298.   Joan Veon, Controlling the World's Monetary System; The Bank for International Settlements. News With Views. August 26, 2003. http://www.newswithviews.com/Veon/joan2.htm

         Andrew Crockett. Financial Stability Forum. Address to the Ministerial Segment of the international Conference on Financing for Development, Monterrey Mexico, March 18, 2002. http://www.un.org/ffd/statements/fsfE.htm (keep trying. It will eventually load)

299.   Carroll Quigley. Tragedy & Hope, A History of the World in Our Time. (New York: The Macmillan Company, 1966), p. 950.

300.   Joan Veon. World Globalization of the Banking & Regulatory Structure, Part I. News With Views, June 29, 2009. http://www.newswithviews.com/Veon/joan165.htm

301.   Joan Veon. World Globalization of the Banking & Regulatory Structure, Part II, News With Views, June 30, 2009. http://www.newswithviews.com/Veon/joan166.htm

302.   Patrick Wood. Carbon Currency: A New Beginning for Technocracy? The August Review. January 26, 2010. http://www.augustreview.com/issues/technocracy/carbon_currency:_a_new_beginning_for_technocracy?_20100125155/

303.   Carroll Quigley, Tragedy and Hope, pp. 551, 553

304. Patrick Wood. Carbon Currency: A New Beginning for Technocracy? The August Review. January 26, 2010. http://www.augustreview.com/issues/technocracy/carbon_currency:_a_new_beginning_for_technocracy?_20100125155/

305. Michael Coffman, ed. Freedom 21 Agenda for Prosperity, Promoting Sustainability through Political and Economic Freedom. (Chicago: Communities for a Greater Tomorrow and the Heartland Institute, 2007), pp 49-50.

306. About Oil Shale. Oil Shale Y Tar Sands Programmatic EIS. No date. http://ostseis.anl.gov/guide/oilshale/

307. Nicolas Loris. Omnibus Lands Bill Restricts Energy Exploration. The Heritage Foundation. WebMemo #2130, November 14, 2005.

308. Michael Coffman. "Has Congress Gone Mad? Range Magazine. Summer 2009, pp 44-46. http://www.rangemagazine.com/features/summer-09/su09-congress_gone_mad.pdf

309. Howard Scott and M. King Hubbert. Technocracy Study Course. New York: Technocracy Inc. 1934. http://www.technocracy.org/images/stories/pdf/studycourse2.pdf (This has been removed from the site) Go to: http://www.archive.org/details/TechnocracyStudyCourseUnabridged

310. Ibid, p 232.

311. Patrick Wood. Smart Grid: The Implementation of Technocracy? The August Review, March 2, 2010. http://www.augustreview.com/issues/technocracy/smart_grid:_the_implementation_of_technocracy?_20100222156/

312. Ibid.

Chapter 9

313. Constitution of the United States. http://www.archives.gov/exhibits/charters/constitution.html

341. William Jasper. Media Jump to Smear Right With Extremist Label. New American, April 26, 2010, pp25-28.

315. Media Double Standard? Fox News Video., April 27, 2010. http://video.foxnews.com/v/4168193/ignoring-immigration-outrage

316. Dana Blanton. Fox News Poll: States Should Have the Right To Make Immigration Laws. Fox News. May 20, 2010. http://www.foxnews.com/politics/2010/05/20/fox-news-poll-states-right-make-immigration-laws/

317. Freedom 21 http://freedom21.org/

318. Cecil Adams. How Do We Get Rid of Whacked Out Judges? Straight Dope, February 9, 2007. http://www.straightdope.com/columns/read/2693/there-goes-the-judge

319. Albert Ellery Bergh, ed. The writings of Thomas Jefferson, 20 Vols. (Washington: Thomas Jefferson Memorial Association, 1907), 15:278

320. United States v. Lopez, 514 U.S. 549 (April 26, 1995). http://laws.findlaw.com/us/514/549.html

321. United States v. Morrison et al., 526 U.S. 687, U.S. No. 99-5, May 15, 2000. http://laws.findlaw.com/us/526/687.html

322. Jay Printz, Sheriff/coroner, Ravalli County, Montana, Petitioner 95-1478 v. United States Richard Mack, 521 U.S. 898 Nos. 95-1478 and 95-1503 (June 27, 1997) http://caselaw.lp.findlaw.com/scripts/getcase.pl?court=us&vol=000&invol=95-1478

323. Patrick Krey. State vs Federal; the Nullification Movement. New American. March 1, 2010 issue, pp 10-16. http://www.thenewamerican.com/index.php/usnews/constitution/2957-state-vs-federal-the-nullification-movement

      Kirk Johnson, State's Rights is Rallying Cry for Lawmakers. New York Times, March 16, 2010. http://www.nytimes.com/2010/03/17/us/17states.html?ref=todayspaper&om_rid=DLGwoH&om_mid=_BLoMcVB8Gc-hwx&

324. Patrick Krey. State vs Federal; the Nullification Movement. New American. March 1, 2010, pp 10-16. http://www.thenewamerican.com/index.php/usnews/constitution/2957-state-vs-federal-the-nullification-movement

325. Joe Wolverton, II. States in Tumult Over National Health care Bill. New American, March 19, 2010. http://www.thenewamerican.com/index.php/usnews/health-care/3162-states-in-tumult-over-national-health care-bill

326. Caress, S. M. The Federal Data Quality Act's Impact on the Environmental Health Regulatory Process. All Academic Research., August 30, 2007, pp 6-7. http://www.allacademic.com//meta/p_mla_apa_research_citation/2/1/2/0/7/pages212079/p212079-7.php

327. Christine Hall. CEI Will File Suit to Block EPA Endangerment Finding. December 7, 2009. http://cei.org/news-release/2009/12/07/cei-will-file-suit-block-epa-endangerment-finding

      Also: EPA Faces New Legal Challenges on GHG Ruling. RechargeNews.com, February 19, 2010. http://www.rechargenews.com/business_area/politics/article207008.ece

328. Tom Head. Summary of Kelo v. New London (2005) – Supreme Count Eminent Domain Case. http://civilliberty.about.com/od/freetradeopenmarkets/p/kelovlondon.htm

329. Summary of Majority Opinion by Justice Stevens. Kelo vs City of New London. Findlaw, June 23, 2005. http://laws.findlaw.com/us/000/04-108.html

330. Ibid.

331. Ibid.

Chapter 10

332.   Fred Kelly Grant. The Coordination Mandate, Bringing Control Back Home. American Stewards of Liberty, http://www.stewards.us/strategies/frameset_strategies.htm

333.   Margaret Byfield. NEPA—Coordination Primer; Protecting the Human Environment, American Stewards of Liberty, P.O. Box 1190, Taylor, TX 76574 (512) 365-2699. http://www.stewards.us/

334.   Ibid.

335.   Ibid.

336.   Fred Kelly Grant. The Coordination Mandate, Bringing Control Back Home. American Stewards of Liberty, http://www.stewards.us/strategies/frameset_strategies.htm

337.   American Stewards of Liberty. http://www.stewards.us/

338.   Margaret Byfield. NEPA—Coordination Primer; Protecting the Human Environment, American Stewards of Liberty, P.O. Box 1190, Taylor, TX 76574 (512) 365-2699. http://www.stewards.us/

339.   Ibid.

340.   Ibid.

341.   Fred Kelly Grant. Coordination; A Strategy for Local Control. American Stewards of Liberty. p 6.

342.   Margaret Byfield. NEPA—Coordination Primer; Protecting the Human Environment, American Stewards of Liberty, P.O. Box 1190, Taylor, TX 76574 (512) 365-2699. http://www.stewards.us/

343.   BLM Internal Working Document, Prepared for BLM Summit on Ecosystem Management March 30, 1994.

344.   Robert Lee. Broken Trust Broken Land, Freeing Ourselves from the War over the Environment. (Wilsonville, OR: BookPartners, Inc., 1994), p. 28.

345.   Robert Lee. Broken Trust Broken Land, p. 29.

346.   Fred Kelly Grant. Coordination; A Strategy for Local Control. American Stewards of Liberty. p 8.

347.   Ibid.

348.   Margaret Byfield. NEPA—Coordination Primer; Protecting the Human Environment, American Stewards of Liberty, P.O. Box 1190, Taylor, TX 76574 (512) 365-2699. http://www.stewards.us/

349.   Ibid.

350.   Coordination is… Standing Ground. March 2009, Vol. II, Issue 1. Special Report. http://standingground.us/sg_march_09/sgmarch09-11.html

Endnotes

351. Fred Kelly Grant. Coordination; A Strategy for Local Control. American Stewards of Liberty. p 10.

352. Ibid.

353. Karen Budd-Falen, Attorney. State Agency Compliance with National Environmental Policy Act. http://www.learn-us.org/Documents/state_compliance. htm

Chapter 11

354. Personal Communication with Attorney Fred Kelley Grant, Stewards of the Range (Now American Stewards of Liberty), 2004. http://www.stewards.us/

355. Fred Kelly Grant. "Private Property Bill Awaiting Passage, The Historic Owyhee Initiative Finally Ready to Become Law," Standing Ground, March 2009, Vol II, Issue 1. http://standingground.us/sg_march_09/sgmarch09-12.html

356. Washington Wilderness Coalition and Philip Brick, v. Walla Walla County and Columbia County. United States District Court, Case Number: CS-94-312-AAM. March 8, 1995.

357. Ibid.

358. Washington Wilderness Coalition v. Walla Walla County. United States Court of Appeals for the Ninth Circuit, No. 95-343454, D.C. No. CV-94-00321-AAM.

359. Jerome R. Corsi. Bus Administration Quietly Plans NAFTA Super Highway. Human Events. June 12, 2006. http://www.humanevents.com/article.php?id=15497

360. Ibid.

361. Ibid.

362. Margaret Byfield. NEPA—Coordination Primer; Protecting the Human Environment, American Stewards of Liberty, P.O. Box 1190, Taylor, TX 76574 (512) 365-2699. http://www.stewards.us/

363. Fred Kelly Grant. Coordination Defeats TransTexas Corridor. American Stewards of Liberty. October 25, 2009. http://www.stewards.us/strategies/frameset_ i35victory.html

364. Ibid.

365. Ibid.

366. Jonathan Elliot, ed. The Debates in the Several State Conventions on the Adoption of the Federal Constitution. 5 vol. (Philadelphia: J.B. Lippincott Co), 3:45. http:// www.quoteworld.org/authors/patrick-henry#

367. Kristie Snyder. Terrorism in America – Coming Soon. Discerning the Times Digest. August, 1999. http://www.discerningtoday.org/members/Digest/1999Digest/ August/Terrorism%20In%20America.htm

368. Ted Flynn. Hope for the Wicked, The Master Plan to Rule the World. (Sterling, Virginia: MaxKol Communications, Inc., 2000)

369. William Safire. "You are Suspect," The New York Times, November 14, 2002.

370. Patrick Henry. Speech to the Virginia Convention Opposing the Constitution, 1788. http://www.milestonedocuments.com/documents/full-text/patrick-henrys-speech-to-the-virginia-convention-opposing-the-constitution/

317. Christopher Swan. "London Still Dominant as Finance Center." Bank of International Settlements, October 10, 2001.

372. See Book of Daniel 2:40-43 and 7:23.

373. Joseph Stiglitz. Globalization and its Discontents, (New York: W.W. Norton & Company, 2003), p. 22.

374. JFK vs. the Federal Reserve. The Federal Observer, Vol. 3, No. 3, January 4, 2003. http://www.federalobserver.com/archive.php?aid=254

375. Geoff Metcalf and Anne Williamson. "Inside the All-Powerful Federal Reserve," WorldNetDaily, March 11, 2001. http://www.worldnetdaily.com/news/article.asp?ARTICLE_ID=21997

376. Fred Kelly Grant. "Private Property Bill Awaiting Passage, The Historic Owyhee Initiative Finally Ready to Become Law," Standing Ground, March 2009, Vol II, Issue 1. http://standingground.us/sg_march_09/sgmarch09-12.html

377. Ibid.

378. United States Code. TITLE 43, Public Lands. Chapter 35, Federal Land Policy and Management. Section 1712 Land Use Plans. http://caselaw.lp.findlaw.com/scripts/ts_search.pl?title=43&sec=1712

379. Peter Coppelman. "The Federal Government's Response to the County Supremacy Movement." Natural Resources & Environment. ABA Section of Natural Resources, Energy, and Environment Law. Summer, 1997, 12(1):30-32. Also see, United States v. Nye County, Nevada, 920 F. Supp. 1108 (D. Nev. 1996)

380. Kleppe, Secretary of Interior v. New Mexico 426 U.S. at 543. (1976)http://caselaw.lp.findlaw.com/scripts/getcase.pl?navby=case&court=us&vol=426&page=543

381. Karen Budd-Falen. "State Agency Compliance with National Environmental Policy Act, "A Legal Opinion http://www.learn-usa.org/Documents/state_compliance.htm

382. Total Maximum Daily Loads Program. U.S. Environmental Protection Agency. http://www.epa.gov/owow/tmdl/

383. Peter Coppelman. "The Federal Government's Response to the County Supremacy Movement," p. 31. Summary paper.

384. United States Code. TITLE 43, Public Lands. Chapter 35, Federal Land Policy and Management. Section 1701General Provisions (notes)(g)(6). http://caselaw.lp.findlaw.com/casecode/uscodes/43/chapters/35/subchapters/i/sections/section%5F1701%5Fnotes.html

Endnotes

385.   Personal communication with Wayne Hage on July 24, 2004 in Reno, Nevada.

386.   Fred Kelly Grant. "Sheriff Issues BLM Trespass Policy." Cornerstone (Boise ID: Stewards of the Range, November, 2000), p. 7. http://www.stewards.us/cornerstone/nov2000/frameset_csnov00-4.htm

387.   Ibid.

388.   Ibid.

389.   Fred Kelly Grant. "Local Sheriff Holds BLM Accountable to the Law." Cornerstone (Boise ID: Stewards of the Range, January, 2002), Vol 9 (1):5. http://www.stewards.us/cornerstone/jan2002/csjan02-5.asp

390.   Ibid.

391.   Sean Fennigan. "Klamath: Pitchforks not required." Sierra Times, Aug. 8, 2001. http://www.sierratimes.com/archive/files/aug/30/arsf083001.htm

392.   US District Court, No. 2:96-cv-099-J. The case was brought by the Wyoming Sheriffs' Association. http://www-2.cs.cmu.edu/afs/cs.cmu.edu/user/wbardwel/public/nfalist/castaneda_v_us_docket.txt It was used as the basis for new legislation in the state of Wyoming: http://www.libertymatters.org/newsservice/2003/faxback/1.8.03antiwolfbill.htm

393.   Jeff Metcalf. "Wyoming Sheriff Analysis," Restoring America. http://www.restoringamerica.org/archive/sovereignty/wy_sheriff_analysis.html

394.   Personal Communication with attorney Karen Budd-Falen of the Budd-Falen Law Offices, Laramie, WY. Bivens v. Six Unknown Fed. Narcotics Agents, 403 U.S. 388 (1979) http://laws.findlaw.com/us/403/388.html

395.   Robbins v. Wilkie et al., 98-CV-201B (Order Denying Defendants' Motion for Summary Judgment, Federal District Court of Wyoming, January 20, 2004).

396.   Ibid.

397.   Ibid.

398.   James Pfander and David Baltmanis. Rethinking Bivens: Legitimacy and Constitutional Adjudication. The Georgetown Law Journal. November 23, 2009.   http://legalworkshop.org/2009/11/23/rethinking-bivens-legitimacy-and-constitutional-adjudication

Index

Index

Index

Index

Q

Index

Index

BUY A SHARE OF THE FUTURE IN YOUR COMMUNITY

These certificates make great holiday, graduation and birthday gifts that can be personalized with the recipient's name. The cost of one S.H.A.R.E. or one square foot is $54.17. The personalized certificate is suitable for framing and will state the number of shares purchased and the amount of each share, as well as the recipient's name. The home that you participate in "building" will last for many years and will continue to grow in value.

Here is a sample SHARE certificate:

THIS CERTIFIES THAT

YOUR NAME HERE

HAS INVESTED IN A HOME FOR A DESERVING FAMILY

1985-2005

TWENTY YEARS OF BUILDING FUTURES IN OUR COMMUNITY ONE HOME AT A TIME

1200 SQUARE FOOT HOUSE @ $65,000 = $54.17 PER SQUARE FOOT
This certificate represents a tax deductible donation. It has no cash value.

YES, I WOULD LIKE TO HELP!

I support the work that Habitat for Humanity does and I want to be part of the excitement! As a donor, I will receive periodic updates on your construction activities but, more importantly, I know my gift will help a family in our community realize the dream of homeownership. **I would like to SHARE in your efforts against substandard housing in my community!** *(Please print below)*

PLEASE SEND ME _____ SHARES at $54.17 EACH = $ $_____

In Honor Of: _____

Occasion: (Circle One)   HOLIDAY   BIRTHDAY   ANNIVERSARY

OTHER: _____

Address of Recipient: _____

Gift From: _____ *Donor Address:* _____

Donor Email: _____

I AM ENCLOSING A CHECK FOR $ $_____ PAYABLE TO HABITAT FOR HUMANITY <u>OR</u> PLEASE CHARGE MY VISA OR MASTERCARD *(CIRCLE ONE)*

Card Number _____ Expiration Date: _____

Name as it appears on Credit Card _____ Charge Amount $ _____

Signature _____

Billing Address _____

Telephone # Day _____ Eve _____

PLEASE NOTE: Your contribution is tax-deductible to the fullest extent allowed by law.
Habitat for Humanity • P.O. Box 1443 • Newport News, VA 23601 • 757-596-5553
www.HelpHabitatforHumanity.org

DISCARD

Breinigsville, PA USA
21 July 2010
242167BV00001B/2/P